W9-CAA-055

What Flavor is your Personality?

Discover who you are by looking at what you eat

Alan Hirsch, M.D.

Foreword by Jan Fawcett, M.D.
and Stanley G. Harris

SOURCEBOOKS, INC.®
NAPERVILLE, ILLINOIS

Published by Sourcebooks, Inc.
P.O. Box 4410, Naperville, Illinois 60567-4410
(630) 961-3900
FAX: (630) 961-2168

Library of Congress Cataloging-in-Publication Data
Hirsch, Alan R.
What flavor is your personality?: discover who you are by looking at what you eat / by Alan Hirsch.
p. cm.
Includes bibliographical references and index.
ISBN 1-57071-647-1 (alk. paper)
1. Typology (Psychology) 2. Food preferences. I. Title.

BF698.3 .H56 2001
155.2'6—dc21

00-066164

Printed and bound in the United States of America
PX 10 9 8 7 6 5 4 3 2 1

Dedication

To my father, who loved to eat.

Acknowledgments

In one way or another, I have been working on the material presented in this book for more than twenty years. During those years many people too numerous to mention by name, have assisted me, and this book is a result of their efforts. I owe special thanks to Denise Fahey and Virginia McCullough; without their efforts and contributions this book would not have been completed. I also want to express appreciation to Dennis Stefancic for his artistic talent. Special thanks go to Noah Lukeman and Hillel Black for their work on this project. I also wish to acknowledge Jan Fawcett, M.D., and Jacob Fox, M.D., whose teaching and encouragement ultimately inspired this and other projects. My children Marissa, Jack, Camryn, and Noah showed patience and understanding when I shared our time together with this book. And, most of all, thanks to Debra for her love and companionship for the last two decades.

Table of Contents

Author to Reader

Almost fifteen years ago, I founded the Smell & Taste Treatment and Research Foundation in Chicago, Illinois, and this book, as well as my two previous books, *Scentsational Weight Loss* and *Scentsational Sex*, result from the studies we've performed over the years. The mission of the Foundation involves diagnosing and treating patients who have lost their ability to smell or taste, a situation that is more common than most physicians and other health care professionals once believed. The consequences of these losses are significant, but to a large extent remain vastly unrecognized by the medical profession and the general public.

In the last decade or so, the sense of smell has gained greater "respect" than it has enjoyed in the past by the medical field and society in general. Today, those who suffer from the loss of ability to smell, and therefore, taste, are not as likely as they once were to remain silent. As a result, our Foundation sees patients that come from all over the United States and Canada, and increasingly we see patients from around the world, including Japan, Europe, and the Middle East. As a neurologist and psychiatrist, the driving force behind the Foundation was and is the desire to find effective treatments for patients whose sense of smell is impaired. In the process of conducting medical research, as well as treating patients, I have had the opportunity and privilege of helping to educate the public about the importance of the sense of smell.

Because both medical and public interest in smell and taste is relatively recent, we find ourselves exploring a new universe, and continue to find that it is much larger than once believed. We stand on the brink of understanding the ways in which the sense of smell influences human behavior, mood, and health. For example, a correlation exists between depression and diminished ability to smell. This knowledge is already opening doors to new diagnostic and treatment techniques, and it may lead to a greater understanding of the causes of depression and other psychological disorders. Although it is outside the scope of this book, the idea for our weight loss study emerged from observations that some individuals with impaired smell gained weight, while others lost interest in food and lost weight. We began to speculate that the nose could be enlisted as an ally in the modern battle waged against obesity, and research confirmed our hypothesis. My book *Scentsational Weight Loss* brought that research to a lay audience for the first time.

Over the years, our Foundation has studied the ways in which the sense of smell influences many areas of human life, including sexual arousal, perception of space, incidence and severity of migraine headaches, the effect of odors on learning, olfactory-evoked nostalgic responses, as well as consumer buying habits. In addition, through the use of surveys and standardized personality tests, we began to establish links between personality and food preferences. This book is a result of enormous public interest in what our food choices say about our personality characteristics.

Most people seek greater self-understanding, and as they move through various stages of life, they attempt to gain insight into their own behavior and the habits of those around them. We've learned that food preferences are not formed only through childhood environment, but may be key indicators of the personality structure with which we were born. Greater knowledge of individual personality characteristics may help us better understand the behavior of our children, life partners, coworkers, and friends. I offer this book as an example that we can unlock the mysteries of human behavior through the pathway of two important senses: smell and taste.

Alan Hirsch, M.D.
Smell & Taste Treatment and Research Foundation
Chicago, Illinois
November 2000

Foreword

Who would have thought that being sure garlic bread is served at a meal may make the conversation go in a more pleasant, maybe even productive direction? Or that a snack of Good & Plenty candies, or a cucumber salad at lunch might lead to an afternoon delight with your female lover? Want to find a risk taker who craves excitement for a partner? Find a man who eats spicy foods and feed him some pumpkin pie! Want to soothe yourself in this frenetic world? Try inhaling some vanilla or nutmeg oil, but don't give up on the chocolate.

We have been conditioned to focus on sights and sounds in our worlds–to rely on the logic or information in what we hear, and the moods of an ever increasing panoply of musical sounds piped to us, from devices from expensive high-fidelity reproducers of sound to that which we hear in elevators. Our appearance, our visual impressions of others, mirrors, images, the *New York Times* magazine fashions, preoccupy and titillate our society. Smell? Odors? Who notices them much—unless they are gross. But then again when did you last relish the smells of the outdoor air, the woods, or a lake?

It seems that as a species we've gotten away from an awareness of the role that smell plays in our lives. We think, talk about, and appreciate the taste of food enough—but as Dr. Alan Hirsch reminds us in this unusual book—90 percent of taste is smell.

Dr. Hirsch is a pioneer in bringing to our attention the importance of our sense of smell. He tells us he wants to entertain and educate with this book. He does both to make this both a fun and worthwhile read. Did you know that our smell-sensing neurons send information directly to our emotion-regulating brain (limbic brain) without our conscious awareness? That means we can be influenced by odors beyond our conscious awareness of their effect. When it comes to pheromones, we learn that we can't even consciously smell these molecules that send influential messages directly to our limbic brain without prior processing. In other words, while we are very aware of the effects of what we hear and see in our lives, we may be even more influenced by the odors that permeate the air about us and by substances we can't even smell. Our moods, outlook, and most important relationships may be affected by our sense of smell without our having the slightest awareness!

Then, Dr. Hirsch asks us to consider that our food preferences (smell preferences) may be related to features of our personality. This book is full of "personality tests" based on food preferences. Are you a potato chip personality or a pretzel personality? What does your preference for ice cream flavors indicate about your sexuality? Sound far-fetched? Read on and decide for yourself. Socrates gave us the wisdom "know thyself"—Alan Hirsch adds to this wisdom by admonishing us to "know thy nose." I found it an interesting place to "nose around"—especially if you maintain an open mind.

Jan Fawcett, M.D.
Stanley G. Harris
Professor and Chairman, Department of Psychiatry
Rush-Presbyterian-St. Luke's Medical Center
Chicago, Illinois

Introduction
Reflecting Who You Are

"When you don't have any money, the problem is food. When you have money, it's sex. When you have both, it's health."
—J.P. Donleavy

"First comes food, then morals."
—Bertold Brecht

At one time or another, everyone expresses a desire for a particular food. Some people may daydream about the hamburger they'll have for lunch; others can't get the thought of cashew chicken, a chocolate shake, or a juicy peach out of their minds. These food thoughts may last until the desired food is found and the "I want..." demand is satisfied. Yet, why do specific foods capture our attention, often to the point of distraction? And why do we choose to eat particular foods? What causes our strong food preferences? What makes us avoid certain foods, and in some cases develop—individually or culturally—an aversion to particular types of food? For the most part, we view likes or dislikes for different foods as "just the way things are." However, current research suggests that desires and preferences for certain foods are more complex than simply reflecting quirky attitudes toward food.

The food preference studies we developed at the Smell & Taste Treatment and Research Foundation helped us gain some wisdom about basic personality structure and food likes and dislikes. For example, we find food preference differences among those who believe they are in control of their own well-being versus those who believe they have no control over their future. The former tend to be concerned with the latest research into healthful eating, while the latter tend to eat what they crave, regardless of the health consequences—after all, their lives are in the hands of the illusive concept we call "fate."

It may surprise you to know that ambitious women who aggressively pursue their own goals typically use less salt and eat more high-fiber foods than women who prefer a more traditional female role. If you reach for eggplant or tomatoes over grapes or bananas, you may be a person who is sensitive to the feelings of others. Or, if you'd choose barbecued meat over a green apple, you may have an optimistic outlook on life. If chocolate ice cream is your favorite, then you may not be much of a risk taker, but if chocolate chip is your best flavor, then you may prefer to serve it in a cup, not a cone. If you pride yourself on your attention to detail and being a stickler for following the rules, then you may reach for a bag of "cheese curls" when you need a quick snack. Since you like to follow the rules, you may choose a companion who enjoys butter pecan ice cream, which may be your favorite, too. A number of different quizzes in this book will help you identify your unique "food personality."

Social and medical scientists, anthropologists, and psychologists currently are learning that our food choices, like our choices of clothes, movies, automobiles, vacation spots, and mates, can provide insight into our personality. Through our food preferences and choices, we reveal inner thoughts, feelings, wishes, and desires. In many respects, the foods we choose provide a window to the unconscious.

More than one hundred years ago, Sigmund Freud developed his theory that dreams are a key road to the unconscious. As we know, dreams can be intriguing, comforting, disturbing, or exhilarating. We may find dreams confusing because they speak to us in a symbolic language not well understood. For the most part, dream content—the images, the individuals, and the plots—seem randomly selected. However, as Freud proposed, dream images are not random events, but reflect the personality and the unconscious, the unseen "force" that motivates our behavior.

Foods we choose reflect our personality in similar ways. Think of a long cafeteria-style line that offers dozens of food choices. We look, we consider, we make our choices. One person may skip the salty french fries and reach for a baked potato instead. Another person scans the food looking for the fried chicken, while another is happy to see an abundance of fruit. Almost everyone considers reaching for chocolate cake. Some choose foods that match the food choices of their companions, while others pay scant attention to what everyone else is eating. The foods we choose provide clues to many things, from health status to the image we want to project to others, but they also provide a window to the unconscious desires and personality characteristics that influence our behavior.

The desire for food—any food—has an emotional component, an emotional investment. This desire requires a "self" to say, "I want...I am important enough to want." When self-esteem is extremely low, a person many not feel good enough to experience "I want," and therefore, the person will not eat. On the other hand, if one is depressed to a lesser degree, then the ability to want may be present, but one may not feel worthy enough to desire good food and an unhealthful or even unpleasant food is chosen.

Beyond individual personality, our food preferences reflect our culture and its underlying attitudes about food. In the prosperous West, the majority of the population has thousands of foods to choose from in supermarkets, natural food stores, specialty markets, and mainstream and ethnic restaurants. This vast array of choices is relatively recent in human history. For thousands of years, what we ate for dinner was almost entirely guided by what was available, geographically and seasonally. However, despite limited choice, anthropologists have established that food rapidly became part of early religious and secular rituals in human culture.

Food and Survival

For many centuries, our evolutionary ancestors wandered from forest to plain to coastal shore in their unending search for food. Of the three essential ingredients for survival—food, clothing, and shelter—food always appears first on the list. When we find enough food or have favorite foods stored in our freezers or pantries, we experience hunger as a positive sensation that invites us to indulge in the pleasures of eating. But when food is scarce, hunger casts a negative shadow over all of life.

For most of human history, cycles of feast and famine represented the norm. The great abundance of food our society currently enjoys is a new phenomenon, and as we have learned, a continuous period of "feasting" brings consequences in the form of expanding waistlines and, unfortunately, serious health concerns.

As much or more than any other survival element, food offers clues to culture. What a family eats for dinner may provide information about many things, including the season, the climate of the country or region, and the family's social status. Depending on the types of foods we find spread across the table, we may guess that it's a special occasion. If no food is visible, we may conclude it's a fast day. We can't forget that how the food is served offers clues about the occasion and perhaps the family's values and economic status, too. In Western culture, if we see plastic forks and spoons we may think a picnic is in the works—or maybe it's moving day. Silver forks and spoons mean something entirely different, and chopsticks sitting by the bowl or plate provide clues about the food or the diners—or both.

Most of us find it easy to accept the notion of food as a window to culture. But jumping to the concept that food is a window to *personality* may be more difficult to understand. However, if food always had been as abundant and easy to pile on our plates as it is today, then undoubtedly, we would know much more about "the potato chip personality" or the "the crunchy food versus soft food mood." The relative affluence Americans enjoy has set the stage that allows extensive investigation into the correlation between specific food preferences and personality types.

American Abundance is Unique in Human History

Less than one hundred years ago in the United States, we could peek into the kitchen or dining room of one hundred homes and see quite different foods featured in each household. In the 1930s, plates of baked beans and cornbread on the table could logically lead us to conclude that the family was strapped for cash. Today, the same dinner might tell us that the family is vegetarian or attempting to follow the U.S. Department of Agriculture's food pyramid. At one time, aromas rising from steaming bowls of pasta and baskets of warm garlic bread might have made us long to be Italian. Today, a family enjoying plates of pasta and bread could just as easily trace its roots to Asia or South America. Only on special holidays might we easily distinguish between one ethnic group and another based on the foods served.

The U.S. remains somewhat unique in the world in that American cuisine developed relatively recently. Actually, some food experts and chefs might argue that there is no such a thing as true American cooking, but rather what U.S. citizens concoct is more accurately described as a cultural hodgepodge. Probably more so than in any society, food plays only a minor role as an indicator of economic or social status. One could say that fast food represents a symbol of democracy because it's surely one of America's great equalizers. A family pulling into the drive-through lane to order their burgers and shakes could as easily be driving this year's BMW as a beat-up "relic" from the '70s.

In the U.S., virtually every kind of food is available year round; a bowl of fresh strawberries on the kitchen table does not tell us it's summer any more than apple pie lets us know it's autumn. In many supermarkets, we can buy salad greens in sealed packages all year round, so we're saved the *backbreaking* work of washing and tearing lettuce! Even in small towns we can shop for a vast variety of food or buy already prepared foods of every description, and we can "hunt and gather" our food twenty-four hours a day.

In her book about food and culture, *You Eat What You Are*, Thelma Barer-Stein points out that Americans plan their schedules around three meals a day; however, because they also have coffee breaks, soft drinks, and hundreds of snack foods at their fingertips, the day is more like one long meal.

Plentiful food and cultural diversity combine to set the stage for studying food and personality. If availability concerns or cultural norms and mores limit food choices, then exploring links between food preferences and personality would prove impossible. America's affluence and melting pot society have allowed us to cross the threshold to a new scientific way of not only classifying personalities but *reading* them, too.

Smell and Taste are Part of Everything We Experience

In addition to focusing on food and personality, this book also discusses the enduring links between food and cultural traditions, religion, and mythology. Also discussed are the many reasons food is closely linked with sexuality and other features of emotional life, including nostalgia. When certain smells and foods remind us of a happier, more carefree time, we may find ourselves unconsciously trying to bring these scents and foods into our daily life. As we learn more about personality and food, we also find that both consciously and unconsciously we seek what is necessary to fill a need in ourselves. For example, certain foods and odors appear to modulate or ease anxiety, and individuals who experience anxiety in its many forms may prefer these foods. On the other hand, those who are more relaxed may show no preference for these anxiety-reducing foods and odors.

More Complex Than We Thought

Our food preferences are influenced by so many factors that we cannot reduce the issue to only one dominant feature. Recent research suggests that food acceptance and preferences may even begin before we're born, and since we're not raised in a vacuum, family life, ethnicity, and the larger culture we live in figure prominently. But, we're learning that the family may not play as big a role as we once believed. We've assumed that we choose from the foods we're presented with over and over, and our preferences will remain true to early influences. That assumption bears out to an extent, particularly when food choices are limited or when special foods or delicacies are offered only now and then. For many families today, though, the atmosphere is quite different.

Interesting research has emerged that suggests a less important family role in food preferences. Not surprisingly, mothers still do most of the food shopping in our society, and the foods they select are based more on their husband's food preferences than their own. The daughters in the family show a slight tendency toward food preferences that resemble their father's favorites, but sons do not show a similar correlation with either parent.

This information is especially intriguing, because we may learn that when choice is, in a sense, wide open, our food preferences are influenced more by innate personality traits or genetic tendencies than by either family or culture. The time never has been better to study the complex link between what drives our attitudes and emotions and what we choose to have for lunch. And we already know that the answer to the simple question "What do you want for dinner?" draws from our evolutionary past, our culture, family, economics, health factors, genetic tendencies, geography, season, personality, the scents in the air, and our mood at that moment.

I hope you will use this book to gain greater insight into your own personality and the personalities of those around you. My two previous books were written to both educate and entertain. I have written this book with the same goal, and I hope you will approach this subject with intellectual curiosity, along with an added dash of good humor and a sense of fun.

Chapter One

Your Personality Rules Your Life

"Tell me what you eat, I will tell you what you are."

—Brillat-Savarin, 1826
(famous French gourmand)

"Regarding food, my grandfather held to an unassailable position: he would not try anything new; he would not mix ingredients; the eggs of his Spanish omelet had to be served on one plate and the potatoes on another; he shook salt and pepper onto his food by the spoonful before tasting it because he believed it was good for the intestines; desserts were for sissies; and instead of wine, he drank large glasses of gin with his meal."

—Isabel Allende

As 1999 drew to a close, Albert Einstein was chosen as *Time* magazine's "Person of the Century." A genius in his work in physics and math, he expanded our thinking and opened new frontiers of science and technology. Future generations will learn about the importance of his contribution to our understanding of the nature of the universe. However, ultimately, Einstein's *personality*, not his intellect, led to his wide acceptance as an influential person in our time and probably to *Time* magazine's designation. For most of us—including the brilliant Einstein—success in life, no matter how great or modest, depends more on personality than on any other single factor.

To gain insight into ourselves and other people, we need to understand this concept—this thing—we call personality. And it has never been easy to define personality, let alone unlock the mysteries of behavior and our unique characteristics and quirks. We often describe individuals as aggressive or shy, go-getters or laid back, optimists and pessimists, and so forth, and then we detect traces of these traits or descriptions in everything they do. Others view us in the same way. Our spouses, parents, brothers, sisters, and close friends see our personality "fingerprints" all over our career choices, hobbies, sports activities, family life, and so forth. Our partners or lovers most certainly reflect our personality traits, which of course, influenced our romantic choices in the first place.

If we make the same mistakes again and again, it is because we have not identified or corrected the particular personality characteristic that guides us to repeat the same patterns.

In psychiatry, we generally accept that it is difficult to change one's basic personality. Certainly, we can attempt to understand personality traits and then help patients modify behavior if necessary, but it is possible that our fundamental personality traits are ingrained in our genes. Just as we're born with eye color we cannot change, some research suggests that personality traits are inborn and unchangeable as well. Genetic or not, personality traits appear to become established by around age seven, which is about the same time food preferences are established, along with other preferences, too. Signs of potential future careers and hobbies may begin to appear very early in life, and our teachers in the early grades often can identify students who are detail-oriented and patient with learning versus those who catch on to large concepts, but become impatient with repetitive tasks. Quite early on, most parents identify different personality traits in their children and adjust their responses accordingly. One child may withdraw

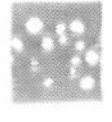

under stress or when angry, and another child may cry and become emotionally expressive. This type of response is in place by age six or seven.

Although we have yet to establish the extent to which basic personality traits are inborn and to what extent we acquire our personality traits through environmental influences, we do know that a biological component of personality exists. For example, damage to areas of the brain affects the functions it controls. The prefrontal lobotomy is one of the most controversial surgeries ever developed, and it involves cutting nerve fibers in the forward portion of the frontal cortex. The damage to the brain results in the loss of certain personality characteristics and renders individuals passive and apathetic. Damage inflicted to areas of the brain that govern emotions may leave the individual unable to read emotional cues, which is a considerable disability and makes normal life difficult.

In one famous case, Phineas Gage, a young railroad worker, was the victim of a freak accident that propelled a long iron rod through his cheek and up through his skull. In a sense, this was an accidental lobotomy. What was most amazing about the accident was that Gage survived it, and apparently never even lost consciousness. After his release from the hospital, Gage was expected to live a normal life—in the medical sense—except for the iron rod that remained lodged in his head! Superficially, Gage was normal. His memory was intact, and intellectually he remained sharp. But in the realm of personality, he was a changed man. Unable to think ahead and plan his future, Gage also lost his social skills. He was unable to discern situations in which profane language was acceptable and where it was not. At one time, Gage was an aggressive worker and interested in getting ahead in life, but after his accident, he lost his ambition and drive. This case illustrates personality changes that result from biological events, and again, shows us that personality characteristics have a biological component.

We cannot forget that twin studies also confirm that personality characteristics and even tendencies toward occupational choices are inborn. The "separated at birth" phenomenon has yielded considerable insight into one aspect of the "nature over nurture" puzzle and has demonstrated that we come into this world with much of who we are already in place. Of course, our environment also influences the way we develop and shape our genetic gifts. Some studies have shown similarities in food preferences in sets of twins not raised in the same family, and these studies offer support to the contention that we have in-born taste tendencies.

Learning to Read–Personalities That Is

If you learn to "read" personalities, you will gain a tremendous advantage in life. We've probably all dealt with the consequences of being unable to do so. For example, the *inability* to spot a potential troublemaker is a liability in any office. Currently, about half of all marriages end in divorce, and perhaps many of these unfortunate relationships could have been avoided had the individuals been able to better read each other's personality. They could have made the decision not to marry at all, or they might have chosen to accept the other's differences rather than try to change a deeply embedded personality trait. Some people are very good at reading personalities, but they use this ability in detrimental ways. The classic con man can spot a "sucker" in a group; likewise, sexual predators can spot women who appear vulnerable and may lack the confidence to fight back.

On the other hand, therapists and physicians often are able to better help their patients when they understand the dynamics of basic personality types. A physician may determine that one patient is independent and self-directed and, therefore, interacts with that patient in a collaborative way, perhaps focusing on treatment options. However, another patient may depend on outside authority and expects exact instructions about how to take a medication, and this patient may not express any interest in how a particular treatment works. On some level, most physicians do read personalities—they offend too many patients if they are unable to modify their behavior to accommodate individual differences.

The athletic arena provides a great example of an area in which the ability to read personalities yields enormous advantages. If competitive runners, for example, understand their opponents, they can make strategic decisions based on personality characteristics. Should they stay behind the principal competitor and then sprint ahead to the finish, or is the opponent more easily discouraged by an early leader so it pays to establish an early lead? One-on-one tennis matches certainly provide examples of opponents "psyching" each other out to gain advantage. To a great extent, baseball can be reduced to the mind-games pitchers and batters play.

Basketball great Michael Jordan's competitive spirit is legendary. More than anything else, that personality trait gives him his "larger than life" aura. Anyone who ever played with him or against him understood his drive to win, and according to well-known stories about him, he takes on every challenge with the same will to come out on top—checkers, cards, and golf included. Opponents who could read his personality were wise enough not to make even the slightest disparaging remarks about any aspect of his game. But pity the hapless fellow who remarked that age had taken the edge off Michael's game! Michael lifted his performance not just to prove the opponent wrong, but to show him up a little, too.

Because the ability to read personality is so critical, an unfortunate gap exists in the way we educate children. We fail to teach children to understand and read personalities, and great disparity exists between our formal education and what we need to live well throughout our lives. In my own case, four years of Latin and knowledge of sophisticated math theorems have had little impact on my ability to practice good medicine. But my ability to read emotions is of great value when I work with patients, and it is a greater predictor of success than my command of Latin.

Far more than intellect, personality affects behavior, and behavior ultimately is the determining factor in success. The smartest kids in the class may not be the "most likely to succeed" because they are unable to read personalities and modify behavior to their advantage. The best salespeople, teachers, physicians, psychotherapists, corporate managers, business owners, lawyers, and politicians may reach high levels of success because they are able to assess other people's personality characteristics. Of course, I don't mean we should learn to read personalities in order to *manipulate* other people in negative and unscrupulous ways. However, understanding people can lead us to spot those we're better off avoiding and also can help us choose our friends, mates, and lovers.

In the workplace, this ability gives us an advantage in determining *how* we do business and interact with another individual, whether that person is a prospective customer, patient, colleague, boss, or employee. Success is correlated with the ability to read personalities far more than with cognitive ability or an I.Q. score. We have all known individuals who do not seem particularly bright or knowledgeable, yet they may head companies or inspire others to succeed. These men and women probably have a superior ability to read personalities, which enables them to manage and lead others.

Most of us learned to read personalities in an informal, haphazard kind of way, and a general belief exists that women tend to have greater sensitivity to emotions and probably read personalities better than men. Remember, though, that this was not always a valued ability or trait. In fact, "feminine intuition" was usually much less prized than the "rational" information provided by intellectual functions, which were presumably the more "masculine" traits. This situation is changing as women continue to move into every field and influence attitudes toward various kinds of interpersonal abilities and communication.

Another Way to Classify Personalities

As you may know, numerous personality classification systems are in use. For example, psychiatrists and psychologists use the *Diagnostic and Statistical Manual of Mental Disorders* (the current edition is the *DSM-IV*). If we use the *DSM-IV*, we are defining personality in terms of one of the recognized disorders, such as the *schizoid personality disorder*. A person with this disorder shows a pattern of detachment from social interaction and relationships with others. A person diagnosed with *narcissistic personality disorder* shows patterns of grandiosity and a need to be admired, while at the same time exhibiting a lack of empathy for others.

In psychiatry, we quite naturally define personality in terms of difficulties and design treatments to help modify an individual's behavior and ability to function in the world. Other systems, such as the *Myers Briggs Type Indicator* defines characteristics such as introvert/extrovert or thinking/feeling, and is designed to help individuals understand themselves and gain insight into others. Another system, the *Enneagram*, is believed to have developed from the Sufi tradition in the Middle East. It classifies nine basic personality types based on ways of viewing the world and coping with life. For example, a person might be described as an "Adventurer," which is #7, or as a "Perfectionist," which is #1.

This book represents the development of a new classification system based on food preferences. As you will see, we can define a potato chip or pretzel personality; personality characteristics can be predicted based on such factors as salt use, favorite types of chocolate, and favorite fruits. As more research is conducted, we discover that what we put on our plates is determined by a complex mixture of physiology, culture, and personality.

It may sound trivial to say that a person is a "pretzel personality," but it is not trivial when we can point to particular traits that describe this type of person. For example, our research indicated that those who prefer pretzels as a snack food are drawn to new challenges and crave novelty. Since they tend to lose interest in mundane things, a career counselor might conclude that an assembly line job or accounting is probably not the best choice. This type of person performs well on jobs where the projects and tasks are short-term and quickly finished, so surgical nursing would probably be a better choice than working in medical research where it might take years to calculate results. Although personality typing based on food preferences is relatively new, this is the kind of information we can expect to emerge in the coming decades as research accumulates.

Eating What and *Who* You Are

Over the last several decades, we've all heard the adage "You are what you eat," which on one level is the nutritional version of "garbage in, garbage out." On another level, it contains the message that we can become what we eat; hence, food has properties beyond its calories. Next, the phrase "You eat what you are" began surfacing, and it refers to the idea that culture and traditions shape us. In this book, I use the phrase "You eat *who* you are," and by that I mean that we bring our personality, along with our cultural traditions and influences, to the dinner table—and the snack counter and the ice cream parlor.

Personality traits tell us much about who we are, and through research, we've gained a preliminary understanding that food preferences—and by implication, the odors we like best, too—tell us much about our personality. This information does not override what we bring culturally to our food choices. For example, the decision to refrain from eating pork is not a function of individual personality

traits, but is a classic example of the way religion and culture shape what we eat—the component that determines that "we eat *what* we are." (The reasons that groups prohibit certain foods and embrace others usually evolve over time and have much to do with environmental—habitat—issues. I touch on these later in this book.)

Culture also determines what foods take on a special, even magical meaning. For example, aphrodisiacs are "magical" foods, and chocolate is probably another food that is "greater than the sum of its 'ingredients.'" While some aphrodisiacs may have chemical constituents that influence sexual performance, belief in the power of the food precedes knowledge. After our study identified pumpkin pie and lavender—and to a lesser extent cinnamon rolls—as stimulating male sexual arousal, these odors began to take on "magical" qualities too. In June 2000, a cosmetic company began producing fragrances based on these arousing food odors—perfumes designed to arouse men and colognes for men based on scents that arouse women.

Religion also endows some foods with special symbolic meaning and applies taboos to others. Many feasts—and fasts—rise from religious beliefs and traditions, and the rituals associated with each festival or holiday call for the symbolic use of food. Over time, then, the food itself seems to take on the essence of the religious and cultural symbolism. Although rabbit was common game meat in the U.S., its popularity has diminished, and for some people eating rabbit for dinner would be like eating the Easter Bunny—and that would be like eating Santa!

Almost every religious group developed practices that involve blessing food. In some regions, a family may say "grace" before a meal, which involves expressing gratitude for the food; in other regions, a member of the family says "the blessing," which also involves giving thanks. The ancient ritual of a communal food blessing increases the value of a meal and elevates the status of the food itself. Blessed food is special, and by implication, those eating it are special too. Traditional blessings and saying grace before a meal—or observing a moment of silence as is done in some spiritual practices—serves other familial and cultural purposes, too. These few seconds tend to calm the atmosphere around the table and remind the group of *who they are*.

More Than Nutrients, More Than Pleasure

It isn't surprising that we would find links with food and personality, or find that food is linked with every aspect of life from the most sacred to the most sensual. For all of human history, food has represented far more than just nourishment and a basic survival element. When you sit down to a plate of food you bring your personality along with past experiences, especially your childhood associations with meals, both happy and sad—perhaps even traumatic. You may bring food aversions and a reluctant attitude toward new foods, or you may bring a sense of adventure and a willingness to experiment with "what's for dinner." But even beyond that, food has strong unconscious and primitive associations.

Our language reflects the desire to take in the essence of food—and we translate that to people. When you play with a baby and say, "You're so cute I could gobble you up," or we tell a lover, "I love you so much I wish I could eat you up," we are expressing our desire to absorb the person, make him or her a part of us. These are verbal manifestations of a primitive way of responding on an emotional level; if we ingest something—take it into our bodies—it becomes part of us. We aren't a cannibalistic culture, but we talk as if we were. Most people don't find it odd when we tell babies we'd like to gobble them up. One of our favorite stories is a frightening fairy tale in which a wicked stepmother threatens to cook and eat the young children, Hansel and Gretel.

The language of love and affection is filled with references to food. We may call children and adults "sweetie" or "honey" and we may extend the reference to sweet things and use specific foods such as "honey bun" or "cupcake" as a substitute for the person's name—usually women. I've never heard a man referred to as a "cute tomato," but during the 1940s and '50s, that was a fairly common lighthearted term of endearment for a woman. Comparisons between animals and people are common in our language. Calling someone a pig or a shark is not complimentary. If we call someone a peach, however, that's a positive remark.

Food has the power to arouse our passions and we say we love chocolate or burgers or lobster, but we do not usually speak the language of love when talking

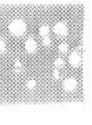

about birds or buildings or trees. Fierce arguments are unlikely to break out over the relative virtues of an oak tree versus a maple, but watch out when people start talking about milk chocolate versus bittersweet. We are far more likely to make passionate noises (those oohs and ahs and other guttural sounds of pleasure we usually associate with sex!) over ice cream or even restaurants than we are over a pair of shoes or a clothing store—and most Americans take great pleasure in their clothing.

Despite how busy we are, most of us spend an inordinate amount of time in our pursuit of food. Each year, hundreds of new cookbooks are released and reviewed, and when a restaurant opens, crowds flock to try it. Food and restaurant advertising is one of the most basic components of our economy, and these industries count on the idea that we will not be satisfied to grab a hunk of cheese and a vitamin pill and call it a meal. People spend extra money on food that looks attractive and tastes good *and* that is served in a desired atmosphere—romantic, social, quiet, intimate, noisy, and so forth. We enter a restaurant with expectations, and when an eatery changes its menu, watch out. A certain number of patrons will become quite upset and may never come back. Make no mistake, most of us are *serious* about hunting and gathering the foods we want. We are equally serious about avoiding the foods we don't like. We are either passionate about eating oysters or brains, or we passionately avoid them.

Festivals, Fairs, and Potlucks

Food festivals exist all over the world, and they continue to grow in popularity. The agricultural fairs of England and other parts of Europe made their way to the United States, where county and state fairs developed as our version of agricultural fairs. We tend to forget that these events had great social significance before transportation allowed rural populations greater mobility. The county or state fair meant an opportunity to experience something outside of the usual routine, particularly a chance to visit with neighbors and make social connections. And we can't forget the neighborhood and church or temple potluck where food is the featured attraction and serves as the social glue that holds these events together.

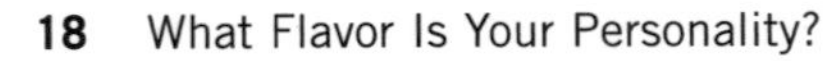

For sure, economic interests drive the extension of various festivals and fairs. Millions flock to the annual Taste of Chicago food fest, and other cities feature similar revenue producing events. These tend to be little more than updated (and very extravagant) versions of county fairs. And what would summer be without the regional festivals, which are almost always centered on food products. New England has its lobster festivals and maple syrup days; pumpkin and cranberry festivals are popular in the Midwest; one county in Indiana celebrates a mint festival every year. Annual garlic festivals are held all over the world, and if you are serious about food, you can travel to Singapore for their annual food festival. We love to celebrate with food, but we also celebrate food itself. In ways not easy to explain or understand, the foods we choose may represent not only who we are, but who we aspire to become.

Who Do You Want to Be?

In New Guinea, a culture that at one time practiced forms of cannibalism, one of the motivations for eating a relative who died was that it was the way to ingest that person's essence and make him or her a part of a living person. This adds another level of meaning to the phrase "You are what you eat." But it also is a way of expressing the idea: "You eat who *you want to be*." When a male ingests the testicles of an animal believed to be powerful and valued, part of the motivation is to transfer the power—the potency—of the animal to himself.

Some examples of ingesting what we aspire to become are dramatic and obvious, but some are subtle. Sales of the breakfast drink Tang rose when astronauts drank it during space flights; certain foods enjoy a blip in popularity during the Olympic Games if they're named "official" foods of the Olympics. These foods become a unifying symbol of something bigger than we are and allow us a vicarious thrill of being part of the experience.

Perhaps we can find no better example of eating who we *want* to become than the famous Wheaties cereal boxes that feature our most accomplished athletes. The face of gymnast Mary Lou Retton or Michael Jordan on a box of cereal sends a message to children that by ingesting the cereal, they are taking in part of the strength and greatness of the athlete.

Using celebrities in advertising is a clever trend, particularly when the famous individuals possess qualities we associate with the heroic. Food and personality studies reveal a tendency to choose foods that in some way provide what we believe we are missing. If we need motivation to reach a goal, we may unconsciously choose a food that a high achiever endorses.

Having Paul Newman's face on Newman's Own pasta sauces, salad dressings, and other products no doubt helps to sell these foods. In the case of Paul Newman's products, the profits are donated to various charities, so the consumer has the additional feeling of becoming philanthropic by buying the product. Consumers buy a *feeling* as well as the taste. Celebrity surveys that tell us that Oprah Winfrey likes potato chips or that Mel Gibson is a fan of jelly beans seem quite trivial, yet unconsciously, consumers may reach for foods their favorite celebrities enjoy in order to be like that person. "Eat like me, become like me," is the message, and it's simply a variation on, "Eat me and become me."

Associations with food extend to qualities of the food itself. In our culture, foods such as caviar, lobster, and champagne are "success" foods and have a connotation of power; black-eyed peas, hush puppies, and chitterlings, for example, may be personal favorites, but they are not associated with success and power. At times, we may seek the comfort of the hush puppies and chitterlings because they remind us of a happy time in the past, but at other times, we may find ourselves needing to feel motivated and successful so we are drawn toward the "success" foods.

I Like What You Like—Vote For Me

Celebrity food preferences tend to have little consequence except as a marketing tool. However, politicians may need to be more careful about what they eat and what they say about food. Running for office means attending numerous functions where food is served, including county fairs and various dinners hosted by civic organizations. Invariably, reporters will film news segments in which a candidate is seen eating—and ostensibly enjoying—a hot dog from a street vendor in a city or Uncle Elmer's award-winning barbecue ribs or fried chicken at a county fair. To be successful, a candidate must walk a tightrope between being perceived as a

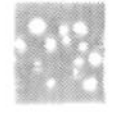

serious leader and a "regular" person. World leaders aren't supposed to be preoccupied with food, but regular people appreciate down home cooking.

When President George Bush made an off-hand remark about not particularly enjoying broccoli, the press reported it and it became one of the campaign jokes. Although it was little more than a sound bite on the evening news, for that brief period, the battle line was drawn, with broccoli lovers on one side and the President Bush camp on the other. We can't ignore the fact that a simple food preference, or in this case, a dislike, was reported along with semiserious speculation about gaining or losing support from broccoli producers!

Later, the "health police" were out in force when news clips appeared of President Bill Clinton buying his breakfast at a popular fast food chain. On one hand, he was perceived as a middle-age man, and a world leader of course, with the food preferences of the average twelve-year-old. However, his breakfast-in-a-bag reinforced a regular person image, and millions of Americans with a taste for fast food combined with a tendency to gain weight identified with him. A politician's food preferences are not a deciding factor in gaining or losing support, but identification with eating habits and food choices is a subtle but important factor in gaining public approval. No politician is unaware of this issue, and no successful politician would ever risk offending a region or an ethnic group by expressing dislike for their "signature" foods.

Love Me, Love My Food

Because we project qualities onto foods under some circumstances, food tends to become quite personal. In many cultures—and in many homes—one of the greatest social "sins" is refusing food. This is the equivalent of rejecting the person offering the food, who may or may not be the same person who cooked it, but it also may signal a lack of respect for a culture. Food etiquette is one of the most difficult social challenges precisely because we can't possibly learn all the variations on what is polite in individual *families*, let alone become familiar with all the culture imperatives that surround food.

In our culture, if we talk about "spitting in the soup" that's an expression of extreme dislike or even revenge—an expression that indicates a silent payback.

But if we are part of the Hua group of New Guinea, then food carries "nu" the life force and characteristics of individuals who prepared it or was in contact with the food. Therefore, eating food that has been prepared by a revered relative adds to the value of the food, which then takes on the prized qualities of the relative. If the relative spits in the food, that adds to the value. (The opposite is true as well. If you dislike Uncle Harry and consider him a scoundrel, then don't touch food he's prepared because those scoundrel qualities can be passed on.)

The Complex Puzzle

As you will see, food preferences have great validity as clues to gain insight into individual personalities. We already know that what we eat tells us much about where we come from, our cultural past, and even our religious beliefs. We are now establishing that identifying the foods we prefer can provide indications about our strengths and weaknesses. In the not too distant future, physicians and psychotherapists will ask about their patients' food preferences in order to understand deeper personality and character structure. We can collect information about personality and food preferences to help ourselves, but we can also use it to help us learn more about others.

As you probably know, taste and smell are closely related senses, and in order to understand the science of food and personality, you need a rudimentary understanding of the way these senses work. So, before we discuss specific studies, the next chapter offers basic information about the anatomy of smell and taste.

Chapter Two

The Ways of the Nose

"Two nerves or appendages to the brain, for they do not go beyond the skull, are moved by the corporeal particles separated and flying in the air—not indeed by any particles whatsoever, but only by those which, when drawn into the nostrils, are subtle and lively enough to enter the pores of the bones which we call the spongy, and thus to reach the nerves. And from the diverse motions of these particles, the diverse sensations of smell arise."

—Rene Descartes

The seventeenth-century philosopher Rene Descartes did not miss the mark by much when he described the mechanism of smell. He—and others—understood the concept that diverse "particles" in the air create the diversity of odors we enjoy. But Descartes was no doubt unaware of the important role our sense of smell plays in regulating many basic bodily functions. Without exaggeration, the ability to smell helps us survive as individuals and as a species, and beyond fundamental survival, it profoundly influences our life experiences. Our ability to taste foods, from the most bland slice of white bread to the spiciest Indian curry, depends on our sense of smell too, because about 90 percent of what we call taste is actually smell.

Interpreting odors as tastes represents a form of *synesthesia*, which means we perceive something as one sensation when it really comes from another sensation. If you push on your closed eye, for example, you will see light–there is no light, but you interpret the pressure as light. Similarly, you perceive the taste of chocolate fudge, but the taste is actually an odor. This is why *olfaction*, the scientific term for the sense of smell, is the initial pathway to understanding food preferences.

As knowledge about human physiology expanded over the last two or three centuries, we learned that odor receptors exist at the top of the nose, and through a complex physiological process we *identify* particular smells and *respond* to them, often with strong emotions. In 1991, two researchers identified genes for odor receptors, leading us to further understand that we have many more genes associated with olfaction than with any other sense. In April 2000, researchers reported having identified a family of as many as eighty genes whose sole purpose is to allow us to detect a wide range of bitter tastes. This makes evolutionary sense because bitter flavors serve as a warning that a substance might be poisonous, an ability that seems less important in modern life, but was critical to our cave-dwelling ancestors. Based on research performed on other mammals, a possibility exists that 1 percent of the human genetic blueprint is comprised of genes used to identify odors. We know this is true in other mammals, and it appears to be the same for humans.

The Breath is the Pathway

Descartes, quoted above, wrote of lively particles in the air. Today, we call those particles odor molecules, and the most direct way to understand how olfaction works is to follow the journey of odor molecules. We inhale and exhale thousands of times each day, and seldom think about the act of breathing unless we are ill and breathing becomes labored. An unpleasant odor—exhaust fumes or smoke, for example—may cause us to consciously hold our breath, or we avoid inhaling deeply in order to protect ourselves from toxic fumes. On the other hand, we may consciously inhale slowly and fully to draw in the fragrance of flowers or the yeasty smell of sweet rolls coming from the bakery we pass on the way to work. The simple act of breathing can block or limit an "odor experience," or encourage and enrich it (see Figure 1).

FIGURE 1

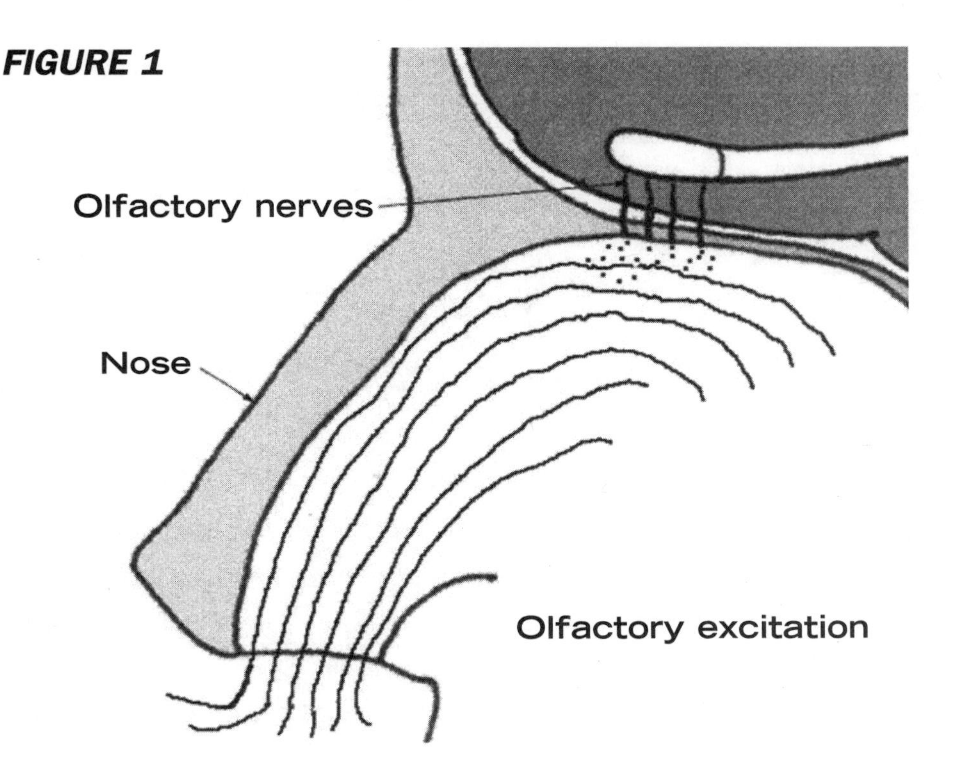

When we inhale, odor molecules enter the nostrils and the air descends into the lungs. However, when air currents develop in the nose, the odor molecules can reach the *epithelia* in the olfactory—or smell—center in the top of the nose, just behind the bone we call the bridge of the nose. Epithelia are protective mucous-coated membranes about the size of a shirt button or a dime. I like to describe these air currents as small gales or tornadoes that develop when you inhale deeply (see Figure 2).

FIGURE 2

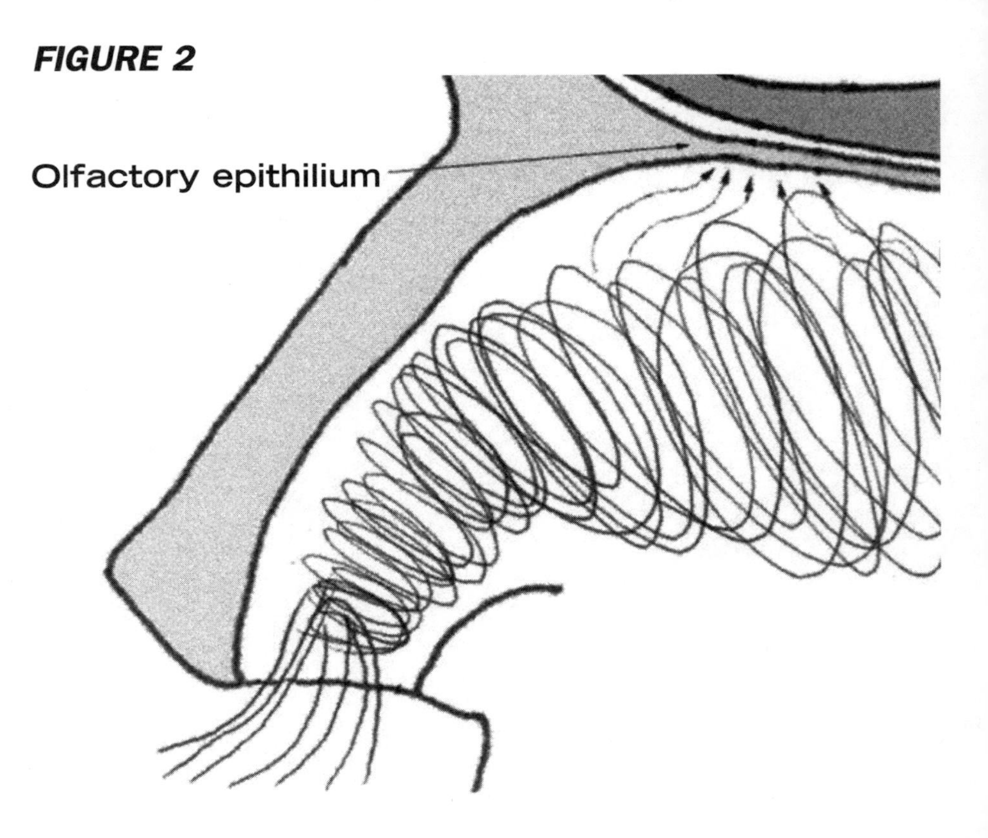

These little nasal tornadoes are actually stronger when the nose is stuffed up. The nostrils are not equally open or closed at any given time, and one usually is open while the other is closed, which constitutes the *olfactory cycle*. In the normal course of things, the olfactory cycle changes every eight hours or so. Test this for yourself by putting your index finger over one side of the nose to close the nostril, and then inhale. Close the other side of the nose and inhale again. You can tell that one nostril is clearer than the other, and your olfactory ability is actually better in the nostril that's stuffed up. If you have a cold or a sinus condition, your nasal passages may become too stuffed up and you can neither smell nor taste food, which is why food tastes like cardboard and you may temporarily lose your appetite. Your ability to detect odors in the air greatly influences your perceptions and sensations of hunger and the desire for food.

Odor molecules make their way to the top of the nose to a pin-sized area of the olfactory membrane, which contains millions of olfactory receptors. The molecules move through a thin area of mucous and bind to receptor sites on the olfactory nerve. Receptor sites may be specifically designed to detect particular odor molecules. Some odor molecules respond better at some receptor sites than at others, which is part of the mechanism that allows us to discriminate between odors and to identify odors that are present in our environment. Each of these receptors—and we have many millions of them—link with odor molecules that match them (see Figure 3).

FIGURE 3

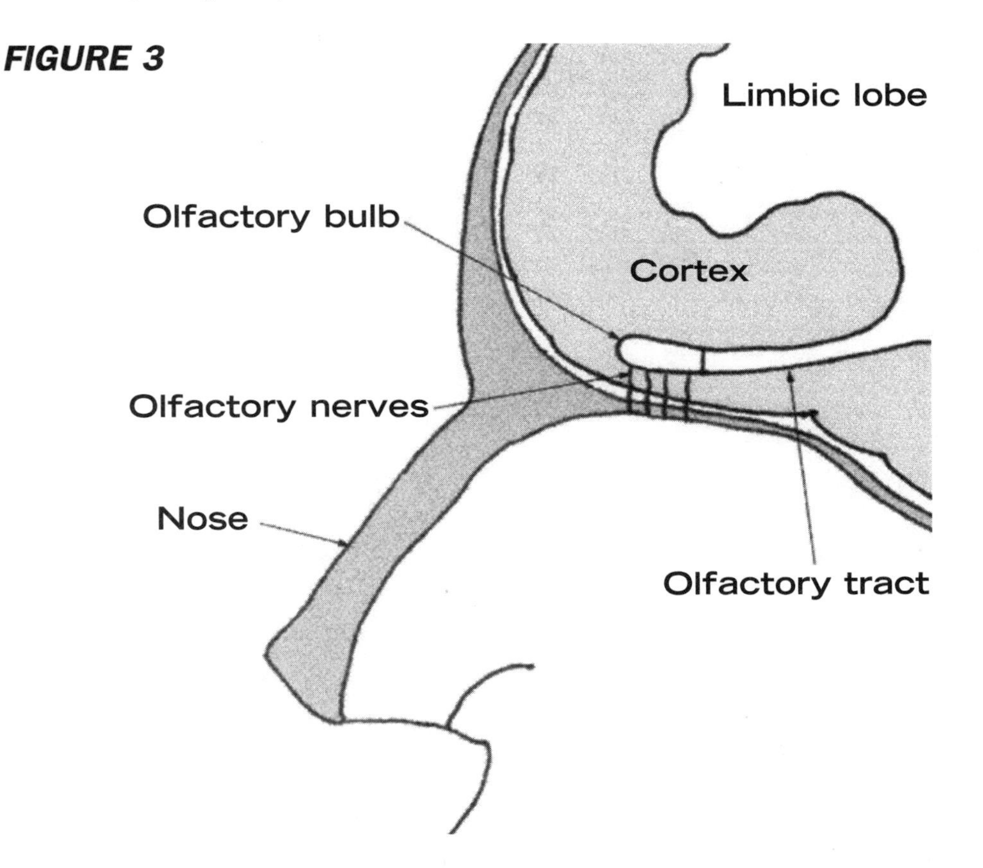

Apples, Gasoline, or Roses

We still don't know exactly how we distinguish odors. We may have a receptor site for every possible odor, or we may have different patterns on the receptor sites, which may help us distinguish specific odors over others in our environment. Once odor molecules reach a receptor site, they stimulate a long thin nerve cell, or neuron, to fire. This neuron is called the *bipolar receptor cell.*

Think of this part of the journey as a stimulus response mechanism whose function is to change the picture or neural image of the odor molecule. This stimulus-response system alters the neural image of the odor by projecting the signal back through the olfactory bulb, where specific cells, *basket and granule cells*, intensify the odor. The original odor stimulus is intensified by a factor of one thousand, and at this point, the odor signal projects through the olfactory bulb again and finally reaches the main components of the brain.

The Pathway to Emotion

An odor signal travels through the olfactory bulb and ultimately reaches structures in the *limbic* portion of the brain, an area we also refer to as the *emotional brain*. The limbic brain sits beneath the *cortex*, the intellectual—cognitive—control center, and is located above the portion of the brain stem that controls unconscious functions such as breathing, digestion, and other survival mechanisms we needn't think about moment to moment. No other sensory receptors or processors have their home in the limbic center of the brain. The sense of smell stands alone as a direct link to emotional responses and emotional life (see Figure 4).

The limbic brain activates the *hypothalamus*, a tiny control center for instincts and drives. The hypothalamus sends messages to the *pituitary*, the master gland that regulates important hormonal functions of the body. A close relationship exists between odors and the physiological systems involved in such basic drives and instincts as hunger, sex, territorial behavior, and aggression.

The limbic lobe of the brain defines us and influences our lives as much or more than our intellectual functioning. Emotional memories are stored in the limbic brain, which also steadily feeds us information about our likes and dislikes. And mood? The limbic brain is an emotional feedback loop, always regulating our mood state. It tells us that we are anxious, depressed, joyful, pleased, surprised, annoyed, and so forth.

The direct link between an odor molecule and the limbic brain helps explain why our sense of smell is such a powerful trigger for nostalgic reverie, for example, it also helps us understand why the presence of a particular food can make us anxious, calm, sad, delighted, or annoyed. Conversely, an understanding of the olfactory-limbic connection offers insights into the reason we crave a bag of chips or a dish of chocolate ice cream after a particularly bad day.

FIGURE 4

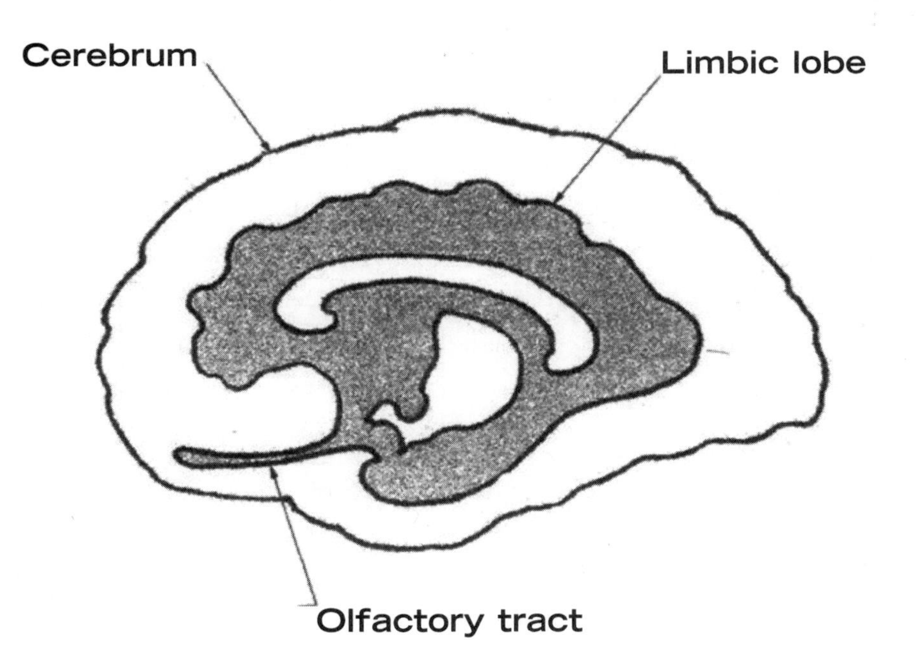

The Chemicals of Emotion

A variety of chemicals in the brain called *neurotransmitters* allow nerve impulses to move from neuron to neuron in the olfactory bulb and on through the limbic lobe. The olfactory bulb contains almost all the neurotransmitters found in other parts of the brain, including *dopamine* (the neurotransmitter that is deficient in those with Parkinson's disease), *acetylcholine*, *epinephrine*, *serotonin*, and so forth.

A part of the brain called the *thalamus* operates as a kind of relay station to and from the cerebral cortex. It plays an important role in sensation, and signals the brain about environmental changes. With the exception of smell—and taste—the thalamus processes sensory information before the limbic lobe becomes involved. For example, I may show you a picture of a mountain, and you determine what it is before you decide if you like it. If I put a handful of pebbles in your hand, you notice their texture and identify them as stones or pebbles before you make a decision about liking them or disliking them. However, if I introduce a scent to your environment, your limbic brain is immediately involved and you decide if you like the odor *before* the cortex identifies the odor as rose or butterscotch or donuts.

Reactions to odors can be so irrational precisely because our responses are independent of logical thought. There's nothing rational about liking or disliking the smell of barbecued beef or a certain brand of floor wax or night-blooming jasmine detected in the summer air. Yet, we make these judgments all the time.

In a more limited way, other senses provide certain built-in responses unrelated to rational thought processes. The sound of fingernails scraped across a blackboard is one example. When you hear that sound, you probably shiver and perhaps even gasp or groan, and you may say your "hair stands on end." You have a physiological reaction, which triggers a hyper-alert or hyper-awake state. Your response falls outside of your powers of reason. You stand ready in full alert—but when was the last time a blackboard attacked you? This represents an unusual reaction to sound, notable only because it's rare. Your olfactory system is designed to react first, identify later.

The Nose as an Early Warning System

Wandering clans and cave families may have adopted dogs as "best friends" because they provided an additional early alert system. Dogs can detect odors and hear sounds humans cannot. In general, your dog's sense of smell is about one thousand times sharper than yours is. However, the human sense of smell is its own early warning system. Remnants of this "primitive" alert system exist today. When you yawn before you sleep, you may be acting from a primitive instinct to detect the odor of dangerous animals lurking about. Yawning is a mechanism by which odor molecules reach the olfactory bulb through the back of the mouth (the retronasal pathway), which increases the chances of detecting potentially

dangerous odors. We associate yawning with increasing oxygen in the body, but yawning also may be part of the early warning system. If this sounds a bit far fetched, remember that Mother Nature doesn't waste effort. Once studied and understood, natural phenomena no longer appear random or accidental.

Some things don't change, and just like our ancestors, we interpret the world through our senses, and even when we can't see, hear, or touch something, we may be able to smell it—even if we aren't consciously aware of an odor in the air. When we say we "smell danger," perhaps that reflects a time when our ancestors were more attuned to their environment and noted sensory reactions, even when the messages weren't completely clear.

Why We Are Olfactorily Repressed

Compared to the rest of the animal kingdom we have a relatively weak sense of smell, and the unwelcome and unpopular cockroach smells one hundred thousand times better than we do. If we examine the olfactory apparatus among mammals, we can see it is much like the human physiological structure. However, relative atrophy exists in the smell apparatus of humans when compared to other animals, particularly dogs.

For many centuries, we've used our canine friends to help us hunt for food and alert us to changes in the environment. Many dog species still work hard for us. With only a few molecules of an odor, trained dogs are able to follow a person through intricate paths, which is why law enforcement has used dogs extensively in manhunts. Dogs can sniff out cocaine, even if it's sealed in airtight containers and packed in garlic or hidden in gasoline tanks.

It's likely that at one time, the human sense of smell was sharper than it is today. As humans evolved, the visual system developed, too, and eventually the ability to see great distances became more important to human culture than the sense of smell. Over time, the sense of smell in humans began to atrophy relative to other species, and became important only in close interactions and to detect nearby dangers. In addition, as societies became more cognitively oriented, the sense of smell became less important than that of vision and hearing, which are processed in the cognitive centers of the brain and linked to components we need to organize societies, such as practical education, building, agriculture, and so forth.

By the time Sigmund Freud began to formulate his theories of human behavior, the intellect already had become elevated in status over emotions. "Rational" thought was considered superior to "irrational" emotions. Because odors have the ability to arouse powerful emotional responses, the nose became suspect, and Freud considered the sense of smell a "primitive" sense, and therefore, not important to so-called civilized society. Because of the link between sexuality and odors, Freud also believed that if the sense of smell were not repressed, humans would walk around sexually aroused virtually all the time. Therefore, in order to live together in groups and concentrate on intellectual pursuits, the sense of smell would need to be repressed and less dominant than other senses. Despite efforts to repress smell or reduce its importance, it remains essential for survival, just as it's always been, in part because odors can have a profound effect on us on the unconscious level. Pheromones represent an important example of this phenomenon.

Pheromones: Nature's Survival Mechanism

Our sense of smell is critical to our survival as individuals and as a species, which is probably why it is processed in the portion of the brain associated with survival mechanisms. Early humans were migratory and roamed their environments in search of food. The ability to detect intruders in our camp or territory by the presence of their odor alerted us to potential danger. At one time, survival probably depended on the ability to smell danger signals before we could see them—or, as we've seen—identify them. In modern life, the generalized odor of fire puts us on alert, and then we investigate to determine the source of the smell. Because survival was a daily issue, our evolutionary ancestors were no doubt more conscious of the array of odors around them than we are.

We also react to odors we cannot consciously detect. *Pheromones*, substances released by one species to influence others of the same species, likely exist throughout the animal world, including the human family. Pheromones provided early

humans with the most basic path to sources of potential mates. (Regardless of the rational reasons we *say* we use to choose our lovers, I believe the sense of smell still largely dictates the "chemistry of love.") Unconsciously, pheromones allowed our ancestors to sense that a human being was walking in the forest nearby, as opposed to a wild boar or an antelope.

Pheromones appear to be a component of nature's intricate design to ensure procreation. Male moths can detect a pheromone released by a female moth a mile away, and the pheromone released by a moth will not attract bees or antelopes or your dog because it is species-specific. Based on current research, we believe human pheromones exist, although the exact substances have not been isolated. Presumably, pheromones are byproducts of reproductive hormones (primarily estrogen and progesterone for women and primarily androgen for men).

Evidence suggests that the apocrine glands, which are located under the arm and around the genitals, produce high-density steroids, which are distributed through the body in various ways, including in the sweat produced by the nearby eccrine glands, commonly called sweat glands. The apocrine glands are sensitive to physical exertion and stress, and they activate during exercise and changes in the physical and emotional environment. Apocrine glands also are sensitive to sexual cues. However, they also activate in threatening situations that arouse fear.

The axillary—underarm—hair traps pheromonal substances and, before we became such a "cleaned up" culture, the underarm area probably carried great concentrations of pheromones. In Elizabethan England, a young woman who wanted to flirt with her lover might place a peeled apple under her arm and let her natural odors penetrate the flesh of the fruit. She then gave the apple to her sweetheart. The man could be have her odor close to him, and he could also eat the apple, thereby taking in her sexual essence. Raising the arms during dancing, hugging, and sexual activity probably releases pheromones and plays a role in heightening sexual arousal.

Pheromones appear to be involved in reproductive cycles. Women's superior sense of smell probably is nature's way of ensuring that they can detect and be influenced by male pheromones. It makes sound evolutionary sense that women's sense of smell is heightened during ovulation, and the phenomenon is probably a built-in mechanism designed to make women more receptive to sex during the fertile period of their cycle. According to sexual surveys, some women report increased sex drive during the ovulatory phase of their cycle as well as increased frequency of orgasm. Unlike other primates, human sexual activity is not dependent on "estrus," which is a specific period during which a female is receptive to mating. Both men and women may be influenced by pheromones at any time, which supports the theory that the formation of a family unit in which the male stays with the female to raise their young is possible because of the absence of estrus.

Remember that one does not need conscious awareness of a pheromone or any odor in order to be influenced by it. Inexplicable sexual attractions, for example, may be related to pheromonal attraction. Rational thoughts or logical events do not rule the nose. Nature provided pheromones and we do not necessarily have conscious control over whom we find sexually attractive, even when such attractions are forbidden. However, because we are rational beings, our values and attitudes usually prevent us from acting on forbidden attractions, but as we all know, men and women can sometimes feel overwhelmed by powerful attractions, whether they act on those attractions or not.

When we look at couples that seem to be mismatched, remember that the secret of their attraction may be found in their "pheromonal compatibility," which is biologically driven and not easily overcome with all the logical reasons two people should not be together. We each have an individual odor, which is determined by our genetic profile, our *genome*. In order to maintain a healthy gene pool, we mate with individuals whose genome is unlike our own. Generally speaking, the odor signature of the individuals we're attracted to is different from our own, which means that successful procreation is most likely to occur. Your genome is unchangeable, and your unique personal odor can't be altered with soaps or perfumes. Your odor signature is genetically determined and is probably at the root of the phenomenon we know as "sexual chemistry." To an extent, it is probably true that we either have or we don't have it, and we cannot manufacture it if it is not present.

Modern Thinking May Be Faulty

In our modern era, vision is considered the most important sense, and surveys have shown that more people dread losing their sight than any other sense. In addition to navigating the world using primarily visual cues, we also assume we "read" other people based on our ability to see them. A person is pleasing—or displeasing—based on visual impressions. In psychiatric training, we are taught that within one minute of meeting a patient we can decide if he or she should be admitted to the psychiatric unit of the hospital. This evaluation is based primarily on sight.

Giving visual cues the upper hand comes from the notion that evaluations are rational and built on a foundation of logic. But first impressions almost always result from emotional responses. We make the emotional evaluation first, and then rationalize our decision using our intellectual abilities.

After studying our sense of smell, it appears more likely that initial emotional impressions of other people arise from olfactory information. In an instant, we are attracted or not attracted to a particular person. I believe we like or dislike certain individuals based on their unique smell, which influences us on an unconscious level. We then call in the intellect to help us rationalize our decision. We may say that our lover has a great voice and a beautiful smile, and we're drawn—even captivated—by those features, but the truth is, we probably felt drawn before our brain processed information about specific characteristics. Our first impression was based on an olfactory event. Our noses might *initiate* our most important relationships.

What We Call Taste Is Mostly Smell

If you close your eyes and pinch your nose and I put a slice of apple in your mouth, you might think you're eating an onion. If you hold your nose and take a bite of the most expensive and delectable European chocolate, you might as well be eating cardboard. As I mentioned earlier, more than 90 percent of taste is actually smell, and taste is a misnomer in most cases anyway. Our taste mechanisms equip us to distinguish four different categories of tastes: sweet, salty, sour, and bitter. Beyond that, we experience flavor, which results from the food's *retronasal* smell.

Odors reach the olfactory bulb in two ways. In the first way, odor molecules travel from the air to the nose, which is called the *orthonasal* pathway. The second pathway starts at the back of the throat and travels up to the olfactory bulb, which is the *retronasal* pathway. We experience flavor through the retronasal pathway when we chew our food and release odor molecules. We seldom think about the retronasal passageway, but most of us have coughed or choked while eating or drinking, only to have the food or liquid come out our nose. Embarrassing though as the experience probably was, it demonstrated the retronasal mechanism in action (see Figure 5).

FIGURE 5

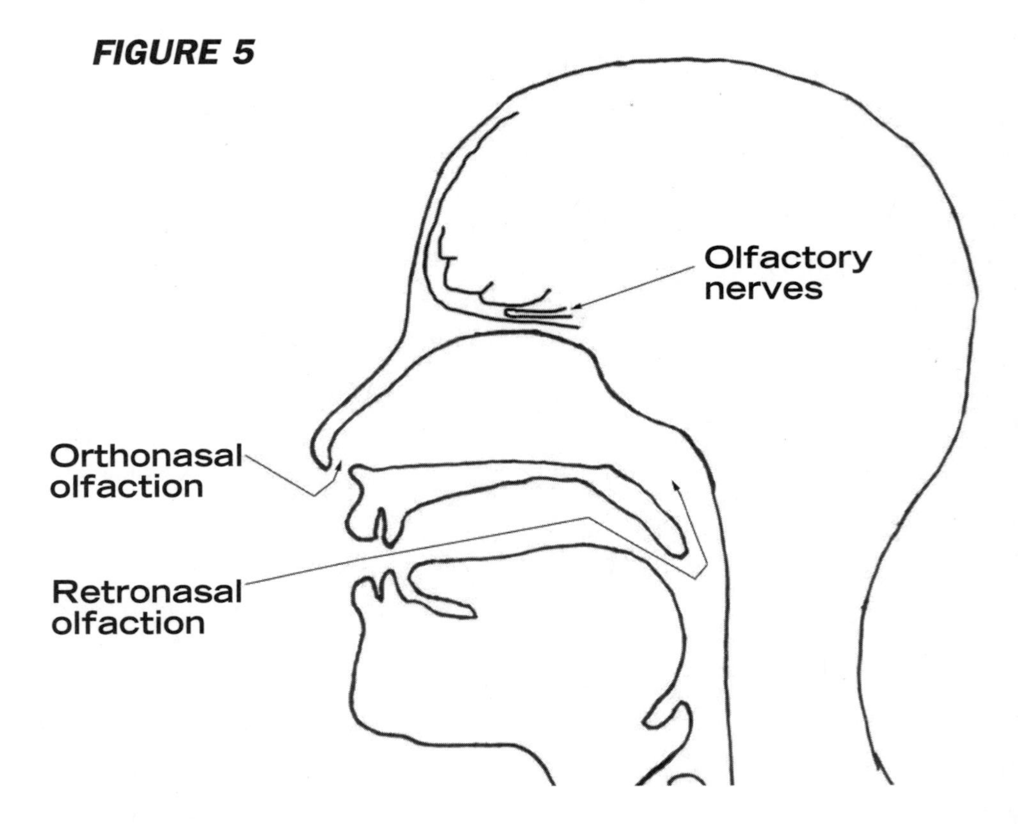

What we typically describe as a smell or an odor is a combination of an odor molecule and a stimulus to another nerve in the nose and face, the *trigeminal* nerve. If you cry, either from sadness or from cutting an onion, the trigeminal nerve is stimulated, thereby causing your eyes to become irritated and burn. This nerve is involved when you sneeze in response to a substance that irritates the nasal passages. A protective mechanism, a sneeze allows us to clear the irritant—purge it—before it can harm us. Even if an individual can't detect the odor of an onion because of reduced ability to smell, the trigeminal nerve detects the odor and responds. In this way, it acts as a back-up system to protect against toxic fumes.

Sometimes those with diminished ability to smell can derive greater pleasure from their meals if they include foods that stimulate the trigeminal nerve. Patients who come to the Smell & Taste Treatment and Research Foundation often are advised to add "irritating" foods such as curry, horseradish, chili peppers, or onions to their diets. They may not notice improvement in their ability to smell, but trigeminal nerve involvement adds sensations to the meal and makes eating less of a chore—and when the sense of smell is gone, sitting down to a meal can seem like a chore.

While the practice is less common today, at one time, some individuals carried smelling salts with them in case they felt faint. Smelling salts, which have a strong ammonia odor, stimulate the trigeminal nerve and activate the part of the brain responsible for keeping us awake and alert. Tear gas is another substance that activates this mechanism, which is why it forces people out of confined spaces and into the air where the molecules are less dense. Exposure to smelling salts and tear gas result in burning eyes and difficulty breathing—physiological responses that are initiated with an odor.

Left-Brain–Right-Brain

As you probably know, the hemispheres of the brain perform different types of functions.

In right-handed people and about half of left-handed individuals, the left hemisphere of the brain controls the so-called logical functions such as calculations and language. The right hemisphere of the brain processes music, art, sexual arousal, and emotions. We sometimes label people "left-brained" or "right-brained," usually based on personality characteristics. Our logical mathematician friend may go through what often appear to be excessively logical thought processes when ordering dinner from a menu, perhaps saying things like, "I had chicken yesterday and a burger the day before, so I should have fish today." On the other hand, our friend the concert pianist will muse about what "sounds good" or "feels right." Of course, we use both sides of the brain in our endeavors. A mathematician may be an intuitive musician on the side, and as you will see in a later chapter, the concert pianist may actually process music in the right side of the brain.

The right nostril projects into the right brain, and the left nostril projects to the left brain. Most right-handed people are right-brain dominant for smell, although the ability to name an odor is a left-brain function. Tests have shown that right-handed people perceive odors as more pleasant when introduced to the right nostril than when introduced to the left, but they are better able to *identify* the odor when it is introduced to the left nostril. These findings correlate with what is known about the function of each side of the brain, and also demonstrates the emotional response to odors that has little to do with identification of the odor. Your right-brain nostalgic response to a fragrance begins before your left brain identifies it and triggers your verbal response, "Ah, my dad's shaving lotion."

The Language of Smell and Taste

Smell and taste disorders are grouped together under the umbrella term *chemosensory dysfunction*, and different terms describe the specific type of problem. *Anosmia* means an absence of the ability to smell and *hyposmia* is a reduced ability to smell. If you are *hyperosmic*, you have an increased ability to smell, and in some cases, this is a symptom of Addison's disease. *Phantosmia* refers to a situation in which a person imagines an odor that isn't there—an odor hallucination—which may suggest the presence of a seemingly unrelated disease state. *Dysosmia* is a distorted smell in the presence of an odor. Taste is similarly broken down into *ageusia*, no ability to taste; *hypogeusia*, reduced ability to taste; *hypergeusia*, increased ability to taste; *phantageusia*, a hallucinated taste, and *dysgeusia*, distorted taste. These chemosensory dysfunctions are symptoms linked to myriad physical and emotional disorders.

Noses Are Not Created Equal

Just as some people can hear or see better than others, wide variation exists among individuals in their ability to smell and taste. The vast majority of people come to our clinic because they can't taste their food due to their diminished sense of smell. Other people spend their lives with a subnormal ability to smell, and they are "odor-blind," the way some people are "color-blind." Often unaware of the deficit, these individuals quite literally don't know what they're missing. Until they're tested for a driver's license, colorblind people may not realize they have a problem. Some young people remain unaware that they lack the ability to smell until they go off to college and learn that their roommates comment on food odors, locker room smells, or cosmetic scents they can't detect.

A small minority of the population may be born with *congenital anosmia*, an inborn lack of the ability to smell. One day, we may learn if this condition is hereditary or appears as an anomaly in a developing fetus. We do know, however, that the ability to smell is by no means equally distributed in the population.

Differences in olfactory acuity cross gender and cultural lines. Many women believe they have a better sense of smell than their male companions do—and they're usually right. Men often think that if they can't detect an odor then the smell must not exist. But men are often wrong when they insist the garage doesn't smell like kerosene. Nothing in evolutionary development results from whimsy, women's olfactory acuity is probably linked to the reproductive imperative, meaning the ability to detect pheromones, particularly during the ovulatory phase of her cycle. And since we know that female mammals can identify their young through odors, women's better olfactory acuity is probably an evolutionary carryover.

Olfactory ability varies among racial groups, too. In general, Korean-Americans have the best sense of smell of the many population groups in the U.S., and both black and white Americans have better olfactory acuity than the Japanese. We don't know the reason for these differences, but tests of olfactory acuity have shown us that the ability to smell can be predicted based on population groupings.

Our Love Affair with the Nose Begins Early

A developing fetus probably detects odors in the womb, and shortly after birth, infants recognize their mothers by smell. Human babies turn toward cotton pads that have been "laced" with their own mother's milk, but react less strongly to a stranger's milk. However, to ensure survival, babies adapt and accept milk from a source other than their biological mother.

To infants, one smell is as good as another. Infants and toddlers taste and smell everything, which is the way they refine their ability to distinguish among odors. Infants accept all smells and tastes as part of the world and put them into a hierarchy of likes and dislikes through the socialization process. We learn that feces smell bad, for example, and in our culture we are not fit for "polite society" until we learn this. As I mentioned before, food preferences, and by implication, odor preferences develop from birth to age seven, which is the same period in which fundamental personality traits develop as well.

When the Nose Ages

As we age, our ability to detect and identify odors diminishes. More than 50 percent of those over age sixty-five and 75 percent of those over age eighty have significantly reduced ability to smell. Some of this decline is comparable to the overall gradual decline in sensory acuity that occurs as a natural part of aging. However, the number and type of medications many elderly men and women ingest adds to the problem. You notice that loss of the ability to smell is not listed as a side effect on the inserts in medication packaging. Pharmacists rarely warn their customers about the possibility that a medication will adversely affect their ability to smell—an oversight that should be corrected.

As a society, we have yet to give more than lip service to the consequences of loss of smell and taste among the elderly population. But we know that gradual loss of appetite is quite common in older people, and little is done to help overcome the problems. For example, as the sense of smell diminishes, food should be more heavily spiced because food begins to taste more and more bland

as we age. However, cooks in nursing homes and home-health workers who prepare meals tend to be young, and the food they prepare may not have intense smells and tastes for the older population. When older men and women prepare their own foods, not being able to smell it increases the risk of food poisoning. In addition, olfactory loss can be downright dangerous. The ability to detect a gas leak depends on the ability to smell the added odorant, but studies have established that many older people are unable to detect the odor at current levels of concentrations.

Diminished ability to smell as we age can be quite confusing, a situation made worse because so little chemosensory testing is performed in current medical practice. Yet, changes in sensory perceptions and abilities may serve as an important symptom of a specific disease. For example, loss of olfactory acuity is seen in many patients with Parkinson's and Alzheimer's disease, both of which affect the elderly population. If smell and taste were tested with the same regularity we check hearing and sight among the elderly, we might detect the onset of these diseases—and others—much earlier.

The Nose Is Worth Protecting

Our sense of smell is unique among the senses in that the olfactory gateway to the brain is direct; no barriers exist to block an odorant from its intricate processing system. The eardrum acts as a barrier between a sound and the auditory processing mechanism, and in a similar way, the cornea serves as a physical barrier between visual stimuli and the visual processing system.

Most of us take the nose for granted. If we happen to break the bone in our nose, our first concern may be the cosmetic consequences. However, the olfactory system is vulnerable. The olfactory nerve travels through minuscule holes in the skull that allow individual nerve fibers to pass through a paper thin area at the top of the nose called the cribriform plate. (The word means "pierced with small holes.") Trauma to the head or nose can damage the nerve fibers that pass through the cribriform plate.

A broken nose or an injury to the head often leads to the loss of the ability to smell, but if the nerve fibers heal fully, the loss may be temporary. If the delicate fibers do not heal, the loss may be permanent. You may not think of seatbelts or bicycle helmets as olfactory protection devices, but efforts to prevent trauma to the head and face protect your sense of smell, too.

For example, as a young medical student, I was hit by a car while riding a bicycle, and sustained a head injury that, among other things, temporarily impaired my sense of smell—for a few weeks, everything smelled like cigarette smoke! My accident happened in the pre-helmet days, and I was fortunate because my injuries were not permanent. However, today, bicycle helmets are available and I urge you to wear one and insist your children use them as well. Like seatbelts in cars, cycling helmets save lives and help to reduce trauma when accidents do occur.

Studies conducted at the Smell & Taste Treatment and Research Foundation suggest that even mild head injuries can cause potential lifelong problems, from weight gain to depression to chronic headaches. Some of these conditions are directly related to loss of the ability to smell and taste. Our research shows that one out of every twenty head-injured patients suffers from a loss of taste and smell, but because these chemosensory losses are gradual and sometimes subtle, patients may not notice their deficits. The results of chemosensory losses often must be dramatic for the deficiencies to be noticed. If you cannot smell the odor of smoke, you may not realize your house is burning, and that calls attention to your inability to detect strong odors. Or, individuals suffer food poisoning because they could not smell or taste the spoiled food. Among the elderly, these situations are not rare, and among head injury patients, they are far more common than generally believed.

Mysterious Links

For reasons not yet fully understood, the inability to smell appears to have psychological consequences (see Appendix 1). At our clinic, we test patients for their chemosensory acuity, that is, the ability to taste and smell, but we also screen patients for depression with a well-known standardized test, the Beck Depression Inventory. About 96 percent of patients demonstrate major psychiatric diagnoses, the most common of which are chronic depression, generalized

anxiety disorder, a form of long-term anxiety disorder. The longer the duration of the problems with smell and taste, the more likely the patients are to have these psychological consequences and the severity of symptoms tends to increase over time. When the sense of smell is diminished over a long period of time, the person is more likely to develop obsessive-compulsive disorder (OCD) as well. Diminished sex drive is also associated with diminished ability to smell.

We were able to correlate the ability to detect a particular odor PE Phenol with the presence of depression, using both the Beck Depression Inventory and the Zung Depression Scale. (Both these tests are widely used in psychiatric practice.) PE Phenol is a neutral chemical odor, and therefore, is not linked with food or normal environmental smells. We found a direct correlation between the inability to detect and identify the odor with the presence of depression. This test further established the link between the limbic system and olfaction, but also helps us remain aware of the importance of smell and taste, not just to quality of life, but to emotional well-being.

The increase in anxiety among those with diminished smell led to a theory that perhaps free-floating substances in the air act like "natural Valium." These natural tranquilizers affect us on an unconscious level; they are *subliminal* odors, which may affect all of us to a degree. For those with a built-in or natural tendency to anxiety, these chemical substances modulate anxiety and, when they are no longer detected, the anxious state increases and eventually becomes a potentially serious problem. The cause of the anxiety may have an evolutionary basis because the ability to detect odors in the environment is essential in order to experience a sense of safety. When that sense of safety is gone, a person may stay in an emotional state that is always on guard and ready to combat unknown dangers and threats.

We Don't Know What We've Got 'Til It's Gone

Perhaps it is too easy to "medicalize" the loss of the sense of smell, and forget that those who have lost their sense of smell tend to miss the little pleasures of life—the smell of a holiday meal or flowers in a garden. And these common pleasures only seem small and perhaps even insignificant until we lose them. One of the most touching accounts of "life without fragrances" comes from physician Brian Elliot, who lost his sense of smell as the result of a head injury. To Elliot, his loss undeniably affected his quality of life. A portion of his article "Practical Management of Head Injuries," published in *Medical Publishing Yearbook* in 1964, is quoted below.

> While reckoning my immunity to unpleasant smells on the credit side, I find that is more than outbalanced by my divorce from a wide range of smell sensations connected with some of the most enjoyable things in life...I could never resist the impulse to smell a beautiful rose. I would cradle the rich-scented blossom in my hand while inhaling the ethereal essence of its silky petals. A walk in the hospital garden on a sunny morning cured me of the habit. Unthinking, I stopped to capture the fragrance of a particularly lovely rose. In one unforgettable moment came the stab of realization that for me the scent of roses could never again be more than a memory. A part of me was dead.
>
> I still have the memory to cheer me. But the memory itself is dimmed when the sense is gone, and only in my dreams do I sometimes recapture the vividness of the reality. A few nights ago I dreamed of lily of the valley and breathed its pure intoxication in my sleep. In the morning it was gone. I was back in my sterile deodorized world, whose roses—by whatever name—smell not at all.

About four million Americans have some degree of olfactory abnormality, and each year about two hundred thousand men and women seek help from family physicians and other specialists due to a diminished or nonexsistant sense of smell. In my practice, I hear the patients talk about their loss in much the same terms as Brian Elliot. The loss of smell indeed affects all of life, and those who cannot smell deserve understanding and compassion. As more medical information accumulates, I hope we can offer increasingly better treatments to help those with chemosensory disorders.

The Results Are In

As you read through this book, you will learn more about food, mood, personality, and even gain insight into cultural influences on food preferences. But for now, answer the following four questions to give you a preliminary glimpse at your olfactory acuity.

Which do you prefer? (Circle *one* item in each pair)

A. chili or hamburger

B. tacos or pancakes and syrup

C. Grey Poupon mustard or yellow mustard

D. café mocha or café latte

If you chose the *first* item at least three of four times, you tend to prefer spicy foods, and that may indicate that you have an impaired or at least slightly diminished sense of smell. Your desire for spicy foods indicates you are seeking greater pleasure from food and blander foods do not provide sufficient smell and taste. Based on other personality correlations, you may have a tendency to have underlying depression, and you may be slightly irritable. You tend to seek comfort in the company of others, and will speak up if you don't believe you are being treated well.

If you chose the *second* item at least three of four times, your sense of smell is probably in the normal range, and you do not need the stimulation of spicy foods. You tend to be an optimist, and you are generally a self-starter and you may work for yourself. An energetic person, you tend to make decisions logically rather than intuitively.

As you will see, we often seek what we need in sensory ways, just as we do on practical levels. If we feel as if we are missing something, we may seek stimulation from foods and smells as well as from other people, but if we tend to feel complete, we may choose the more bland smells and tastes. This is the most basic correlation in food and personality studies.

I recommend noting if you find a change in your food preferences. If you are choosing spicy foods or adding more spice to dishes you prepare, your ability to detect odors, and therefore, taste various foods, may be diminishing. (Your basic personality is not changing, however.) It is my hope that this book impresses upon you the importance of the sense of smell to your quality of life. Medications, vitamin deficiencies, and numerous medical conditions contribute to loss of olfactory acuity, so I suggest you see your family physician to determine the reason your sense of smell is not as sharp as it once was.

Taste Has Its Own Quirks

Like the sense of smell, our sense of taste is essential for survival. Just as we are able to "smell danger" by our ability to detect smoke and gas leaks and spoiled food, we have built-in mechanisms to taste potentially harmful substances as well. The mechanisms by which we develop food preferences include physiological pathways as well as extensive social conditioning. When we say we desire or even crave a food, it is the taste we think of, not the smell.

Cravings and Pregnancy

According to common folklore, women have odd cravings during pregnancy. For example, in typical sitcoms, pregnant women develop a sudden yearning for pickles, ice cream, or chocolate cake. As these stories go, husbands are expected to run off to the store to get the food that will satisfy his wife's craving because pregnancy is a special time, after all, and a woman should have whatever she wants.

When food cravings are measured, however, no increase in cravings during pregnancy exists. The number of cravings women experience tends to remain stable before, during, and after pregnancy. The difference does come down to women's special status during pregnancy, which makes them more likely to indulge in the craved food.

Many women tend to develop aversions to certain foods during pregnancy, which is a result of a mechanism that protects the fetus from potential fetal toxins. For example, some pregnant women develop aversions to coffee, which has a bitter taste, and to certain meats. In nature, many toxic substances have a bitter taste, which is one way we protect ourselves from poison. So, while coffee is not a toxic substance, it temporarily triggers an aversive response because of the built-in protective mechanism.

It is essential that we have the ability to develop food aversions. If we didn't, we would not learn which substances are potentially harmful and we would repeat food mistakes. In animal studies, we know that if rats fed a poisonous substance become ill, they then avoid that substance again because they have learned a particular taste that alerts them to danger. If they were unable to develop an aversion, the rat species would have died out long ago. The same is true for humans.

Once you develop an aversion, it may become permanently learned. Just as I developed an aversion to curry, perhaps you developed an aversion to a food that made you ill. It isn't logical that the thought of pizza or tuna salad makes you ill. But if eating those foods resulted in food poisoning, then the aversion is learned and it is very difficult, if not impossible, to overcome. When college students were surveyed about food aversions, researchers found that permanent aversions were likely to develop to foods that were unfamiliar or less preferred foods in the first place. In other words, if pizza is one of your favorite foods, you are more likely to overcome an aversion that developed after a single incident of food poisoning. Likewise, if a woman was a dedicated coffee drinker prior to becoming pregnant, she is more likely to start drinking coffee again once she gives birth and the aversion is no longer present.

Maybe Your Children Really Were Born Picky Eaters

While we cannot explain all likes and dislikes that appear among babies and young children, some evidence exists that the food a pregnant woman eats influences the fetus. For example, if the mother eats garlic, it becomes part of the amniotic fluid and the newborn will be oriented toward the odor of garlic. One study demonstrated that when women consumed carrot juice while pregnant and/or while nursing, the infants were more accepting of carrot-flavored cereal, even when they had been weaned from breast milk. The exposure to the taste and odor of carrot juice from either the amniotic fluid or the breast milk was sufficient to influence later acceptance and enjoyment of the food. If we think in global terms, we can see that cultural influences may start even before we are welcomed into the world.

Can You Taste This Chemical?

Taste sensitivity may be correlated to a built-in ability to taste particular chemicals. For example, the ability to detect the taste quinine and a chemical called *6-n-propylthiouracil*, or PROP (a bitter tasting chemical used in chemosensory testing), in foods was related to liking or disliking certain foods. In a study using college-age subjects, both males and females who were sensitive to the taste of quinine and PROP showed a preference for mild-tasting foods. The ability to detect quinine is associated with disliking spinach. Heavy smoking was associated with insensitivity to PROP, as was the presence of duodenal ulcer. In some women, sensitivity to quinine and PROP fluctuates with the menstrual cycle, just as the smell acuity changes throughout the cycle.

The ability to detect the bitter tasting chemical phenylthiocarbamide (PTC) is a genetically transmitted ability. Sensitivity to PTC may help explain why some individuals like certain kinds of vegetables and others do not. In simple terms, if you are a PTC taster, then you are unlikely to prefer bitter tasting vegetables such as watercress or turnips. Research suggests a significant variation in the way food tastes among individuals, so if you crinkle your nose at a turnip, it may be because you have an innate ability to detect the bitter taste. Or, put another way, the bitter taste of certain foods may be perceived as more or less bitter depending on your sensitivity to PTC. Other substances, such as caffeine and saccharine taste more bitter to the PTC tasters than to those who are not sensitive to the chemical. Variations in the ability to perceive different tastes in foods may eventually explain some of the broad differences in food preferences.

Changing Perceptions

The perception of a particular taste may change based on many factors, including temperature. A study conducted at the Yale School of Medicine found that changing the temperature of the tongue results in changes in flavor perceptions. For example, warming the front of the tongue induces a sensation of sweetness; cooling the same area induces a salty or sour taste. If we cool the back of the tongue, we induce a sour or bitter taste sensation. Researchers concluded that these are false tastes, and the way this affects the flavor of foods remains unknown. However, the study suggests that our perceptions of food may vary based on temperature.

Context is Critical For Smell and Taste

In general, we are conditioned to prefer food that smells, tastes, and looks a certain way. We will make exceptions in certain circumstances, such as drinking green beer on St. Patrick's Day or adding blue food coloring to cake batter or frosting even though no food exists of that color. These foods are novelties—perhaps our child longs to eat some blue birthday cake. While most of us can adjust to occasional food flukes, for the most part we like our foods to look "normal."

Elderly individuals who are given pureed carrots may not be able to identify the vegetable because it doesn't look the way it's supposed to, so therefore the smell and taste are not perceived as related to carrots. Most of us reject the idea of putting a meal of salmon, asparagus, and pasta, for example, into a blender to make a "dinner shake." Yet, the nutritional value is the same regardless of how the food is presented. Likewise, if we take a bite of turkey that is shaped to look like broccoli and dyed green, too, the sensation we perceive will likely not be broccoli, but we may not recognize it as turkey either. We expect the movie theater to smell like popcorn. If it smells like fish, we're likely to leave.

The importance of context is well illustrated in Mark Twain's short story "The Invalid's Story." When a hobo hops aboard a train, he finds himself in a car with a large box that is giving off a terrible stench. It's dark in the car, and he can't see the box, but he is certain that a rotting body in a coffin is responsible for the sickening odor. When he can no longer stand to be in the car with the body and the smell, he jumps off the train and into a snowbank. The poor guy then develops pneumonia, and when he's found, he's taken to a hospital. Unfortunately, he isn't expected to live. However, for his last meal he's served some cheese that came from the crate he identified as "rotting flesh." Had he recognized the odor, he might have happily had lunch in the boxcar rather than allowing a perceived stench to lead to his demise.

We're on a Threshold of Knowledge

Scientific understanding of smell and taste is relatively recent, but on an instinctive level, human societies have always incorporated odors into their cultural life. As we discover more about the way olfaction works, we also gain insight into the ways it influences behavior, from choosing dessert to falling asleep.

The next time you find yourself thinking about a particular food, or lost in a memory from the past, or even wondering about ways to improve communication in your family, consider the fragrances and foods that surround you. Subtle shifts in your mood and the atmosphere around you could be triggered by an odor molecule that made its way to the limbic brain, the seat of your emotional life.

Chapter Three
You Are What You Munch

"Americans, like most of the Western world, love to snack. Coffee breaks and coffee parties, the easy access of the corner store for candy, soft drinks, and chewing gum, or the fast-food outlet with ethnic specialties such as tacos or pizza as well as hamburgers, hot dogs, ice cream, and french fries, all seem necessary to keep the American fueled. More and more, the pattern of three meals a day is blurring into a day-long fest of nibbling or "grazing" from breakfast to the late-evening show on television."

—Thelma Barer-Stein

When we released the results of our "snack food" study in 1999, we expected a degree of media attention, but we didn't necessarily think that the public would show more interest in the "potato chip" personality than they did in aromas that promoted sexual arousal. When reporters and columnists heard that a whiff of pumpkin pie had greater power to sexually arouse men (as measured by penile blood flow) than the most expensive perfume, they wrote *hundreds* of columns about it. Even now, several years later, I am still invited to participate in radio and television shows to discuss the link between odors and romance. But after we went public with the snack food study results, Americans showed their true preferences—they are more interested in food than in sex! To date, the snack food study has generated the most attention, with the ice cream flavor preference study following close behind.

Reporters invariably ask why we would choose snack foods to explore in the first place. The answer lies in the larger issue of personality and food and why food preferences offer a window to the unconscious mind. We started with the premise that a desire for a particular food is not a random event. At one time or another, you thought about a food and probably decided you wanted it. You might daydream about what you'll have for lunch, and if you begin to think about cashew chicken or a cheeseburger or turkey and swiss on an onion roll, the specific food soon becomes all you can think about until you satisfy the desire.

Sometimes, certain foods capture our attention to the point of distraction. Our food choices, like the clothing we buy, or the cars we drive, or the significant life choices, such as the mates we select, provide insight into our personality and character structure. Through our food preferences, we reveal inner thoughts, feelings, wishes, and desires. This is what is meant when we say that food preferences provide the window to the unconscious.

Personality Testing Isn't New

Personality testing has been around since the days of Sigmund Freud, and the early measurement tools that still exist today are *projective* tests, which means that an individual responds to questions or material by "projecting" his or her perceptions and thoughts onto the presented material. There are no right or wrong answers in this type of test, but responses are believed to reveal personality characteristics. Projective personality testing was once widely used to diagnose psychiatric disorders. Currently, however, psychiatric illnesses are primarily diagnosed by documenting objective signs of disease, but a variety of projective

tests are still used, too. You've probably heard of the Rorschach test, sometimes called the "inkblot" test, in which we present inkblot patterns and ask patients to report what they perceive in the patterns. Using a standardized scoring technique we tabulate the responses, which provide clues to thought patterns, perceptions, motivations, and so forth. The Thematic Apperception Test (TAT) is another projective test. It uses pictures and elicits a narrative or a "story" from patients. The story the patient creates—"projects"—is analyzed for clues into conflicts, attitudes, patterns, and perceptions.

These projective psychological tests are based on the assumption that personality characteristics can influence sensory experiences. If I show you a photograph of a dense forest, you will form an impression of this picture based on how you interpret what you see as well as how you *feel* about what you see. You might interpret the photograph as a serene depiction of the natural world and feel a sense of longing to go camping in the woods; or, you may interpret the forest as a lonely place where frightening creatures live and you dislike the photo and everything it represents. The only landscape you care to look at is one filled with skyscrapers. You have brought your personality to a sensory event, and by asking you to respond to various stimuli, clinicians and researchers are able to categorize your personality traits.

Projective testing has generally been based on visual clues, but we can obtain similar results using other sensory systems, including touch, for example, but also using smell and taste. The sense of smell is particularly relevant because of the established link between olfaction and the limbic system—the connection between odors and emotions. Remember that an odor can influence your emotions, even when you cannot consciously recognize the smell. Potentially, projective testing based on taste is equally useful because, as explained in chapter two, 90 percent of what we perceive as taste is actually smell.

I believe that perceptions of the taste and smell of food are a more appropriate measure of emotional and personality characteristics than a visual interpretation of inkblots. Looked at logically, why would the ability to distinguish a bat from a butterfly on a Rorschach inkblot card reveal underlying personality characteristics? The foods we prefer, including all the complex factors that guide our choices, from prenatal influences to our cultural conditioning, provide greater insight into our basic personality structure and emotional life than choosing between a bat and a butterfly when presented with an ambiguous picture. Smell- and odor-preference measurement tools remain in the category of projective testing in that we bring our unique history to our choices and perceptions, but our food preference studies have shown clear delineation between personality types. In other words, the results of our studies tend to correlate with other personality testing and with results of our group of food preference and personality studies.

Explaining Food "Hedonics"

You may know individuals you think of as hedonists—pleasure seekers. In our society, calling a person a hedonist is not necessarily a compliment because we tend to be suspicious of anyone that has too much fun. We're not supposed to eat candy bars and ruin our appetite for green beans at dinner, but if our weak character drives us to it, we should feel guilty about it. A food's hedonic value is defined and measured by the degree of pleasure with which it is received or viewed, and it is more than a simple matter of taste.

The reasons a particular food is considered hedonically positive may include past conditioning, perceived nutritional value, cravings, and olfactory-evoked nostalgia, along with the inherent taste and smell properties. Some factors will overpower any inherent features of the food. If you are conditioned to believe that grilled snake meat is unacceptable, the inherent flavor of the meat will not change your decision. Likewise, if you have become ill after eating a particular food, then you may have a permanent aversion to it. This happened to me decades ago with curried chicken, and to this day, I am unable to eat any dish seasoned with curry.

A particular food may bring pleasure to the consumer because it carries with it an image of health and vitality. For example, many people assign high hedonic value to certain vegetables and fruits because they perceive them as promoting health. Nowadays, a bottle containing a pint or two of water—with a price tag that may be higher than a gallon of gas—may have hedonic value because it is perceived as pure and natural. Consumers may feel good about themselves when

they drink it. Based on additional factors, "good for you" foods may or may not be placed high on the hedonic value scale. You may enjoy butter, for example, but you have been told that because it is a saturated fat, you should avoid it as part of a total dietary and lifestyle plan to prevent cardiovascular disease. Some people may lose their desire for butter because it has become a "tainted" food and, therefore, its hedonic value drops. Others among us think butter just as wonderful and tasty as we always did, even as we avoid using it on our morning toast.

The nutritional value of food is a *cognitive* issue, so a perception that foods such as chicken, salmon, whole wheat bread, or carrots are positive is an intellectual decision. Beyond that, a preference for one brand of bread over another or enjoying carrots that are cut into a particular shape represents decisions based on emotional associations. The aura surrounding many foods is defined and imprinted by advertising. We bring many influences to the supermarket and our preconceived evaluations about one brand over another cannot be overestimated.

At first glance, we may assume the actual smell, taste, and texture of food have the greatest influence on our food choices. Generally speaking, humans prefer sweet or salty tastes and avoid bitter or sour ones. But consider the global phenomenon of coffee. Throughout the world, so much coffee is consumed that it is the primary export crop of many countries, and where once we contended with competing *brands*, today we have competing *flavors*. We routinely talk about coffee drink concoctions our grandparents never heard of, and they probably wonder what happened to the twenty-five cent cup of coffee served in white cup and saucer. Despite its bitter taste, we savor coffee and flavor desserts—even ice cream—with it. Entire cookbooks are devoted entirely to recipes for coffee drinks.

Rite of Passage Foods

Coffee once was a right of passage in that it is considered an adult food, and enjoying it meant that one had reached the age to acquire a taste for what is essentially a bitter substance. Of course, because of caffeine, coffee has an effect on the brain and tends to stimulate an awake and alert state, which is why we determined that young children shouldn't have it. At one time, drinking one's coffee black had a "macho" connotation, similar to, "I drink my whiskey straight

and eat my one pound steak rare." Adding cream and sugar was considered a more "feminine" and genteel way to drink coffee. However, this is no longer the case. The advent of frothy coffee drinks, with their whipped cream or milk and sugar and other flavorings, has changed that. Today's coffee drinks are more like infant formula than a macho rite of passage.

Chili peppers can be agonizing to eat, yet they enjoy immense popularity, and for some, they are a rite of passage food. Hot chili peppers can even cause damage to areas of the tongue called *fungiform papillae*, small protrusions on the tongue that contain taste buds. But, as much as they burn the mouth, for young men in Latin American culture, the ability to tolerate the unpleasant sensation of chili peppers is the equivalent of the bar mitzvah, the rite of passage ritual for young Jewish males. As you can see, inherent sensory properties alone do not account for the differences we see in the perceived pleasure derived from food.

We also cannot ignore the "Pavlovian" response to food. Caffeine wakes us up, alcohol removes our social inhibitions, and a candy bar is quick energy. We can remove the caffeine and the sugar and we may still respond the same way to the idea that we are consuming a stimulus or an "energizer" food. Alcohol-free beer and wine have a market because individuals may want the ambience associated with alcohol, but without the side effects associated with it—namely, the risk of getting drunk.

Some emotional responses to food are not conditioned. If you have pumpkin pie for dessert and then enjoy a romantic encounter with your lover, you may rate pumpkin pie high on the hedonic scale. The reverse is also true. Many males associate chipped beef dishes with some military experience. Perhaps they ate their chipped beef lunch and then were ordered to take a ten-mile hike. Through no fault of its own, so to speak, the chipped beef has developed a bad reputation and women are unlikely to seduce their lovers using chipped beef as their lure.

The nostalgic association with food is so strong that I devoted an entire chapter to it. In brief, nostalgia is an idealized memory of the past, and it includes idealized sensory experiences as well. *Olfactory-evoked recall* is a universal phenomenon, and the term describes the ability of an odor to induce a memory from the past. Foods that are associated with pleasant times and events of the past tend

to rate high on a hedonic scale. In some cases, these odors tend to be personal and are relevant only to individuals. A mother's perfume and the odor of a particular room in one's childhood home are personal memories. The odor of roasting turkey or the pine scent of a Christmas tree or scented green candles tend to have a wider ability to evoke a nostalgic response because the fragrances are associated with cultural holidays.

Other influences on food hedonics include our place of origin and to some extent our ethnic background. In the previous chapter, I mentioned that olfactory ability tends to fall into cluster groups, and preferences tend to be the same. Age also influences our ability to smell, and it also affects the foods we choose because we do not enjoy foods we are unable to taste. In some cases, an elderly person may enjoy heavily spiced foods where once he or she preferred bland dishes. This does not mean that the individual's personality has changed, but it does indicate a loss of olfactory acuity.

Most of us have experienced food cravings, which are strong urges for specific foods or categories of foods. Cravings for sweets and salty items are among the most common cravings. In some cases, a craving is an emotional response to an event. "I'm sad, only chocolate can cheer me up," or, "I'm exhausted, but I'm sure that a double-iced cappuccino will restore me."

Some food cravings may result from internal nutritional demands, neuroendocrine imbalances, or certain psychological factors. If you are deficient in salt, you body may crave salt and you feel hungry for salty foods. Hypoglycemic individuals may crave sugar. Of course, you may crave sugar when you are angry or upset. Sugar is a component of many of the so-called "comfort foods," and chocolate cravings are seen in women who have premenstrual sadness or lethargy (dysphoria). Sometimes, when you are under stress and feel anxious, eating is one way you stabilize your emotional state. Sniffing the odors of certain foods—and inhaling non-food odors, too—may improve your emotional state, even without eating.

Since eating or smelling food may reduce psychological tension, craving a food may then indicate an underlying psychological conflict, and the particular food craved may tell us quite a bit about inherent personality structure. Taken as a whole, long-standing food preferences may form the basis of a projective personality test that will one day augment or replace the traditional projective tests in use today. Our snack food study added to my belief that your food preferences reveal considerable information about your personality.

The Snack Food Personality

Before reading further into this chapter, take the following quiz:

Which do you prefer? Choose one.

Potato chips
Tortilla chips
Snack crackers
Pretzels
Cheese curls
Nuts
Popcorn
Meat Snacks

These were the same items from which our study participants chose their preference. Our snack food data was gathered from two groups of participants: the first group included eight hundred men and women, and the second group included a total of 18,613 volunteers. Before we asked any questions about snack food preferences, the participants underwent a series of psychological tests, including the MMPI (Minnesota Multiphasic Personality Inventory-II), the Millon Clinical Multiaxial Inventory-II, the Beck Depression Inventory, and the Zung Depression Scale. These personality tests and the screening tests for depression are standardized tests, which provide accepted personality groups and definitions, against which we can correlate our results. We used the depression screening tests because the presence of symptoms of depression often correlates with sensory losses and/or preferences for certain kinds of foods. (Note: Unless otherwise

noted, the personality groups and types that correlated in the other quizzes that appear in this book are based on responses and findings of the same eight hundred individuals in our first snack food study.)

Once the personality testing was complete, our volunteers were questioned about their snack food preference and the hedonic—pleasure—value they assigned to these foods. We also queried spouses and mates of our volunteers about their snack food preferences. Eight different snack foods were included in the forced-choice questions. Forced choice simply means a multiple-choice format in which only one answer was allowed. The snack foods used in the study were *potato chips*, *tortilla chips*, *pretzels*, *snack crackers*, *cheese curls*, *nuts*, *popcorn*, and *meat snacks*. We then analyzed the data and came up with what has popularly been called the "potato chip personality."

1. If **potato chips** are your preferred snack food, then you are probably an ambitious and successful person, and a high achiever. You enjoy the rewards of success both at work and at home. Not a selfish sort, you enjoy the successes of your spouse and children, too, and you seek nothing less than the best from them. You also tend to be impatient with less than the best, and you are easily frustrated by life's little blips—traffic jams make you crazy, and you consider waiting in line a huge imposition.

   Note: If you want to do business with a potato chip lover, or you are in a competitive situation with this personality type, be prepared. Potato chip lovers are always worthy and prepared adversaries, and you may lose if you don't bring your best to the situation.

2. If **tortilla chips** are your preferred snack food, then you are probably a perfectionist, with high expectations for yourself. If it's less than perfect, you'll redo it, and the phrase "let it go" is not one you often use. Not satisfied with a mere A, you want an A+. These individuals are not selfish about their concerns, so if you want a partner to help you fight injustice, then look to the people with their hands in a bowl of tortilla chips.

Invite them for the weekend, too, because they are likely to be good houseguests. Punctual and sticklers about time and schedules, the tortilla chip lover is not tolerant of those who show up late for appointments. Generally, these individuals are socially and personally conservative and staid. A male tortilla chip lover can slip into a tux or feel just as comfortable in an old tee-shirt, but don't look for a tortilla chip loving woman to dress provocatively—she is rather sexually restrained.

Note: Because these men and women are responsible types, they will always make sure the car is running and the insurance premiums are paid—and if you are choosing the person to be marooned with on a desert island, then look for a tortilla chip lover. They're so responsible, you'll all survive.

3. If a bag of **pretzels** suit you, then you are a lively sort of person, who loves novelty and are easily bored with the same old routine. You look for new challenges at work and at home, and you can spend hours mulling over abstract concepts while you munch on your pretzels—too bad you forgot about dinner. You are probably flirtatious and like to dress in a provocative manner, but you quickly tire of a clothing trend and are off to find the latest style. You may be a collector, too, with a herd of "beanie babies." Now you're looking for the next fad. Pretzel lovers are intuitive and make decisions based more on emotions than on logic, and they may be overly trusting in romantic relationships. While they may be a wonderful party guest, and great fun to be with, they are vulnerable, too.

   Note: Pretzel lovers have a tendency to move on to new projects before they finish the old ones, and they may overcommit to work projects and deadlines—they may take on more family chores than they can handle, too.

4. If you always have your hands in a box of **snack crackers** then you're probably thinking out a problem using a rational logical approach. In fact, you think a lot—some people would call you contemplative. You tend to be

shy, and avoid arguments because you do not like to hurt another person's feelings. Chances are you have many projects going at the same time, and they are all competing for your attention. It's no surprise that you feel pulled in many directions because you have so many interests. Snack cracker lovers tend to be loners who prefer private time, so you probably value and protect those times that you can relax alone without responsibilities and interruptions.

Note: Those who prefer snack crackers may easily find themselves involved in an on-line romance.

5. If you regularly stain your fingers with **cheese curls**, then you are a conscientious, principled person, who is always proper and expects others to be, too. You tend to occupy the moral high ground with your colleagues and family. With your finely tuned sense of right and wrong, you treat everyone in the same just and fair manner. Most people would say you have great integrity. You may appear rigid to others, but in reality you're just conscientious and know enough to plan ahead. In your house, the spare batteries and the Band-Aids are right where they belong—just like everything on your desk.

   Note: If you're dealing with a cheese curl lover, be sure to put everything back where it belongs—they love order. If you're in someone's home, and you think you could eat off the floor, then you're probably visiting with a cheese curl lover.

6. Those who reach for the jar of **nuts** tend to be easygoing, empathic, and understanding. Nut lovers can be counted on to stay clam, even in the midst of upheaval, so even a screaming spouse or a disapproving boss won't ruffle these individuals. Because they have an "even keel" nature, they are good in jobs that involve dealing with the public. Nut lovers may not be outstanding leaders, but their overall demeanor and willingness to lend a hand contribute to a peaceful home and an effective office.

7. The **popcorn** people know how to take charge of a situation, and these individuals are usually quick to take on extra work or pick up the slack if the need arises at work, at home, or in social situations. While these men and women have great self-confidence, they are rather modest and humble, and no one would ever call them showoffs. Popcorn lovers may hide their success so well that they may appear to be a "poor relation," while they squirrel away their treasures. If you inherit money from a relative you thought was flat broke, he or she was most likely a popcorn muncher.

8. If you munch on **meat snacks**, then you probably prefer to be with other people while you indulge. Meat snack lovers are at their best in the company of others because they are so gregarious—and sometimes generous to a fault. If you want a true friend, pick the meat snack lover. These are trustworthy people and always loyal. They will go all out for their friends and family, even to the point of making extraordinary sacrifices.

   Note: These men and women are so overly trusting that they are predisposed to emotional turmoil. For a meat snack lover, breaking up is particularly hard to do. And these individuals must be careful to avoid those messy rebound romances.

Mix and Match

You may have come down clearly in one of the above categories, but of course that does not mean that you cannot see some traits in the other "snack categories." We all have considerable overlap in personality characteristics, although the loner usually is not mistaken for the "life of the party." Regardless of the personality system we use to classify individuals, we always see that most people are combinations of traits, with one dominant type emerging.

Although the issue of sexual arousal and the link between foods and sexuality are discussed later in this book, the snack food results can be mixed and matched to link our snack food personalities with romantic personality types. In other words, we can speculate about who your best romantic match might be.

Here's what we came up with:

1. If you're an ambitious **potato chip** lover, you would be most compatible with a person who also prefers potato chips and is a high-achiever, too. As an alternative, an always-on-the-go pretzel lover might be a good match.

2. You say you prefer **tortilla chips**? Then you will probably be most compatible with a tortilla chip lover—you're both such perfectionists and are so responsible, anything less might be too hard for you to handle.

3. The **pretzel** lovers would be happiest with those who prefer potato chips, pretzels, or cheese curls. Sometimes you need a detail person and someone who follows the rules, and a cheese curl lover may be just right.

4. If **snack crackers** are your choice, you may need someone who brings you out of your shell. Stick with the flirtatious, lively sort who prefer pretzels.

5. When you curl up with your bag of **cheese curls**, your companion should be someone who's munching on potato chips because he or she has taken care of all the responsibilities at hand and now it's time to relax. Or, you could go for the tortilla chip type and talk about improving the world as you munch.

6. If you prefer **meat snacks**, you would be most compatible with another meat snack lover who can keep up with your need for company and is as loyal as you are, or you may enjoy the competitive spirit of one whose hand is in a bag of potato chips.

Doing What You Love

Choosing a life partner is one of the most critical choices we will ever make, and a very close second is our career choice. School and career counselors, as well as employers, often use personality testing in their attempts to find a good match between individuals and jobs. Personality testing as a tool to assist in job placement and career counseling came into wide use in the mid-twentieth century, which coincided with a period in which career choices were "democratized" to a great extent. Men and women in our society have greater freedom to choose careers than any other society ever has experienced. For most adults today, a career means more than a paycheck—we view our jobs and careers as an important path to self-fulfillment.

In addition to offering great latitude in choosing careers, our culture tends to define us based on our careers. We often use language that identifies us with the work we do. We don't tell others that we "work as an accountant" or "hold a job wiring houses." Instead, we say, "I am an accountant," or, "I am an electrician," as if our career gives us our identity, just as gender, religion, and ethnic background help define us.

As we link food preferences with personality types, I am confident we will see questions about food and odor preferences included in batteries of vocational testing. Our snack food study showed that indeed a correlation exists between what we munch and what we do. This phase of the snack food study involved 18,613 adults from Illinois, Florida, North Carolina, and Washington, D.C., with thirty-five occupations represented (a minimum of five hundred people were in each occupational group, with the exception of race car drivers, which had thirty-three representatives in our study). When we look closely at the results, we see:

- Men and women who are lawyers, tennis pros, police officers, or CEOs tend to reach for the potato chip bowl more than any other snack.
- Gathering around the pretzels we find firefighters, journalists, flight attendants, veterinarians, and pediatricians.

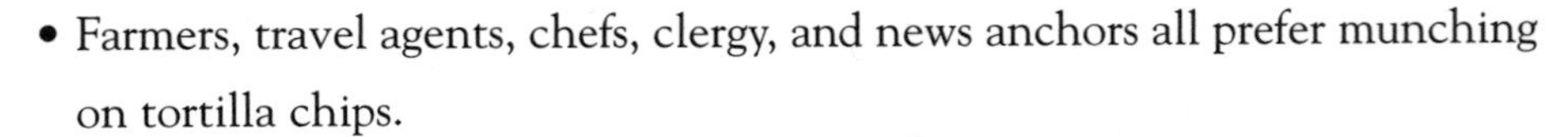

- Farmers, travel agents, chefs, clergy, and news anchors all prefer munching on tortilla chips.

- If you like cheese curls best, you may be a real estate agent, a psychiatrist, or a producer.
- The smell of popcorn at the movies has the strongest pull on artists, teachers, truck drivers, nurses, judges, and neurosurgeons.
- If we want to win the hearts of cardiologists, politicians, sanitation workers, plumbers, and architects, then we'll pass them the bowl of nuts.
- Reach for the box of snack crackers and you may be a stockbroker or a race car driver.
- Those who prefer meat snacks are likely to be bartenders or dentists.

I Am...Therefore I Like...

When we look at the overall personality characteristics we identified with the snack food groups, the career correlation makes sense. For example, according to our study, potato chip lovers are driven and success-oriented, which are traits we certainly associate with attorneys and CEOs, and, of course, competitive athletes like tennis pros. One could certainly argue that police officers must be driven in order to do a good job at one of society's most difficult jobs. We want our chefs and travel agents to be perfectionists and it isn't surprising that news anchors share that trait. Those perfectionists reach for tortilla chips. Farmers and clergy don't have much "margin for error" either, and we find them gathering around the tortilla chip bowl, too.

Some personality traits may not appear to match at first glance, but you may find that the results are compatible with your personal experience. For example, pretzel lovers tend to be fun-loving and life-of-the-party types, which may not match your stereotype of a journalist. However, individuals who have worked in newsrooms may heartily disagree. The stereotype certainly affirms my social experience with firefighters, veterinarians, and pediatricians. Perhaps firefighters, for example, need to be fun-loving in order to cope with the long periods of relative calm in the fire station.

I can't say I ever imagined politicians favoring cashews or peanuts, but in actuality, a successful politician must be able to react competently in emergency situations, which is certainly true for cardiologists and plumbers alike.

Those partial to popcorn tend to be self-confident, a trait that we want to see in our neurosurgeons and nurses. Then too, teachers or artists must have great faith in themselves because they tend to come up against many personal challenges and considerable rejection in order to succeed. We tend to think of race-car drivers and stockbrockers as risk takers, but in order to succeed, these individuals must also be thoughtful, careful people, which correlates with the profile of snack cracker lovers.

Meat snack lovers share the ability to be a true friend, which fits the stereotype of a bartender, who can cope with people under stress. A trip to the dentist is one of the most stressful events, and dentists generally know their patients are afraid and need reassurance. And while real estate agents, producers, and psychiatrists seem like professions with little in common, they do share the need for a high degree of integrity. So, when we look at the personality traits associated with particular professions, a logical link exists between these traits and snack food favorites.

Just One Category

At the present time, we cannot make specific recommendations about career choices based on the snack food you prefer, but as you can see, early research reveals patterns on which we can build. The Smell & Taste Treatment and Research Foundation continues to look at a variety of food preferences, and our results suggest that the foods we enjoy can tell us much about underlying personality structures. This snack food study represents just one category of foods. We have studied ice cream and fruit flavor preferences, too, which are discussed in the following chapters.

Chapter Four

Not So Plain Vanilla: The Ice Cream Personality

"We dare not trust our wit for making our house pleasant to our friend, so we buy ice cream."

—Ralph Waldo Emerson

"Dolley Madison used ice cream to make her famous White House dinner parties special; a guest enthusiastically described one such occasion when "an Air of Expectancy" which Mrs. Madison had propagated among those present was gratified by the sight, in the centre of a lavishly set table and high on a silver platter, of 'a large, shining dome of Pink Ice Cream.'"

—Margaret Visser

Ice cream stands out as one of the major products resulting from the pursuit of ice, which was motivated by the quest for cool drinks to refresh even in the hottest weather. The Chinese had underground ice houses at least as early as 1100 B.C., and ice and snow hauled from the Alps were prized by the rich and powerful in early Mediterranean empires. In nineteenth-century Peru, Indians chopped ice blocks from the glacier formations in the Andes and hauled them into Lima to make iced drinks and ice cream.

In the mid-nineteenth century, an American woman named Nancy Johnson invented an ice cream maker using salt and paddles. Johnson's invention started the "democratization" of ice cream, but refrigeration made ice cream almost universally available. Refrigeration changed the world in many ways, not the least of which was its ability to allow just about everyone to enjoy cold drinks and frozen desserts, the most popular of which is ice cream in all its forms. High status ice cream is essentially a function of cost because, like fast food, ice cream is enjoyed by nearly everyone in the culture.

Ice cream stands unique among foods in that we consume it as a prized dessert or as a quick snack, and for many people it seems like a treat no matter how often we have it. Part of the pleasure of eating ice cream is making decisions about what flavor to choose. Vanilla has a plain image—solid and basic, but not too exciting. With all its variations, chocolate hangs on to a bit of an exotic image, and some people are just die-hard fruit lovers and almost always return to strawberry.

Our foundation conducted research on personality and ice cream flavors using flavors provided by Dryer's and Edy's Grand Ice Cream, Inc. Most children love ice cream, but so do adults. Most of us never outgrow our desire for an ice cream cone or a sundae with whipped cream. As often as many of us consume it, it never loses its image as a special treat. And ordering an ice cream cone in a mall or in an ice cream parlor always reveals something about us. We may be the adventurous type and try new flavors, or we may resist change and go back to those we consider tried and true—they will never let us down. Because of the range of choice, ice cream is one type of food that lends itself to personality testing.

Initial assumptions about ice cream flavors and personality type follow along stereotypical lines. Vanilla is the quiet, steady flavor, so wouldn't those whose first ice cream love is vanilla have quiet and steady personalities, too? And the double chocolate chunk types would probably still be kids at heart. As with the

snack food study, most people see this project as a lighthearted look at food passions rather than a serious look at personality. However, we found the same kind of valid correlation between favorite ice cream flavors and results of standardized personality tests. We also were in for a few surprises when we looked at the ice cream personality.

The Ice Cream Personality

Forty women and twenty men, ranging from age twenty to sixty-nine (the average age was forty-five) participated in our study, which involved completing four standardized tests, basically the same tests used in our snack food study: the Minnesota Multiphasic Personality Inventory-III, the Millon Clinical Multiaxial Inventory-II, the Beck Depression Inventory, and the Zung Depression Scale. The quiz below is identical to the one our participants took.

Which one of these six flavors is your favorite:

vanilla
double chocolate chunk
strawberries and cream
banana cream pie
chocolate chip
butter pecan

We also asked if they prefer one or two scoops, and if they prefer ice cream in a cup or a cone, and they expressed a preference between sugar and plain cones. Decisions, decisions. Still, these are the choices we make when we stand in line and look into large "vats" of ice cream, and as we all know, it can be difficult to choose from the available flavors, perhaps even several dozen nowadays.

We found that all sixty individuals liked ice cream, and in addition, distinct personality types emerged based on ice cream preference.

1. The **vanilla** personality does not match its plain image. The vanilla lover is a colorful person, a gregarious risk taker with a hectic schedule—perhaps

even overcommitted. These individuals may pack their calendars because they tend to be impulsive and suggestible. They don't like to say no to a request or a chance to see friends. Vanilla lovers tend to set high goals and ideals, especially for themselves. They are romantic and expressive and enjoy close relationships. And as gregarious as they are, they prefer a close secure romantic relationship. The women vanilla lovers may enjoy indulging in a romantic novel or relaxing with their favorite soap opera.

2. Don't try to keep the **double chocolate chunk** lovers down, because they really are the life of the party, and in some ways fit the image of the grown-up with a kid's heart. These chocolate lovers like to be the center of attention, and because they are charming and lively they often are. Their flirtatious nature makes them easily seduced into romantic fantasy, and other people easily influence them. Despite their extroverted nature and dramatic persona, which would make them good actors, these individuals do not seek leadership, but usually trust and follow the lead of others. This makes them somewhat vulnerable in relationships, but they enjoy intimacy and romance. The double chocolate chunk lover relies on intuition and plays "hunches" rather than relying on logic. These individuals represent the prototype of their sex: the macho man and the very feminine woman are probably double chocolate chunk lovers.

3. If you consider yourself an introvert, and perhaps at times find life a bit overwhelming, you may prefer **strawberries and cream**. These individuals are emotionally robust despite their shy demeanor, and they have high standards for themselves, which is why they can seem cranky and irritable. Unfortunately, they are pessimistic personalities who frequently feel guilty. Still, if you need a curmudgeon around—a newspaper columnist or a bureaucrat—then call on the strawberries and cream lover.

4. We all enjoy being around those whose favorite ice cream is **banana cream pie.** Easygoing, well-adjusted, good listeners—of course the rest of us enjoy

them so much. If you want the perfect mate, choose a banana cream pie lover, and if you notice your toddler enthusiastically eating that flavor, you may have lucked out.

5. If you chose **chocolate chip**, then you are best described as a visionary who goes by the motto: I came, I saw, I conquered. These are the competitors, the go-getters, and the types who can't stand losing. They are also charming and generous on their journey to the top, but they are not pleasant to be around when they suffer a defeat.

6. If you generally play by the rules, then you like the nutty flavor of **butter pecan**. These are detail individuals, who set high standards for themselves and others. They plan ahead and do not waste time as they take charge of their projects. However, they can be rigid and not particularly expressive. If you want to know about a butter pecan lover's feelings, be prepared to wait, because they may be afraid of hurting your feelings. The competitive component of the butter pecan personality makes them aggressive in athletics, but they are ethical and fair individuals, more likely to be critical of themselves than of others. Their efficient nature makes them good accountants, executive secretaries, or office managers.

Cups and Cones

When we interviewed the sixty study participants, we asked them if they ever ate ice cream straight from the carton, and every person denied ever doing that. I wonder though, if some of the individuals might have been reluctant to admit they pulled out a carton of ice cream from the freezer and skipped putting it in a bowl.

We did find that only chocolate chip lovers preferred eating their ice cream in a cup, and all the flavor-personality types preferred sugar cones to plain cones. We also found that those who favored vanilla and chocolate chip preferred a single scoop, while those whose favorite was strawberries and cream or butter pecan chose two scoops. The double chocolate chunk and the banana cream pie lovers were equally divided between one and two scoops.

The Ice Cream Romance "Horoscope"

Men and women interested in astrology, even in a casual way, are curious about romantic compatibility among the twelve signs of the zodiac. Most people find it amusing to read about their ideal mate, at least according to the "stars," even if they question the validity of astrology. Now that we can link personality types with food preferences, specifically, a food as ubiquitous as ice cream, we may be able to establish potential compatibility using clues such as one's favorite ice cream flavor.

When we matched the ice cream flavors with principles of romantic compatibility, we found the following:

1. If your favorite ice cream flavor is **vanilla**, then you like to stay busy achieving your goals. Never one to waste time, you would be most happy with another vanilla lover who is as romantic and expressive as you are.

2. If **double chocolate chunk** is your first choice, you may recognize the need for some stability, so you'll likely be most compatible with the stable and kind butter pecan type or if you're feeling adventurous the go-getter chocolate chocolate chip lover may motivate you to stay focused.

3. Those who prefer **strawberries and cream** may need someone to give them a sense of hope and optimism, so they would likely be happy with chocolate chip lovers who can match their high standards, but do so with a lighter touch.

4. If you love **banana cream pie**, then you are have many choices—you're likely to be compatible with all other flavor favorites. You are such a good listener and so easy to be with that the other types may seek your company, so you are never without a date.

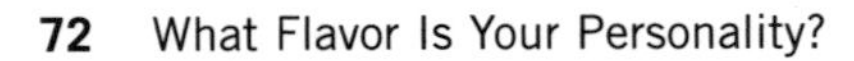

5. **Chocolate chip** lovers will most enjoy their ice cream in the company of either butter pecan, who will identify with their high standards, or with the double chocolate chunk lovers, who appreciate their charming nature.

6. **Butter pecan** lovers are most compatible with others whose favorite is butter pecan because you both set such high standards that you can admire each other's good taste. Besides, another butter pecan type won't be pestering you to express your feelings all the time.

Looking for Connections

As we delve more deeply into the link between personality and food likes and dislikes, we notice that sometimes our hypothesis is not just wrong, but the results turn out to be the opposite of our initial assumptions. For example, "vanilla" has a bland image, and erroneous as it turns out, we may believe that those who favor vanilla ice cream may have bland personalities. Double chocolate chunk has a more "daring" image, so we assume those who name it as their favorite ice cream flavor must be daring people. As it turns out, the opposite is true. If we want to meet a risktaker with big dreams and goals, we'll seek a "vanilla" person; while the double chocolate chunk personality is lively and charming, they tend not to be particularly daring.

The results of the ice cream flavor test tend to correlate with results of other food preference surveys, which show that when it comes to food, we eat from *who we are*, and just as important, *who we want to be*. If I'm a risk-taking, goal-setting vanilla ice cream lover, I do not need the daring flavors of ice cream because I already have those qualities. But if I don't take enough risks, and I need to develop that in myself, then I tend to choose the ice cream flavor with the more daring image.

Some of the links are not so clear, and we cannot explain why these results occurred. However, as you will see, the desire to fill an inner need or choose our foods based on what we want to become occurs too frequently in research to ignore.

Chapter Five

The Fruit in Your Life

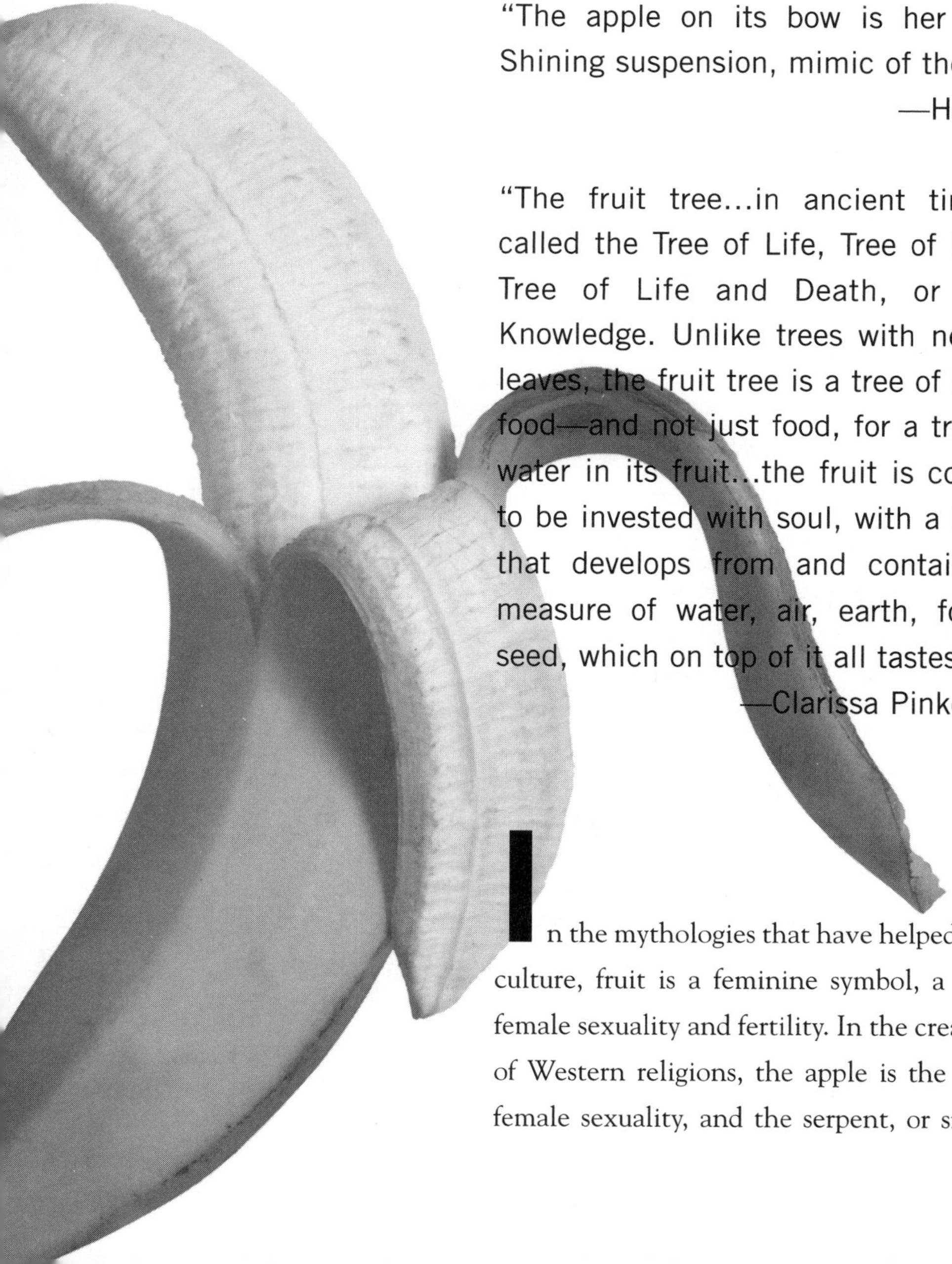

"The apple on its bow is her desire—
Shining suspension, mimic of the sun."

—Hart Crane

"The fruit tree...in ancient times was called the Tree of Life, Tree of Knowing, Tree of Life and Death, or Tree of Knowledge. Unlike trees with needles or leaves, the fruit tree is a tree of bountiful food—and not just food, for a tree stores water in its fruit...the fruit is considered to be invested with soul, with a life force that develops from and contains some measure of water, air, earth, food, and seed, which on top of it all tastes divine."

—Clarissa Pinkola Estés

In the mythologies that have helped shape our culture, fruit is a feminine symbol, a symbol of female sexuality and fertility. In the creation story of Western religions, the apple is the symbol of female sexuality, and the serpent, or snake, that helps lure Adam is the phallic symbol. In cultures influenced by Freud, the snake is associated with the phallus or the male, but in other non-Western cultures, the snake is symbol of feminine wisdom. Both tend to work in the myth, so take your choice.

In traditional folktales, flowering fruit trees are linked with fertility, and in the spirit of eating who we *want* to be, we can ingest feminine wisdom and creativity when we eat from a fruit tree. In a symbolic sense, the fruit trees offer the wisdom of intuition and instinct—qualities often associated with women. Peaches and apricots have been viewed as resembling female genitalia, while figs are considered representative of male sexuality, the testicles filled with the "seeds" of life. For centuries, the mystery of birth has been connected with fruit, and the womb is said to bear its fruit just as land bears its fruit in the form of crops. While it would be considered politically incorrect by modern standards, the word "barren" has been commonly used to describe both an infertile woman and land that does not produce crops.

In Chinese philosophy, the concept of yin and yang are loosely comparable to the masculine and feminine principles, or in modern terminology, the right-brain/left-brain analogy. Fruit is generally considered a yin classification, and is associated with the expansiveness and creativity of the right brain, or feminine principle in nature; hard, dense foods are classified as yang foods and linked with the left brain, or masculine principle in nature.

When we talk about fruit and personality, we include vegetables, because we are talking about the foods that are "fruits" of various plants, regardless of how modern culinary and nutrition sciences classify them. (Some common foods, such as tomatoes are popularly called vegetables, but are actually in botanical terms fruits because they produce their fruit from a blossom and contain seeds.) In the following food quiz, you will notice a variety of plant foods used for preference comparison, and they indicate personality characteristics among people who prefer certain kinds of fruit to other types of foods. In this study (which used the same eight hundred participants from the snack food study), as in the others, distinct personality characteristics clustered and matched with individual food choices.

The Fruit Personality Test

1. Which group of fruits do you prefer?
   a. Oranges, Bananas, and Grapes
   b. Eggplant, Corn, and Tomatoes

2. Of these pairs of fruits, which do you prefer more? (You must choose one of each pair)
   a. Applesauce or Fresh Apples
   b. Pineapple Chunks or Pineapple Glaze
   c. Creamed Corn or Corn on the Cob

3. Do you like (circle those foods you like):
   a. Bananas
   b. Broiled Fish
   c. Fruit
   d. Honey
   e. Tapioca
   f. Nuts
   g. Hot Curry

4. Do you like spicy pickles? Yes/No

5. Which do you prefer?
   a. Green Olives or Black Olives
   b. Pecans or Almonds
   c. Pickles or Cucumbers

6. Which do you prefer?
   a. Lemons or Oranges
   b. Potatoes or Yams
   c. Grapefruit or Tangerines

Fruit vs. Vegetables

In the first question, if you prefer the first group, the fruits (1a), this indicates that you are a strong-minded, ambitious, aggressive, dominant individual, who is a natural leader. If you favor the second group, foods we know as vegetables (1b), you tend to be an introspective, self-searching person who is sensitive to the needs of others. You tend not to be impulsive in your decision-making processes, but rather weigh all the alternatives in question before making your decision.

In the second question, if at least two of your choices are the first item in the pair (applesauce, pineapple chunks, or creamed corn), then you tend to be a passive, easygoing, agreeable sort, who tries to solve problems without raising a commotion. But if at least two of the above are the second choice (fresh apples, pineapple glaze, or corn on the cob), you tend to be an aggressive "go-getter" who will not take no for an answer. You work hard and play hard.

Optimist or Pessimist?

In the third question, we determined an overall outlook on life based on the types of foods chosen from the list. If you like five or more of the listed foods, then you are a natural optimist and view life through rose-colored glasses. You are a pleasant coworker and would make a good friend. But if five or more of your answers are no, you tend to be pessimistic. Before becoming involved in social interaction, you tend to be careful and you may even doubt the intentions of others. The fourth question measures optimism and pessimism, too. If you like spicy pickles, then you tend to be pessimistic. If your answer was no, you tend to be optimistic.

Do You Assert Yourself?

In question five, if two or more of your answers are the first choice (green olives, pecans, or pickles), you tend to be assertive in your relationships and an enthusiastic person in everything you do. Although anxious at times, you are a decisive and resilient person, and prone to *act* rather than *react* to dilemmas in your life. If two or more of your answers are the second choice (black olives, almonds, or cucumbers), you tend to take responsibility for your own actions. You are self-confident and a natural leader.

Introvert vs. Extrovert

In the sixth question, if two or more are the first choice (oranges, yams, or tangerines), you tend to be reserved, quiet, and contemplative, and are generally not an impulsive person. You tend towards introspection. If two or more are the second choice, you are likely an outgoing, gregarious person who enjoys a stable relationship. Your sense of humor would make you a good disc jockey, and because you are an extrovert, you would be a good used-car salesman or politician.

Chapter Six
Spices, Salt, and You

"Awake, O north wind; and come, thou south; blow upon my garden, that the spices thereof may flow out. Let my beloved come into his garden, and eat his pleasant fruits."
—Song of Solomon, 4:16

At one time, asking about favorite spices and engaging in a discussion of the personality types linked with specific spices would not have been particularly useful—flavorings or seasonings for food were unavailable except in places where they occurred as indigenous plants. However, one of the primary motivations for exploration and expansion of global horizons was the search for spices. As you remember from grade school, Marco Polo explored the Orient in search of spices, and Columbus went in search of the Indies to find a shorter route with which to bring home spices. At one time, cinnamon, curry, and ginger were as valuable as gold. When methods to preserve food were lacking, spices masked rancid tastes and helped make food more palatable. In a sense, spices represent the ultimate "hedonic" search and a by-product of the quest for new ways to season and enjoy our food in a shrinking planet—the proverbial "global village."

Today, we can find seasonings such as cilantro, turmeric, cardamom, or any of the spices used in ethnic cooking as easily as we locate peanut butter and jelly. It is no exaggeration to say that the availability of spices has allowed us to import and export *culture*, and glancing at the spice shelf in many homes is much like taking a world tour of ethnic cooking. It isn't unusual for a household to eat Mexican tacos one night and Chinese vegetable stir-fry the next. In addition, many cooks are blending the cuisine of one country with that of another, so now we have restaurants offering a variety of ethnic foods on their menus. An Indian curry dish may be offered in the same restaurant as linguini and clam sauce and B.L.T.s!

Even with the variety available, a top ten list of spices (excluding salt and pepper) in the U.S. was determined by Spice Islands, which is one of the largest companies that package and distribute seasonings and spices, including ethnic blends of spices. The list itself reveals the kind of breadth of the multicultural landscape of cooking in the modern world. The top ten list, which was not ranked in a specific preference order, includes:

Basil: This sweet herb is popular in Italian cooking and often used to flavor meat, poultry, and fish.

Rosemary: Also popular in Italian cooking, rosemary is sweet, with a hint of mint flavor and is often mentioned in the medieval folklore of courtship and romance.

Oregano: Found in both Mexico and the Mediterranean countries, oregano has a strong flavor. Americans use it in all kinds of cooking, including their favorite Italian dishes.

Garlic: Almost every major cuisine, from Chinese to Italian, uses some form of garlic in everything from spreads for bread to sauces to flavorings for meat. Garlic appears frequently in folklore, and in almost every culture in which it is widely used, it is said to have healing properties. In the folklore that surrounds garlic, it has been used to ward off evil and disease, and it has been used to "purify" the blood.

Cayenne Pepper: If you like the famous Cajun cooking of New Orleans, then you probably like the strong taste of cayenne pepper. Barbecue sauces and chili popular in the American Southwest also use cayenne pepper.

Thyme: This is one of the old stand-bys in American and European cooking, and is popular in the traditional cooking of the American South.

Vanilla: Almost everyone loves the odor of vanilla, although the strong sweet smell we associate with common vanilla used in baking and to scent household products, candles, and so forth is actually an artificial vanilla scent. Vanilla is used in all types of baked goods, and in the U.S., it is becoming increasingly popular as a coffee flavoring.

Cinnamon: Once considered an exotic spice and sought after by explorers, cinnamon is one of the most popular flavorings in the world. It is used in desserts and coffee, but also as a part of a spice combination for dishes using game meats such as venison.

Dill Weed: Northern Europeans use dill for fish and in cream sauces for vegetables. Snack crackers and chips are often served with dips seasoned with dill.

Curry Powder: Indian cooking uses curry liberally in many of its main dishes, but in this country, many of us are introduced to mild curry in dishes such as chicken curry salad and curry-based dips.

Obviously, this is not a complete list of popular spices. Americans also use great quantities of ginger, paprika, nutmeg, anise, sage, bay leaves, and so forth in their cooking, and the blended spices, such as pumpkin pie spice and poultry and fish seasonings are popular, too. For some people, spices tend to be one area where they need to work up some courage to try new things. For example, as popular as curry is today, for example, millions of people have not tried it.

The Spice Islands Personalities

This study used eight hundred participants, the same women (73 percent) and men (27 percent) ages seventeen to seventy-seven who participated in the snack food study. Their answers were then correlated with the results of the personality tests. Just as our study participants did, choose your preferences from following five groups of spices.

Which do you prefer? (Circle *one* from each group.)

1. a. Cayenne Pepper
   b. Garlic
   c. Lemon Peel
   d. Parsley
   e. Onion Salt
   f. Caraway Seed

2. a. Red Crushed Pepper
   b. Pepper
   c. Dill Seed
   d. Chives
   e. Celery Seed
   f. Fennel

3. a Curry Powder
   b. Cloves
   c. Sesame Seed
   d. Paprika

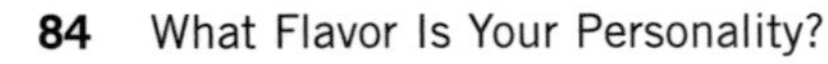

e. Celery Salt
f. Mint Leaves

4. a. Chili Powder
b. Sage
c. Oregano
d. Bay Leaves
e. Garlic Salt
f. Nutmeg

5. a. Mixed Peppers
b. Saffron
c. Thyme
d. Sweet Basil
e. Pickling Spice
f. Anise Seed

As you go through the following information, refer to your choices to see what your favorite seasonings say about your personality.

Look at the five questions and tally your answers.

A. If you chose spices from the (a) group (cayenne pepper, red crushed pepper, curry powder, chili powder, mixed peppers) for at least four of the five questions, then the results suggest you are a person who needs and likes order, and your friends may call you a perfectionist. You are good at detail work because you have a tendency to check your work many times and you will catch your mistakes. But you may find it difficult to delegate tasks because you want complete knowledge of every part of a project. You were probably one of those students who started term papers weeks ahead of the due date because you wanted to allow ample time for rewrites. You are enthusiastic about life and consider it worth living, but you don't like to waste time and you work so hard your social life could suffer. Your family and friends may tell you to "lighten up" because you even take your hobbies very seriously—you like to be the best, whether you're collecting stamps or raising pedigree dogs. If you have anything to say about it, your house will always be clean and organized, although you do hang on to papers and even old clothes—you never know when you might need them. You consider yourself thrifty, but a person who is not fond of you might call you stingy. Pity the waiter that doesn't give you good service—you might leave a penny tip just on principle, so you aren't above dropping an insult or two. In general, you are a logical thinker and tend to make decisions based on intellectual reasoning, more than on intuition. Because you engage in black and white thinking, even your friends might think you're rigid. Your mate may wish you could express affection more easily, and you aren't likely to be caught kissing in public—you like to keep your romance private.

B. If you chose spices from the (b) group (garlic, pepper, cloves, sage, saffron) for at least four of the five questions, then the results suggest you like to gather many opinions before making decisions because you doubt your ability to think independently and function well alone. This is a self-confidence problem, however, because you actually function quite competently on your own. You have a tendency to lean on other people to direct you and make decisions for you, but you can overcome that with practice. Some might call you a pessimist because you seem to have fears that influence your behavior. You enjoy tight-knit family relationships and social groups, and you don't care much about being a standout leader. You don't spend time picking fights or criticizing your friends—you enjoy close friendships and do not like to alienate other people.

C. If you chose spices from the (c) group (lemon peel, dill seed, sesame seed, oregano, thyme) for at least four of the five questions, the results suggest you tend to carry the weight of the world on your shoulders more than other personality types, so some may call you a worrier. You want things to go well, so you tend to worry that they won't, and your concerns extend to work, family, health, and so forth. You do not confine your worries to yourself, so no one can call you selfish or self-centered. You are as concerned about the health of your loved ones as you are about yourself. You are a stickler about being on time, and you are not the type to forget to check the oil in your car, and you rotate your tires right on time. Looking outside yourself comes naturally to you, so you are concerned about world events. You tend to be a perfectionist and expect others and yourself to bring in a perfect performance. Your friends would not call you carefree, but you see yourself as concerned. Shouldn't everyone worry about their children's grades and global warming?

D. If you chose spices from the (d) group (parsley, chives, paprika, bay leaves, sweet basil) for at least four of the five questions, the results suggest your personality would be considered "well-adjusted," in that you are adaptable and easygoing. If you want a marriage partner who won't pick fights with you, then give potential mates this spice test and choose a group (d) member. These individuals tend to be good workers, although if you need a perfectionist or a person who attends to detail—and checks and rechecks the work—these carefree individuals would not be such a good choice. A group (d) personality may be a good politician because they are pleasant and do not have obvious negative traits, but other personality types may be better at drafting legislation or developing an impressive knowledge of current affairs. These individuals do not seek the limelight and they do not care about such things as being dramatic—they just have a good time in their pursuits and are not image-conscious.

E. If you chose spices from the (e) group (onion salt, celery seed, celery salt, garlic salt, pickling spice) for at least four of the five questions, the results suggest you are a dramatic, theatrical person, who enjoys being the center of attention. You tend to be lively and enthusiastic, flirtatious and perhaps seductive, even sexually provocative—you aren't shy about kissing in public.

You tend to be intuitive and you may cry easily at movies because you have a strong sentimental streak. You trust authority figures, develop strong relationships, and you easily find yourself in romantic fantasies. You probably become bored with routines and seek new stimulation. A repetitive desk job is probably not for you and because you like change, you become dissatisfied with projects not long after you've started them. If you like to participate in sports, you're an aggressive athlete, and if you're also a woman, you may appear quite feminine in your style. If you are in love with a group (e) member, then be generous with your compliments because they enjoy that kind of attention.

F. If you chose spices from the (f) group (carroway seed, fennel, mint, nutmeg, anise seed) for at least four of five questions, the results suggest you tend to enjoy power and success, and people who love you may think you're brilliant—and probably beautiful or handsome, too. You tend to strive to be the best, and you like the idea of being special and unique. You surround yourself with people who you think are superior. You tend to seek out the best—the best lawyer, the best doctor, the best hairdresser—others may find that tendency tedious or irritating. You like to be at the top and you demand to be treated that way, too. The little annoyances of life bother you, and you become easily disgruntled if you have to wait in line. These individuals expect respect for their talents and abilities, but to a degree they lack empathy. Group (f) types tend to use the power of logic over emotions in the way they express themselves. If you are this personality type, others may accuse you of being a snob or patronizing. Your ambition, success, and competence give you great confidence. You are a winner.

Once you see the patterns, you can assess your personality, even if your answers tended to be mixed and do not fit neatly into types. In fact, many individuals will see a mixture of personality types within their results. This isn't surprising because, as you may have seen by now, you cannot be defined only within one clear type. However, our results were surprisingly consistent, and definite "Spice

Islands personalities" emerged. As you can see, each personality type has strengths and weaknesses. So, this food preference test may be especially valuable for assessing areas in which you perhaps need or want to alter your behavior. It is certainly possible that your family, friends, and associates were quite sure they knew the outcome of the test for you, and maybe you thought you could predict the outcome for them as well.

While it is true that our basic personality traits are stable, each has positive and negative potential. Use your results to guide you in working on your weaknesses and enjoying your strengths.

Salt and Personality

Nowadays, many of us share a suspicious and standoffish relationship with salt, primarily because media headlines continue to alert us to the dangers of overdoing our sodium intake. Food producers have responded with a new breed of processed foods that boast "No Salt," "Salt-Free," and "Low Sodium." Even the traditionally salty chips, pretzels, and snack crackers are available in reduced-sodium varieties, usually made to fit the low-fat trend, as well.

As essential a role as it has played in shaping human culture and history, eating salt from external sources, that found in the earth or sea, is not necessarily essential for a healthy human body. Some groups have survived—and thrived—entirely without using any external salt. The Inuit in North America and the Aborigines in Australia do not incorporate external salt into their diets. Cultures that use salt will go to great lengths to get it.

Anthropological research suggests that people began craving salt, in the form of the loose grains we use in cooking, when their societies began cultivating vegetables. Apparently, the combination of an increased intake of vegetables, plus the shift to consuming boiled and cooked foods, creates a desire for rock salt. This is easily explained. Animals, human and otherwise, whose diets consist largely of animal meat, obtain sufficient salt in animal blood to satisfy their body's needs. Herbivorous animals, on the other hand, seek salt externally. Deer, horses, cows, and other domesticated grazers gather at the salt lick, where they ingest other minerals they need along with the salt.

Since most present-day humans consume substantial amounts of plant foods and cooked foods, salt has become slightly more important to the diet. Keep in mind, however, that the actual amount of salt needed for a normal human being is a mere 1.1 to 3.3 grams per day—modern Westerners often consume up to ten times or more of that amount.

The Love/Hate Relationship with Dietary Salt

Rather than having the esteemed place in Western culture it once held, salt has entered a period where it is labeled as unhealthy. This doesn't necessarily stop individuals from consuming it, but when a food has been "medicalized," the next step involves labeling it "bad" or "good." The food then becomes endowed with moral connotations. Foods such soybeans, broccoli, and sweet potatoes are considered "super foods" in that they are nutritionally rich and valuable. They become filled with virtue, like a virtuous person. Green leafy vegetables are the "Mother Teresa" of foods. On the other hand, salt (along with its pals, sugar and fat) has fallen out of favor, although some consumers still cling to it.

The amount of salt that satisfies you is an acquired taste. If you were raised on salty gravy and heavily salted scrambled eggs served with bacon or sausage, you may find food without a considerable amount of salt bland—perhaps too bland. On the other hand, if salt was used sparingly in your childhood household, a piece of bacon may seem much too salty for you to eat.

In the last part of the twentieth century, high sodium intake was linked with hypertension (high blood pressure), the presence of which increases the risk of stroke, cardiovascular disease, and kidney failure. The amount of sodium present in our bodies is one of the most important of all the fluid and mineral regulatory functions. Too much sodium can cause edema, a situation in which fluid is retained in the tissues, thereby adding to the load carried by heart and the kidneys. Edema on a short-term basis is not always serious, and pregnant women may experience periods of edema, which usually can be quickly reversed. (However, although not always indicative of a serious condition, do not ignore swelling in the hands, feet, and ankles, because it is a signal that the sodium balance in the body is amiss.)

Too little sodium in the body is serious, too, and leads to weakness and disorientation. Athletes who become dehydrated (lose excessive amounts of sodium through perspiration) are at great risk for sodium deficiency. Excessive weakness and fainting are obvious symptoms that sodium is needed. In a study of college students given a low-sodium diet and then diuretics that made them salt-depleted, the study participants began to crave salty food such as olives and ham. Their interest in fruit and ice cream dropped. They craved what their body needed most, which was salt. Again and again, we say that cravings stem from nutritional demands in some cases, just as they stem from emotional demands in others. While adequate salt intake is important, most of us are at greater risk for excessive sodium intake.

Before reading on, answer the question below to determine the nature of your "salt personality":

Which do you prefer? (Choose one from the pair.)

Salty chicken soup

or

Chicken soup prepared with little or no salt

One View: Pour the Salt and Seek Excitement

Some studies that compare personality traits to attitudes toward salt and salt use suggest that the salt-lover seeks outside stimulation and a tendency to be an extrovert, but other studies did not clearly show these tendencies. However, individuals who use salt in cooking and at the table—two different salt "behaviors"—did show what researchers called "tough poise." As defined by a personality test called "16 Personality Factors," tough poise is associated with decisive, resilient individuals who tend to act quickly and perhaps, on the downside, do not give sufficient thought to their actions. These characteristics are consistent with an unwillingness to take seriously nutritional information that discourages salt use—at least not at the moment when the salt is presented. We can think of a person who for the moment throws caution to the wind and on impulse grabs the salt shaker. Using this supposition, individuals who don't add salt as they cook or at the table, tended to show characteristics of the "worry wart," and they are not impulsive individuals.

Another View: Hold the Salt—Stay in the Driver's Seat

Correlation with other personality tests provides an additional and different way of viewing salt preferences. If you like salty chicken soup, you may believe others control your fate—and you may look in the morning paper and read your horoscope to find out what kind of day you'll have. You tend to believe in fate and do not have firm ideas of your own, which means you sway with public opinion. Perhaps these individuals use salt, not because they are impulsive, but because they do not believe they have control over their health.

If you don't like salty soup, you have an internal locus of control, meaning that you have adopted a "I'm the master of my fate" attitude. You take charge of situations, and tend to aggressively pursue your goals. You are a leader, not a follower. These individuals may not use salt because they believe that, at least to some extent, the state of their health is their own hands.

What Conclusions Can We Draw?

Some people become convinced that foods are either going to ruin their health or almost assure them good health and a long life. A faddist generally adopts beliefs about certain foods that aren't based on scientific evidence. On personality scales, these individuals tend to be rigid, which fits the subjective impression most of us have about those we call "food fanatics." I suspect food faddists tend to fear foods they believe do not promote health.

In a general way, it seems to make more logical sense that individuals with an *internal* locus of control would heed the advice of medical professionals and use less salt. Rather than being considered "worry warts," these men and women are more likely to take charge of their diets so they can avoid worrying about their health. The fatalistic among us are less likely to heed medical advice because they think their future might literally be "written in the stars."

Because of our affluence and the abundance of food at our fingertips, we are in a position to make more decisions for ourselves about the foods we eat that current information tells us builds health, versus foods that may be detrimental. It makes sense to listen to medical advice, and you should follow the salt guidelines recommended by your doctor. However, we can take sound advice without assigning labels to food that makes them either good or bad. As you can see, with salt and other foods, it's a relative issue anyway.

At first glance, the quiz below may not appear related to other information in this chapter, but take a minute to answer the questions and see how the information fits.

Which do you prefer? (Circle one choice from each pair.)

Rice Crispies or Alphabits
Raisin Bran or Lucky Charms
Baked Potato or Boiled Lobster
Tuna Fish or Pizza
Banana or Banana Split
Mixed Salad or Shrimp Cocktail
Raisinettes or Milk Duds
A Granola bar or a Snickers Bar
Black Coffee or Café au Lait
A Hamburger or a Cheeseburger

If seven or more of your choices were the *first* food item, then you show an internal locus of control. You believe that you are responsible for your own choices and that you control your own destiny. For this reason, you tend to choose the foods with the healthier image based on current medical thinking. As an adult, you have moved beyond the "kids" cereal, for example, and you would be more likely to buy the leanest cut of beef for your burger—and hold the high-fat cheese please. If you are a woman, you are probably ambitious and independent, perhaps aggressive, and you believe you have control over your life and your goals, and you watch your diet by consuming less salt, fat, and sugar than your more traditional sisters tend to enjoy.

If seven or more of your choices were the *second* item, you may have heard about healthier food choices, but you act on impulse at the grocery store—you'll eventually clean up your diet, but not today. You haven't outgrown the taste for kids' cereal and you love cheese too much to pass it up on your burger. If you're going to order a burger, it might as well be the way you like it. If you're a woman, you may have followed a more traditional path to fulfillment and may not consider yourself ambitious. Regardless of sex, you may have doubts about your power to control your own destiny, which is why you turn to the horoscope in the newspaper. You may say you don't believe it, but still…

Perhaps you show a mixed result, 50–50 or 60–40. Many people do, and this simply means that you are not all one type or another. In fact, many of us believe we have control over some areas of our lives, but not every area.

The issue of locus of control is an important one because life decisions often are related to the degree to which we believe we have control over our lives. Those who believe they have control are more likely to make healthful choices, at least most of the time. Employment tests exist that measure locus of control and they attempt to help choose appropriate people for certain kinds of jobs. For example, if a job involves danger, then an employer may prefer an employee who believes he or she has control and that accidents are not mere destiny. One day, food preferences may be added to this kind of screening tool.

Chapter Seven

The Sweet Scent of the Past

"Ho-Hos and Twinkies, Swanson's Turkey TV Dinners, with the cute little baked apple section in the middle...steaming brown gravy, jiggly cranberry sauce—every day could be Thanksgiving. I made hors d'oeuvres by spreading frosting from the can on Triscuits....Kids from our apartment building loved my mother—she was beautiful, she was single, played Beatle records and taught us how to do the frug and the jerk. She made root beer floats, knew how to spray a shaken-up bottle of club soda into a glass with Hershey's syrup and half 'n' half, plop in a scoop of vanilla ice cream and make real ice cream sodas at home."

—Valerie Ann Leff

From an early age, we associate food and food smells with comfort and a sense of security. In Maurice Sendak's classic children's story *Where the Wild Things Are*, a little boy is sent to bed without supper. Alone in his room, he takes a "journey"—a dream—to the place where "the wild things are." But as Sendak says, when "all around and far away from across the world he smelled good things to eat" he returns to his bedroom and finds his supper waiting for him. And his meal was left by "the one who loves him best of all," his mother, of course.

In one short children's story, Sendak touches on both the fears and pleasures of childhood, and the feelings of security and love the scents evoked, which brought the little boy "home." When we fully comprehend that our sense of smell is a powerful influence on our emotional lives, we grow more curious about the role of olfaction in our view of the past, which, at least in part, shaped the individuals we are today.

At our foundation, we have a fascination about a phenomenon called olfactory-evoked recall. A nearly universal experience, most of us have an immediate recall of childhood memories when a particular odor is present. Most often the smell is associated with pleasant feelings and the flood of memories that appear unbidden may bring about a nostalgic state. And our poets and writers bring us example after example of this powerful experience. One of the most powerful passages that associates smell with emotion in all of literature comes to us from Marcel Proust's *Swann's Way*:

> One day in winter, as I came home, my mother, seeing that I was cold, offered me some tea...soon, mechanically, weary after a dull day with the prospect of a depressing morrow, I raised to my lips a spoonful of the tea in which I had soaked a morsel of the cake. No sooner had the warm liquid, and the crumbs with it, touched my palate than a shudder ran through my whole body. An exquisite pleasure had invaded my senses....And the vicissitudes of life had become indifferent to me...this new sensation having had on me the effect which love has of filling me with a precious essence....I had ceased now to feel mediocre, accidental, mortal. Whence could it have come to me, this all-powerful joy? I was conscious that it was connected with the taste of tea and cake but that it infinitely transcended those savors....
>
> ...I put down my cup and examine my own mind....

> And I begin again to ask myself what could it have been, this unremembered state which brought with it...only the sense that it was a happy, that it was a real state in whose presence other states of consciousness melted and vanished.
>
> ...Undoubtedly what is thus palpitating in the depths of my being must be the image, the visual memory which, being linked to that taste, has tried to follow it into my conscious mind. But its struggles are too far off, too much confused...
>
> ...And suddenly the memory returns. The taste was that of the little crumb of madeleine [cake] which on Sunday mornings at Combray...when I went to say good day to her in her bedroom, my aunt Leonie used to give me, dipping it first in her own cup of real or of lime-flower tea. The sight of the little madeleine had recalled nothing to my mind before I tasted it...But when from a long-distant past nothing subsists...still...the smell and taste of things remain poised a long time, ready to remind us...in the tiny and almost impalpable drop of their essence, the vast structure of recognition.

For better or for worse, the sensitive version of nostalgic recall Proust provided can be transported into the commercial world in which every retailer knows that nostalgia sells. What would the winter holiday season be without the smell of cinnamon and pine floating through the stores? Add red and green decorations and some holiday music, and shoppers are surrounded by the sensory triggers for nostalgic reverie. Nostalgia is what motivates us to bring the past into the memories we're creating in the present.

Would we remain deeply attached to our family and religious traditions if they were not so strongly linked to the scents we associate with them? If we saw a pumpkin pie but couldn't detect its spicy odor, would we immediately think about Thanksgiving, perhaps a specific Thanksgiving Day twenty or thirty years ago? When school children are told our cultural story of the first Thanksgiving, it is essentially an intellectual rendition. But the emotional attachment to the holiday, along with the individual traditions families duplicate year after year are created at home. The scent of turkey stuffing or of cranberries is forever linked

with that holiday. Patients who have lost their ability to smell often tell us that holidays are particularly difficult because they cannot match the festive mood of others around them.

What Is Nostalgia?

Nostalgia is usually thought of as a simple longing for a bygone time. But the psychiatric understanding of the experience is more complex. Looked at psychologically, the capacity for nostalgia results from natural and appropriate passages through developmental stages. As we advance to a new stage of life, we inevitably feel some sadness as we give up the old and make way for the new. We may be reluctant to give up the playthings we have outgrown and they end up stored in cartons in the attic. When we cry at our high school or college graduations, we are acknowledging that we are giving up the security of being young students. If we are anxious about the next stage of life, the school we grumbled about begins to look better and better—we may even ramble on nostalgically about how great it was to live in a dorm. Doesn't it surprise us when men and women who have been through hellish combat experiences talk nostalgically about their "military days?" But even that difficult life passage has contained within it the potential for nostalgia.

Memory tends to enhance the positive things of the past and screen out unpleasantness. So, once the sun sets on the old life we leave behind, we may look back and see it in a rosy glow. Intellectually, most of us know the "good old days" weren't necessarily all that good. Psychologically, nostalgia is a yearning for an idealized past, not the one that actually existed.

The details of an event or situation are not as important as the emotional states shaped by a complex combination of sensory impressions. A woman recalls a summer evening at grandmother's house and talks about the sound of the insects, the taste of the lemonade, the smell of the rose bushes, and the feel of the old wicker porch furniture. These sensory details characterize a time and a place, and she may unconsciously attempt to gratify the nostalgic longings by recreating this idealized past in the present. For this woman, the fragrance of roses might stimulate a bout of nostalgic reverie, and current concerns are temporarily dis-

placed with a flood of memories from the past. She might soon linger in the furniture department of the store and gaze longingly at wicker porch furniture. Suddenly, she has a compelling urge for a frosty glass of lemonade. Without question, nostalgia influences behavior.

When the present is painful or troublesome, we tend to increase our idealization of the past and the nostalgic yearnings grow stronger. It's as if we think of the past as "paradise lost," even if we know that the past wasn't really paradise at all. When Thomas Wolfe titled one of his novels *You Can't Go Home Again*, he struck a chord in the human psyche. We "can't go home again," not only because we have changed, but because the place we call "home" never existed in the first place. The past is always filtered through a screen that leaves behind what we'd rather not include. Similarly, the nostalgic journey that a smell evokes is always reshaped because a memory of the past is essentially a reconstructed experience or a combination of experiences.

Taking the Research to the Street

Few researchers disagree that olfactory-evoked nostalgia is nearly universal, but some doubt remains that smells are more powerful than other sensory experiences in bringing up these stream-of-consciousness memories. In other words, the poets and sages may know that an odor is more powerful than a visual image or a sound, but it's up to scientists to demonstrate how profound this phenomenon is and the ways it may drive our behavior.

One step in establishing the relationship between nostalgia and odors is organizing anecdotal information and then examining the data to find patterns. In order to look at odors and nostalgia, our Foundation sent researchers to a large shopping complex in downtown Chicago. We stopped people on the street and asked them if they would be willing to participate in a study about odors and memory. This method meant that our participants were randomly selected volunteers, people who just happened to be passing by when we were there. Although all of our nearly one thousand participants were English speaking and most came from the Chicago area (51 percent), forty-five states and thirty-nine countries were represented. Slightly more than half of the subjects were women

and the majority of participants were born after 1940, although more than two hundred were born between 1900 and 1940 (see Appendix 2).

We asked our volunteers if they had ever had the experience of detecting a particular odor that then evoked a childhood memory, and 85 percent said yes. Then we asked what odors stimulated their memory, but we didn't offer any sample choices or give a list of odors to choose from. The answers people gave were spontaneous and personal. As might be predicted, baked goods comprised the largest category of smells mentioned, with 18 percent mentioning odors such as baking bread, cookies, and cakes. Apple pie, bacon, soup, cooking meat, popcorn, spaghetti, fish, chicken, and general cooking odors each received 2 percent of the responses. Other foods mentioned included: blueberries, hot chocolate, figs, Cracker Jacks, meatballs, cinnamon, candy cigarettes, tacos, Sweet Tarts, tuna casserole, and Cocoa Puffs. Perhaps you, too, have associations with these foods.

Among the older population, those born before 1930, the odors of nature—pine, sea air, horses, flowers, meadows, hay, and so forth—had the greatest ability to evoke nostalgic recall. This group also was more likely to mention things like burning leaves, the specific odors such as tweed, clover, or honeysuckle. (These specific odors were not mentioned with great frequency, but rather represented the category of odor the older individuals were more likely to remember.)

We also considered it important that among people born after 1930, and increasing in number among those born after 1960 and 1970, artificial smells were mentioned often. This group tended to name specific products, from the odor of plastic (in general) to scented markers to Pez to Play Dough. Some older individuals within this group mentioned odors associated with automobiles or industries such as motor oil, factories, or refineries. The younger men and women were likely to mention chlorine or fabric softener, mosquito repellent, and even marijuana.

I believe the shift in odor preferences from natural smells to artificial ones represents a shift in values. Our society's concern about preserving endangered species and protecting our natural environment from overdevelopment and pollution is at least partially dependent on our nostalgic feelings about an unspoiled green world. But are those who have grown up in an urban environment and who

favor manufactured smells over natural ones going to place the same value on environmental issues as those whose nostalgic responses are closely linked to the smell of hay fields or budding trees after a spring rain?

It could be argued, of course, that the impetus for the environmental movement has come from the generation born after 1940. For this generation, creeping urbanization intruded into the natural environment. These individuals may have seen their small towns turned into densely populated suburbs—the site of their childhood home might be a strip-mall today. They span the generations of rapid commercial expansion, but may emotionally yearn for a return to a time when life was simpler—and greener. The trend toward wilderness vacations and activities such as rock climbing and white water rafting might indicate that the nostalgia for the natural world is strong indeed.

Age and experience influenced nostalgic recall, too. For example, those born before 1960 liked the smell of newly cut grass, but those born between 1960 and 1979 disliked the smell because they associated it with having to mow the lawn, a chore they didn't enjoy. It's possible that as younger people age, their memories will change and one day they too will look nostalgically back to newly cut grass and screen out the drudgery they associate with it. But, human memory being what it is, these men and women might deny ever having the negative association. Nostalgia is like that.

About 91 percent of our study participants reported having a happy childhood. We had anticipated that people whose early lives were unhappy would not have olfactory-evoked memory recall because they would not experience nostalgia, by definition a positive feeling state. However, we were mistaken. This small group reported unpleasant smells associated with childhood memories, from sewer gas to dog waste. Those with an unhappy childhood also mentioned menstrual and body odors as reminders of unpleasant scenarios.

We know that odors can stimulate flashbacks among those suffering from post-traumatic stress disorder, where the desire to eliminate memories is strong. This is the antithesis of a nostalgic state. For many Vietnam veterans the stimulant odor is burning diesel fuel, and in some cases, seafood; Korean War veterans reported flashback episodes stimulated by the odor of wet canvas or beaches.

When we look at the power of odors to stimulate memories, it isn't so surprising after all that an unpleasant odor will cause psychological pain especially for those whose childhood was characterized by deprivation or abuse and which lacked a sense of security. The more positive nostalgic response tends to recreate an entire scene from the past and all the emotions that went with it. It is then filtered in order to isolate the idealized memories, making it possible for the person to mentally return to a safe, secure time.

Many people who read about our study expressed surprise that such a large percentage of people reported a happy childhood. Popular psychology and pop culture would have us believe that most of us came from dysfunctional families. Our finding doesn't surprise me, however. Our study was self-selected, in that people had a choice to participate or not and individuals were not screened out by age, sex, region, or country of origin. In addition, these men and women were not offered a product, as in a marketing study, or a treatment, as in a medical trial. We didn't probe deeply into the happy childhood issue. Besides, most people answer a question a researcher poses in the simplest way and provide a response that allows the least degree of personal disclosure. If these men and women had told us their childhood was unhappy, they might have anticipated a question that required them to explain what they meant, thereby exposing information they would just as soon keep private.

In reality, the majority of adults, chosen from any random sampling, had a childhood that was a mixture of pleasant and unpleasant memories, but for the purposes of our study, we didn't offer a range of choices. We asked a general question and given that choice, the majority chose the less complex answer.

The Past Drives the Present

We all tend to filter out unpleasantness, so our memories can fool us in ways we don't understand. In addition, the natural urge to recreate the past within the present is a driving force in our behavior. We participate in family holiday rituals that are recreations of the past; we may practice a religion that repeats the same rituals year after year—in some cases century after century. Great resistance to change often arises in these areas. Religions splinter off into new sects and

families end up resentful and angry over even slight alterations in the rituals that have become nearly sacred (let's face it, sometimes too sacred) to some members of the family or religion.

Some nostalgic drive is quite subtle. We frequently marry spouses with characteristics reminiscent of our parents, and we may adopt our parents' attitudes and beliefs because they are familiar and part of a secure environment we attempt to recreate. Odd as it might sound, the nostalgic urge also explains why many abused children marry abusive spouses, or children with alcoholic parents marry spouses with the same disease. They may talk about the unhappiness of their childhood, but at the same time they have their own idealized and sanitized nostalgic memories that manifest in a symbolic way in their adult partners.

Using the Information

Potentially, olfactory-evoked recall could play an important role in psychotherapy because the elicited information is rich with associations from the past and provides clues about the memories we have allowed to slip through the filter of experience. By understanding nostalgia and the way it nudges us to recreate the past, we are given glimpses into our own personalities and life choices, as well as societal trends and customs. What is the custom to name a first born son after the father but an action driven by nostalgia, an attempt to recreate an idealized version of the past? When we have a revival of old television programs or movie sequels or we bring back Broadway productions that originated half a century ago, we're trying to satisfy a yearning to bring back something that made us feel safe—even if that version of the past never existed.

Although nostalgic reverie isn't necessarily an accurate recreation of a past situation, that doesn't render the experience meaningless or insignificant. In fact, olfactory-evoked recall can often help us gain insight into our problems and be part of a coping mechanism we use. For example, when a smell reminds us of a person, perhaps a loved one who has died, the wave of memories that wash over us have to the power to both delight us and trigger sadness. We may long for the person while at the same time, the warm associations provide us with memories we cherish. Writing in *National Geographic*, Boyd Gibbons recounts an incident

where he took his grandfather's deerskin hunting vest out of a closet and pressed it to his face as he smelled it. A flood of emotion and memory washed over him:

> No longer was I an adult squinting across a chasm of years at dim events: Suddenly I was a boy again....This was no hazy reverie. I could feel his whiskered cheek against mine and smell his peculiar fragrance of age, wool, dust, and a touch of Old Grand-Dad. Momentarily I was once more on the floor of my grandparents' breakfast room, the linoleum cool against my belly as I sketched B-17s, then sneaking down the hall into my great-uncle's gloomy bedroom hung with mounted pheasants and deer heads—musky and mysterious. The epoch slowly faded as I lay curled up on the backseat of my grandfather's Ford, returning from a long hunt in Mexico....All this from the whiff of a vest. I was not consciously trying to recall my boyhood. Such is the involuntary power of the sense of smell, my boyhood was recalling me.

So, a scent can put us in an emotional state where even subtle details are part of the memories. For Proust, it was madeleine cake, for Gibbons, it was a hunting vest, and as odd as it seems to many of us, plastic toys or scented markers have the power to evoke the same effect. When this kind of memory comes upon us, sometimes so suddenly, we are in a paradoxical situation in that we cherish the memories but may shed tears over them nonetheless.

These experiences most often symbolize both great love and great loss. Ask any man or woman who has lost a much-loved spouse or child about the power of an odor when they are in the early stages of grief and we may be told about an article of clothing that carries the scent of the lost loved one. At this stage, people in mourning may be able to give away many of the lost person's belongings, but they will hang on to items they can smell. It's as if the person isn't quite gone as long as the scent is still there.

Shared Experiences

Some nostalgic memories are dramatic and illustrate nearly universal experiences. However, some nostalgic experiences seem quite ordinary and mundane, and if we pay attention to our thought processes we might notice how many of them repeat. The smell of apple pie, for example, reminds us of the same neighbor again and again. We used to eat pie at the neighbor's house and we were happy to be invited there. That thought leads us to wonder about the whereabouts of that neighbor. Later that day, we order apple pie for dessert. We may or may not have made a conscious connection between the thoughts and our desire for a piece of pie.

Many individuals mention that the smell of varnish reminds them of a classroom on the first day of school; the smell of a new book might momentarily hurtle them back to that same first day. If we pay attention, we'll find that during any given week we may have dozens of such events, all triggered by a scent. If we're with another person, we might comment on it and share what we're recalling.

Paula Dranov opened an article in *Cosmopolitan* magazine about current smell research with a personal anecdote that illustrates how common these nostalgic experiences are:

> The smell of chlorine inevitably transports me back to the YWCA where I learned to swim. In a cinematic flash the pool appears, a shimmering rectangle of blue-green water. Just as clearly, I can see the dinky diving board and hear the hollow echo of the little-girl splashes and squeals. Before the image fades, more details converge: the slimy feel of the changing-room floor, scratchy white towels, droopy regulation tank suits.

Millions of women read that article, and the mere mention of a chlorine smell may have transported readers back to their own experience of swimming pools and locker rooms. In this country, we can mention certain kinds of experiences, from holiday smells to swimming pools to movie theater popcorn, and be fairly certain that we are talking about shared experiences. No two people perceive the odor exactly the same way or react the same way, but the similarities are sufficient to allow us to understand each other. A friend of mine went to Korea with her husband, who had worked there twenty-five years earlier. He had often talked about the unique and pleasant smell of the air in the small village

he'd lived in, but there was no way to describe it because our language is so limited. Once she had smelled the same odor, she knew exactly what he had been talking about. They had crossed a bridge into a shared experience.

Societies always have some shared odor experiences, but our nostalgia study revealed some regional differences. People from the eastern seaboard mentioned flowers as a smell that triggered nostalgia; those from the South named fresh air; Midwesterners mentioned farm animals; and those from the western part of the country said that the smell of meat cooking on a barbecue evoked nostalgia.

In general, odor preferences are thought to follow along ethnic or cultural lines, resulting in shared regional similarities. Yet, research has confused this issue somewhat because odor preferences don't appear to fit neatly into geographical regions. In one study, sample populations from twenty nations were asked to evaluate twenty-two different fragrances. One group with similar preferences included people from Japan, West Germany, Taiwan, Canada, the Philippines, and Italians in Brazil, Taiwanese natives living in California, and Americans residing in California and Kansas. Another group included residents of Australia, Sweden, Norway, East Germany, Finland, Mexico, and people from Japan and Africa living in Brazil. So much for neat clusters.

At the time this odor preference research was conducted, less information existed about personality characteristics and odor preferences. While this would obviously be a huge undertaking, I can foresee a time when there is a personality map of the world, which is constructed at least in part with information about odor and food preferences. We are on the brink of a human gene map of the planet, so it is not so far-fetched to imagine a personality map using food preferences as one of the determining factors.

Your Choices, Your Memories

As you can see, your favorite foods may arise from your memories of the past, and your "food mood" may be influenced largely by foods that provided comfort and security to you as a young child. Choosing our comfort foods is a form of self-medicating. While we know, for example, that individuals suffering from depression often crave carbohydrates, day to day fluctuations in mood not linked

to clinical depression may lead to the same types of cravings. However, the foods you choose to satisfy the cravings or, quite literally, comfort yourself, may depend on what you are attempting to recreate from the past.

In her book *The Best Thing I Ever Tasted*, author Sally Tisdale offers her ideas about the role of food in family and society. One passage in particular captures the emotional essence of nostalgia:

> On summer evenings, when the sky begins to pale and the crows fly singly and in pairs across its white face, I can still taste the hand-cranked vanilla ice cream, every other mouthful flavored by tiny drops of salty water. On cold winter nights, my face dry as papyrus near the hearth flames, I can feel the smooth cream of tiny marshmallows melting into Swiss Miss instant cocoa. And this on cool spring days: slices of canned mandarin orange that seem like the best thing I've ever tasted. The bright light sweetness tinged ever so slightly with a hint of aluminum explodes gently in my mouth as I suck the small cells open one by one. I am sitting in a puddle of sun and watching my mother stir sour. She is making my favorite: Campbell's cream of mushroom.

So, if you choose mashed potatoes or chocolate pudding or meat loaf, perhaps it's because you associate these foods with your mother, who represents your source of safety and security. Maybe you choose ice cream or chocolate chip cookies or angel food cake because you remember eating those foods with your family around the dinner table. You may have the strongest—and strangest—feeling that your current case of the blues will be soothed *only* with these foods.

If you pay attention, you may notice that your cravings may not only be linked to a present mood, but your desire for a particular food is linked to a mood state you'd like to recreate. Too often, we feel weak or guilty about cravings, but in reality they are as natural as physical hunger. And if you find yourself with a sudden shift in mood and do not understand why, think about the odors in your environment. Olfactory-evoked nostalgia may be at work.

Chapter Eight
Taming the Dinner Table Monsters

"Coming together to share food is a behavioral pattern we have in common with many other creatures. The word "companion" derives from the Latin word for bread, panis. Breaking bread together both establishes and symbolizes a fundamental social bond. A Japanese phrase for 'intimate companion' is 'one who eats rice from the same bowl'...The social importance of food and eating, like their association with pleasure, must be honored by anyone advocating eating well."

—Andrew Weil, M.D.

"A meal is an artistic social construct, ordering the foodstuffs which comprise it into a complex dramatic whole, as a play organizes actions and words into component parts such as acts, scenes, speeches, dialogues, and exits, all in the sequences designed for them. However humble it may be, a meal has a definite plot, the intention of which is to intrigue, stimulate, and satisfy."

— Margaret Visser

Several years ago, a friend told me about a scene from a story that took place during the Great Depression. The details of the story were long forgotten, but she remembered that a character in the book kept an onion, along with other spices, simmering on the stove all day. Then, after a day of job-hunting, the woman's husband would smell the odor of cooking food when he walked into the house. This young wife believed the scent of the food would send a subtle message that implied security and abundance, thereby reassuring her husband that he was a good provider—even during hard times. By the time the family sat down to the table for their evening meal, no matter how sparse, the odor likely would have taken the edge off the husband's less-than-happy mood. As it turns out, the notion of filling the house with food odors in order to "tame" a bad mood or encourage a pleasant mood state may be scientifically sound.

In the United States today, both men and women are economic providers in most families, but it appears that the mood of the husband/father still has power in setting the tone of the family dinner hour. Research also shows that women still do the majority of the shopping, and her purchases are influenced more by her husband's preferences than her own. Vestiges of the patriarchal underpinning of our society remain—apparently the dinner table stubbornly resists change. However, food odors and, potentially, specific foods may in subtle ways contribute to improving family relationships.

Garlic Bread and Family Harmony

In a study conducted by the Smell & Taste Treatment and Research Foundation, we measured the effects of the odor and taste of Pepperidge Farm frozen garlic bread on family interactions (see Appendix 7). If you are wondering why we would embark on such a study, consider that currently the family is under great stress. Divorce rates are high, and even intact families may find communication difficult because both parents often work outside the home. Most single parents work, too, of course, which creates additional pressure in these families. Then add to adult work hours and commuting time the children's seemingly endless activ-

ities, and it is amazing that families have time together at all. Despite the struggles, many families attempt to preserve the family dinner hour, which at one time was considered a hallowed institution of our society's family life. But as you may know, "hallowed" doesn't necessarily mean easy. In fact, family tensions may manifest in the atmosphere around the table. Although I cannot prove this idea, I believe that eating together as a family is extremely important and has an enormous influence on the quality of family relationships.

Those who are fortunate recall their childhood dinner table as generally pleasant. Overall, they have positive associations with their parents' behavior, the emotional climate around the table, and the smell and taste of the evening's fare. Unfortunately, some adults have quite different memories. For many individuals, gathering around the table meant listening to family members bicker, or always being on guard for a stressed-out parent (usually, but not always, the father) to complain about the quality of the food. And in some families, a mealtime is viewed as an opportunity to lecture the children or constantly correct their behavior, a situation that does not lend itself to happy memories of the family gathered to "break bread" together.

Perhaps in your childhood specific rules set the tone of the dinner hour and those rules were strictly enforced. One of my patients mentioned that she was not allowed to talk during any meal. Her father considered the dinner hour as a time for eating, and talking, he claimed, interfered with digestion. Because of her memories of this cold silence, she now makes a conscious effort to improve the atmosphere around her own family's dining room table—and she likes the conversation lively.

The point of our garlic bread study was to see if introducing certain odors and tastes would change the mood and emotional tone around the table. Would family interactions be influenced, one way or another, by the odor of garlic bread? And, taking the long view, do foods and/or odors possess the power to alter the course of family communication? (See Appendix 7)

Our study included fifty families. During one phase of the study, twenty-five families were provided with a spaghetti dinner that included garlic bread. The other families were provided an identical dinner, but minus the garlic bread.

Family size ranged from two to twelve individuals, with the average family size being 3.9 persons. (A total of 182 individuals participated.) Participants ranged from age one to age eighty-four. The mean age was 29.2. Ninety of them were male and ninety-two were female. The majority (72 percent) reported that they liked the odor of garlic bread very much. Only a small percentage (about 8 percent) disliked garlic bread, and the remaining group were somewhat ambivalent.

In order to record and rate family interactions, we used three-minute intervals for each dinner. The first minute served as a baseline. During the second minute, the garlic bread was presented at the table and family members could smell the aroma, and during the third minute, they tasted it. Our observers recorded the number of both positive and negative interactions during the three minutes intervals. The observers also noted the positive or negative reactions to garlic bread and whether an olfactory-evoked nostalgic response occurred.

All fifty families had two identical spaghetti dinners, one with the garlic bread and one without the bread. We had two dinner events to compare, and in general, our results indicate that if we want to improve the tone of our family interactions during dinner, we'll serve up a warm basket of garlic bread. The presence of garlic bread not only reduced the number of negative family interactions, but also increased the positive interactions during dinner. We rated the interactions by family member, so that one particularly positive or negative person would not skew the results.

In the presence of the garlic aroma and taste, the average reduction in negative interactions was 22.7 percent. The increase in positive interactions was 7.4 percent. It was particularly noted that the negative interactions of the "dominant" male showed the most reductions. In addition, the older the participant, the more likely it was that the garlic bread increased pleasant interactions. Those who liked garlic bread in the first place also showed the greatest increase in positive interactions.

The Pleasing Aroma of Garlic?

The results of this study intrigued us for a number of reasons. When we consider the aroma itself, garlic is considered a pleasant odor only in the right context.

When was the last time you bought room deodorizing sprays, scented candles, or cosmetic items that feature garlic as the appealing fragrance? The word "fragrance" is never used in reference to garlic. You are more likely to use a room spray to mask the odor of garlic. However, more than one-third of our study participants stated that the odor of garlic induced an olfactory-induced nostalgic response. For the most part, the odor of garlic is linked with food, and if nostalgia is involved, it is probably linked with pleasant associations of group gatherings such as family meals.

A number of possible explanations exist for our results. One is very simple: if the family members liked the taste and smell of garlic bread, then their mood elevated. In a more positive mood state, they were less likely to be critical of, and confrontational with others. In particular, this was true among the males, who tended to be more negative and domineering at the dinner table. While criticism does not lead to positive interactions, pleasant moods tend to enhance generous, expansive feelings while reducing aggressive emotions.

The positive response to garlic bread could be related to a concept known as state-dependent learning. Put simply, this means that recall of information is easier if we repeat the conditions under which we learned the information in the first place. For example, if you drink hot chocolate while you memorize French verb forms in preparation for an exam, you will recall the information more easily if you drink hot chocolate while you take the test. So, in a similar way, if you experienced pleasant family interaction in the presence of an odor, introducing the same smell may influence your mood in a positive way. The odor of garlic may have had this effect among our study participants because of past associations—or learning.

Some men and women in our study said that the garlic bread made the meal special, and this added to the pleasant mood and positive response. It then follows that for at least some participants an olfactory-evoked nostalgic response was in part responsible for the elevated mood. Garlic bread may have consciously or unconsciously triggered a mood that was reminiscent of a happy time in the past.

We do not yet know if garlic itself has a direct effect on the brain and, therefore, changes behavior by changing brain wave activity or brain chemistry. But our study indicates that if you and your family enjoy garlic bread, then by all means serve it often. Its aroma and taste add a special element for many people and anything that elevates mood and leads to positive interactions creates pleasant associations and memories.

Logically, we can ask if garlic bread is one of only a few foods that would show similar results. The taste and smell of garlic is pleasant only in the context of food and meals, which is one reason why studying its effects is possible without other variables potentially interfering. For example, the odor of pumpkin pie was found to be sexually arousing in men, even in the absence of an actual pumpkin pie. Garlic has no similar associations of which we are aware.

Garlic bread is associated with Italian food, one of the most popular ethnic cuisines in our country. But many other types of ethnic cooking call for garlic, and it is widely available in commercial products. Garlic bread is a popular complement to pasta, which currently enjoys great popularity as dinner fare. This made it a logical food to study when looking at dinner table interactions.

More studies are needed to determine which foods may influence family or group interactions, specifically the combination of socializing and eating. At this point, I can't tell you what foods will have a positive effect on your family. However, common sense tells us that if we share food we all enjoy, whether that's pot roast or tofu or pasta, the mood around the table is likely to improve.

Why Study Family Interactions and Odors?

As a psychiatrist, I believe that studying elements of family life at this particular time in our society is a worthwhile undertaking. Despite all the pressures on it, families remain one of the most important influences in childhood. I realize that school, social activities, and television appear to exert even stronger influence, but the fact remains that we learn much about human interaction within our families. In addition, family meals often set the tone for the overall quality of interaction among family members. Many people do not have pleasant childhood memories of family meals eaten in a nurturing environment, and in these individuals, the dinner hour can provoke feelings of anxiety and dread. This is one

reason that holidays often provoke confusing emotions; excitement and anticipation may coexist with anxiety and dread.

Even when family life is working fairly well, meals are often rushed affairs, which are not the conditions we need to create positive associations and memories. This concept becomes important when we look at the future of food and the marketing possibilities behind new food products. It is likely that one day soon "dinner in a tube" will become available. We already have "dinners for one" we can microwave in individual trays, and if that's too much trouble, we can open a can of a liquid "meal replacement" shake—we have our choice between several flavors. Pressures to eliminate some of the time spent shopping and cooking real food, not to mention, shortening actual eating time, logically leads to the notion that we can consume a nutritional paste of some kind and pop a vitamin pill. No doubt, this concept will be marketed as a way to "simplify" our lives. In other words, in a society whose pace is increasing rapidly, sitting down to eat a meal can appear to be just another waste of time. What a huge mistake.

If we look at our evolutionary past, we can see that the family is organized around obtaining, storing, and cooking food—"bringing home the bacon and frying it up in a pan." Throughout human history, meals have been ritualized and organized to include feasts and holidays. Even fast days are an acknowledgment that food and eating have significance and are important enough to sacrifice for a greater purpose. In some homes, meals even add a predictable element to the day. It's Tuesday, it must be roast chicken, or since it's Sunday, dessert is a special treat. In modern life, we may designate Sunday for pizza and Friday for Chinese takeout and maybe Monday for fast food. (I'm not saying this is the best way to plan meals, but the reality is, some families do eat this way.)

In our society, where families tend to live in small nuclear groups rather than in large compounds or houses with extended family present, a meal is a central, unifying symbol. Generally speaking, rather than working together, our modern families spend their days apart. We work, study, play, and so on in different locations. However, our concept of home includes the idea that the place we live is our refuge and where we gather together again after a long day. Even when family members are too busy or too tired to cook, they may meet at restaurants for an

evening meal. Much of the fast food and family restaurant advertising focuses on providing an easy answer to the question "What's for dinner?"

Although this may sound dramatic or a bit far out, I believe we are poised on the brink of doing away with the family meal. Television has changed the way America eats in more ways than one. We know it has changed what we eat, but perhaps even more important, it has changed how we eat. In many homes, meals are no longer opportunities to talk and catch up with each other because the television is on while the family is eating. Even when no children are in the home, many couples fall into the habit of eating their meals on trays in front of the television. When a television dominates a room, one-on-one communication is at a premium. Sex therapists generally advise removing the television from the bedroom, and I believe family therapists should offer the same advice about the dining room or kitchen.

Thinking About the Future

Much has been written about the social element of eating and the symbolic meanings of gathering together. But in only a few words, Leon Kass, M.D., expresses both the positive and negative potential that exists within this superficially simple ritual of the family dinner: "Not surprisingly, incivility, insensitivity, and ingratitude learned at the family table can infect all other aspects of one's life. Conversely, good habits and thoughtful attitudes regarding food and eating will have far-reaching benefits."

It is ironic that at the same time vast amounts and variety of foods are available to us, many families are allowing—little by little—their dinner hour to fade away. I suggest that more research into food, mood, and family atmosphere is needed precisely because we may soon unthinkingly sacrifice an important custom. Furthermore, no mystery exists about the phenomenon. The more activity we pack into a day and the harder we work, the less the time we spend relaxing around the table at the end of the day. Do you remember a time when dinner was meant to signal the end of the day's work?

One important aspect of our garlic bread study involved exploring family interactions. Research using garlic bread or other foods is helpful only if we take seriously the idea that the atmosphere, including the odors of the foods we serve, can influence interpersonal communication while we engage in the ancient ritual of, as Dr. Andrew Weil mentioned, "eating from the same rice bowl." I hope our study stimulates more research into this area of family life. Perhaps our garlic bread study will help to remind you that the atmosphere around your table today is creating the memories that your children carry with them for life.

Chapter Nine
Sexy Nose, Sexy Food

"In the game of food and erotic play, the most desirable shapes, for obvious reasons, are phallic and rounded: carrots and peaches; fleshy, moist textures, like tomatoes and avocados; the sensual colors of skin and the most personal orifices, pomegranates and strawberries; and lingering scents like mango or garlic....No one who has lived to adulthood and has held a fresh tomato in the palm of his hand and bitten into it, feeling its flesh in his mouth as juice streams down his chin, can escape the temptation to compare it with other oral pleasures."

—Isabel Allende

"I have perfumed my bed with myrrh, aloes and cinnamon. Come let us take our fill of love until morning; let us solace ourselves with love."

—Proverbs 7: 17-18

In the 1950s, William Masters and Virginia Johnson, the famous sexuality researchers, suggested that odors influenced sexual arousal, but several decades ago, no accurate way to test this theory existed. Sigmund Freud also understood the connection between sexuality and odors, but he speculated that the sense of smell should be repressed because if it were not, men—but not necessarily women—would live in a constant state of sexual excitement. Freud also linked the sense of smell with his concept of the Oedipal conflict. Freud believed that during a boy's development, he eventually grows to dislike his father's odors, but will have positive associations with the mother's scent. When discussing the Electra complex, a developmental conflict in girls analogous to the oedipal conflict, he did not mention the significance of the parents' odors.

Psychology and child development aside, the world's poets have been writing about sexuality and odors for thousands of years, and this makes sense because we respond to odors on many levels and the sexual responses are direct. The nose is one of our most important "erogenous zones," and during sexual arousal, the nose becomes stuffed up. Most books about sexuality fail to mention this "stuffy nose" phenomenon, and you may not notice it. However, it exists and results from a built-in physiological mechanism.

In chapter two, I described the air currents that form in the nose that allow you to perceive greater concentrations of odor molecules. As the air currents form, the subliminal scent of pheromones and other odors associated with sexuality heighten arousal. We may think of the scents of sex as "intoxicating" and they fuel our passion, but on another level, the odor-arousal mechanism is one of nature's important ways of promoting reproduction and preserving our species.

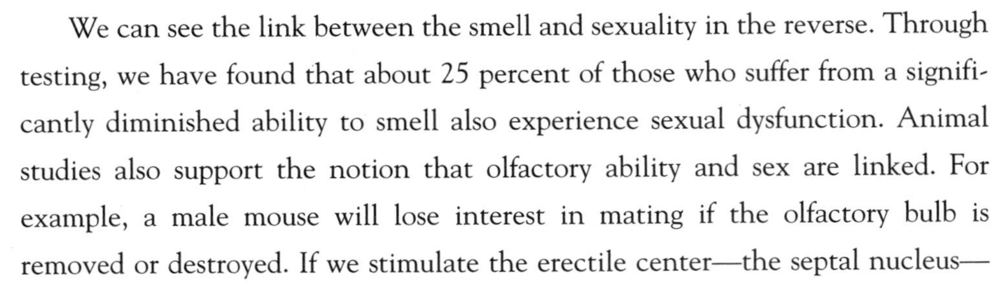

We can see the link between the smell and sexuality in the reverse. Through testing, we have found that about 25 percent of those who suffer from a significantly diminished ability to smell also experience sexual dysfunction. Animal studies also support the notion that olfactory ability and sex are linked. For example, a male mouse will lose interest in mating if the olfactory bulb is removed or destroyed. If we stimulate the erectile center—the septal nucleus—

in the brain of a male squirrel monkey, an erection is induced. A direct pathway connects the olfactory bulb to this part of the brain in both squirrel monkeys and humans. When an odor can act directly on the brain and cause a physiological response, this means that the odor has a neurophysiological action.

Understanding that odors influence sexuality raises many questions, some of which take us into the area of personality characteristics and differences. The research projects conducted by the Smell & Taste Treatment and Research Foundation suggested gender differences in connection with sexual arousal and also provided insight into the types of odors that stimulated the strongest sexual response. And despite the billions of dollars women and men spend on cosmetics and perfumes, it appears that food odors elicit the greatest sexual response. However, we didn't know this when we started our research, and we used a number of different types of odors in our studies.

Food, Sex, and Odors

We continue to speculate about our results—and specifically the response to food smells—and it is possible these odors may have induced a Pavlovian-conditioned response. On a somewhat primitive level, the smell of food reminded the men of their lovers, and the reminder stimulated penile blood flow. In most people, the aroma of baked goods stimulates olfactory-induced recall, which resembles a Pavlovian response to stimuli (see chapter seven). These recalled events usually are positive, and may alter one's mood. Food odors may have been perceived as positive and therefore induced a positive mood state. While in a good mood, the men may have experienced pleasant thoughts, some of them sexually related.

We remain uncertain about the reasons the sexual responses to food odors occurred, although many of the odors are known to have a relaxing effect. For example, the odor of lavender increases alpha waves in the back of the brain. Alpha waves are associated with relaxation and sexual experiences are most enjoyable when you are feeling relaxed. Nothing can kill sexual desire like a hypervigilant state, usually induced by stress and worry.

On the other hand, some smells, such as jasmine, stimulate an increase in beta waves in the front of the brain. Beta waves are associated with an alert state.

In folklore and popular aromatherapy, jasmine is associated with sensuality and sex. We tested peppermint, which is also associated with inducing an awake and alert state.

Are we certain that the responses were directly sexually related? While we believe they are, we are aware that some odors may induce an aggressive response, which in male squirrel monkeys—and probably in human males as well—increases blood flow to the penis. If this were the case, the response would have been involuntary and not resulting from consciously aggressive feelings.

We are still left with the question about why food smells stimulated the greatest increase in penile blood flow. Perhaps it is related to our evolutionary past, which included definite periods of "feast or famine." Reproduction occurs in a predictable pattern when food supplies are abundant. Most of us do not dwell much on that issue because in the West, finding enough food is not an issue for the majority of individuals. (I realize exceptions exist.)

Early human beings roamed their territories in search of food and they tended to gather at the site of animal kills. Since their ability to preserve food was limited, they most likely ate large quantities of food during times of availability. These occasions offered opportunities for procreation, and hence, the link between food and sex was established. Even when humans became tied to agricultural villages, the association between plentiful food and sexuality remained.

For conception to occur, women require a minimal percentage of body fat, and menstrual cycles may stop for a time when food supplies are inadequate. When conditions are such that new life can be supported, then fertility cycles return. In the ways of nature, the procreative imperative is strong when conditions are favorable and the imperative not to reproduce is equally strong when conditions are unfavorable. So, over millennia of evolution on the planet, plentiful food odors equal a favorable time to procreate.

In modern times, food odors do not necessarily make us think about reproduction—they induce a sexual response, which is apart from procreation. While we go to great lengths to control fertility, we do little to discourage sexual pleasure. We have biological mechanisms that urge us to reproduce and keep our species going.

Measuring Male Arousal

The traditional method of assessing sexual arousal in men involves measuring penile blood flow, by means of a small blood pressure cuff attached to the penis. (This is the method used to measure impotence and other male sexual dysfunction.) In our study, we also attached a blood pressure cuff to the arm because we wanted to determine if the odors we introduced caused generalized changes in blood pressure.

We conducted our first study of odors and male arousal in 1994, using twenty-five male medical student volunteers. The study was double-blind and randomized, meaning that neither the research team nor the research volunteers knew which odors were used or the order in which they were introduced. This removed any potential bias on the part of the investigators, or the medical student participants.

Each subject wore an odorized surgical mask, with each odor introduced individually. The odorized mask was worn for one full minute. (This one-minute interval allowed us to eliminate a phenomenon called the "novelty effect," which simply means that any new stimulus brings about some kind of response. By keeping the masks in place for a full sixty seconds, the changes induced by the novelty had time to wear off.) After one minute, we measured changes in penile blood flow resulting from each odor. We maintained three-minute intervals between the introduction of each new smell, and no mask was worn during this "wash-out" period, which allowed the nose and the penis to return to baseline.

You may wonder how anyone could become sexually aroused when hooked up to blood pressure machines in a laboratory. However, the way the body reacts to odors and penile blood flow are involuntary responses. Changes in blood flow to the penis can be induced by a variety of tactile, visual, or olfactory stimuli.

The Macho Cinnamon Roll

We tested a variety of scents, including, of course, common floral scents and perfumes. Because we needed what is known as a "control," we added in the scent of baked cinnamon buns. We thought of it as a control item because we didn't

expect the odor of cinnamon rolls to have an effect on sexual arousal. Therefore, we could measure how it performed when compared with fragrances typically associated with sexual or romantic settings. Our assumptions were incorrect, however, because the cinnamon rolls turned out to be the sexiest odor—at least as measured by penile blood flow.

Our results formed the basis for all kinds of jokes and speculation about what Grandma really meant when she talked about the "way to a man's heart." On the other hand, we had to determine if what our study actually "proved" was that male medical students are always hungry—looking at it from a scientific viewpoint, that's what our results might well have meant.

In 1995, we conducted a second study that included thirty-one men drawn from the general population in the Chicago area, and they represented a wider age range (eighteen to sixty-four) than our first study. Demographically, our study subjects were fairly typical American men (see Appendix 8).

We isolated thirty odors, which represented different categories of smells, including perfumes and food. However, we combined some odors and ended up with a total forty-six tested odors. The method of testing was identical to that used in the first study. Of the forty-six odors and combination of scents, the lavender-pumpkin pie mixture resulted in the greatest degree of measurable sexual arousal. In fact, this combination increased penile blood flow by an average of 40 percent. We retested cinnamon rolls, too, of course, and that odor again ended up in the "winning" group.

Other "virile" odors in our study included a combination of licorice and doughnuts, which increased penile blood flow by a median of 31.5 percent. A pumpkin pie and doughnut combination was also a winner, with a 20 percent penile blood flow increase recorded.

It appears that some odors do not "measure up." If you're thinking about romance during Thanksgiving dinner, inhale the pumpkin pie, but leave the cranberry sauce alone because it increased blood flow by only two percent, the lowest percentage of any odor used in the study. Chocolate, generally considered a romantic giant among foods, also showed little power to arouse, whereas licorice, which is not considered a sexual food or odor, showed considerable abil-

ity to increase blood flow. We tested some odors because we wanted representative odors from different categories, even if no logical reason existed for their inclusion. For example, we tested baby powder, which came in near the bottom of the list.

Some men responded moderately to the odor of buttered popcorn, orange scent, and musk, and the combination of licorice and cola increased penile blood flow more than either odor alone. Overall the combination odors produced the strongest responses, which makes some sense when we consider that food odors tend to occur in groups.

We found that our older participants had a stronger response to the odor of vanilla than that among the younger men. Those who expressed the most satisfaction with their sex lives showed a greater response to the strawberry scent. The men who had the most active sex lives, that is those who reported the greatest sexual intercourse frequency, responded most strongly to the odor of lavender, as well as to Oriental spice and cola. No odor diminished penile blood flow.

Although various media personalities and columnists had great fun with this study, the press failed to mention that the man who showed the strongest response to the lavender and pumpkin pie combination was asleep throughout the testing. Remember that blood flow response is involuntary, and obvious sexual cues were unnecessary. We also know that the brain's response to odors is not controlled by rational thought processes—our sleeping subject shows us that the brain does what it does, with or without us, so to speak.

Measuring Female Arousal

Once we learned that odors influence penile blood flow, it logically follows that odors would influence female arousal. In 1997, we recruited thirty volunteers between ages eighteen and forty. We chose women within this reproductive range, but not pregnant or actively trying to become pregnant, although we attempted to perform the tests on individuals around the time of ovulation (see Appendix 9).

We excluded anorgasmic women—that is, women who do not experience orgasm—because we wanted to test a group whose experiences fall into the large

normal range of sexual response. In addition to establishing the effect of odors on orgasmic women, researchers would later be able to isolate certain odors and test them as a treatment modality for women with orgasmic or arousal disorders. (The results of our male study led us to speculate that odors could be useful in treating sexual dysfunction. We knew this was a possibility in our female study.)

The thirty women were instructed not to have sexual stimulation, either by a partner or through masturbation, for forty-eight hours prior to testing. During the testing process, a sterile monitoring gauge, a photophlethysmograph, similar in shape to a tampon, was placed in the vagina. This device measures pulse pressure, which indicates any change in blood flow to the vagina. The gauge was hooked up to a computer, which recorded changes in pulse strength.

Odorized masks with different individual and combined odors were presented to each woman. (Neither the examiner nor the study subject knew which odors were introduced and in what order they were presented.) Just as in the male study, the odorized masks were in place for one minute, followed by a one-minute period when no mask was in place, during which blood flow was measured.

We tested the following odors individually and in combinations: charcoal barbecue smoke, mesquite barbecue smoke, cucumber, cherry, lemon, banana nut bread, pumpkin pie, lavender, Good & Plenty candy, cranberry, baby powder, sweet pea, parsley, coconut, green apple, baked cinnamon bun, peach, Oriental spice fragrance, grape, chocolate, root beer, cappuccino, gardenia, and some popular perfumes and colognes. Some of these odors had been used for other studies, such as our odor and weight loss study. Good & Plenty candy is a popular non-chocolate candy product and we had it in the lab. We tested chocolate because it is purported to be a "sexy" food, and we included some perfumes and colognes because they have a reputation for contributing to sexual arousal. Obviously, we had hundreds of odors to choose from, and our sample was representative of food scents and popular cosmetic products. Our combination odors were representative as well, but we did not have preconceived ideas about which combinations would yield particular results.

Following the one-minute measurements, each woman was asked if the odor was familiar, if could she identify it, and if she liked or disliked it. We also included a series of tests of olfactory ability. This group of tests allowed us to establish olfactory acuity and identify those who had a normal sense of smell and those with lesser—or no—ability to smell.

The female sexuality study was designed to gather as much demographic and personal data as possible, so each woman completed a questionnaire that asked for information about such things as favorite colognes, favorite food, least favorite food, number of sexual partners and encounters in the previous thirty days, sexual preference, and so forth. We also asked if a particular odor caused the women to recall their childhood.

In addition, we asked about orgasmic functioning, including frequency of sexual activity in the previous thirty days and previous six months. We determined the number of women who experienced orgasm infrequently, and we identified a group of women who were multiorgasmic. We didn't know if this information would make a statistical difference when measuring response to odors, but we wanted it to be available for comparison. As it turned out, these data helped us analyze complex results.

The final group of questions was very personal and explored the study subjects' experiences with and attitudes toward various types of sexual activity. Each activity was rated for its ability to arouse or to inhibit arousal. Using a scale from -1 to 5, participants were asked if particular activities were either very arousing (5) or adversely affected their arousal (-1). These activities included such activities as seeing a lover nude, kissing of the breasts and nipples, a lover stimulating the genitals with the mouth and tongue, making love in an unusual place, and so forth. Answers to twenty-eight questions were used to rate sexual anxiety. Participants rated not only what did and did not arouse them, but also what activities induced anxious feelings, which were defined as extreme uneasiness or distress.

As was true in our male study, almost all our participants were heterosexual; very few reported ever having same-sex partners. A correlation existed between the overall enjoyment of sex and the frequency of orgasm (almost 90 percent of the time) with frequent sexual activity, from several times a week to several times a day. These same women also reported experiencing multiple orgasms several times a week.

As you can probably see, we collected more data from women than from men. This was not a case of discriminatory medical testing, however. Female sexual arousal, as measured by blood flow, has not been as extensively studied as male arousal. We attempted to gather as much information as possible about an area of female sexuality that needs more research. In addition, for many reasons, female blood flow studies are more costly to carry out and, in just one study, we were able collect information that covered a number of different areas.

A Complex Female Response

While no odor decreased blood flow in the men's study, this was not the case with our female study subjects. In fact, as a group, several smells impaired arousal. The baseline blood flow measurement actually decreased when cherry (18 percent reduction) and charcoal barbecue smoke (14 percent reduction) were introduced. Some smells showed minimal effect. For example, male colognes actually decreased vaginal blood flow by 1 percent, and female perfumes increased it by only 1 percent. A combination of baby powder resulted in a 4 percent increase.

The pumpkin pie and lavender combination increased vaginal blood flow by 11 percent, but the odor that had the greatest power to induce female sexual arousal was a combination of Good & Plenty candy and cucumber, which increased blood flow by 13 percent. While the Good & Plenty and cucumber combination was arousing to most women, differences occurred based on preferred sexual behavior and activities. For example, the women could be subgrouped into those who were extremely sexually aroused when a lover manually stimulated her genitals and those who were not. Women who found manual genital stimulation arousing showed a 12 percent increase in vaginal blood flow in response to pumpkin pie and lavender and averaged an 18 percent increase with the Good & Plenty-cucumber combination.

On the other hand, no odors induced sexual arousal in participants who were not extremely aroused by manual genital stimulation. Among this group, many odors inhibited arousal, including male colognes and perfumes, both of which decreased blood flow by 14 percent. Among the women in this group, even Good & Plenty and cucumber decreased blood flow by 13 percent.

Differences appeared between women who found masturbation arousing and those who did not. The women who reported that masturbation was extremely arousing were also the women for whom every odor had an arousing effect. The greatest effects were found with Good & Plenty and banana nut bread combination (28 percent increase) and the Good & Plenty and cucumber combination (22 percent). Among these women, popular perfumes showed an 18 percent increase in vaginal blood flow, as did baby powder, which was nearly as arousing at a 16 percent increase.

Among women who were frequently multiorgasmic (one-third of the time), the odor of baby powder reduced vaginal blood flow by 8 percent; the mono-orgasmic were aroused in response to baby powder with an average increase of vaginal blood flow of 15 percent.

It is possible that, like the men, the women in our study had a Pavlovian response—a conditioned response to the familiar odors we presented. If that were the case, then our results suggest that baby powder, cucumber, banana nut bread, and Good & Plenty reminded the women of their partners! But it's also possible that the odors evoked a nostalgic response. Some participants reported that baby powder made them recall their childhood, and we know that nostalgic responses tend to induce a more relaxed mood and remove inhibitions.

Some of the odors may have stimulated the reticular activating system of the brain, which makes one awake and alert. The noise of an alarm clock activates this system. In an alert state, the women may have become more aware of sensory stimuli in the environment, including sexual cues. In addition, the odors may have acted directly on the brain to reduce anxiety, a connection made in other research.

Women's responses to food odors were not as homogeneous as men's responses, but overall the Good & Plenty-cucumber combination was the most effective odor. Subgroups of women responded quite differently to the same odors and we linked their responses with their preference for various sexual activities and behaviors.

After our male sexuality study, we were not surprised to find that food odors induced arousal, at least among certain groups of women. In short, sexual arousal in

the presence of food odors makes evolutionary sense. Furthermore, it does not make good evolutionary sense for one sex of the species to be aroused when the other is not. Our female sexuality study showed a combination of food odors as the most sexually arousing, which further supports the link between food odors and sexuality.

From the Lab to the Perfume Bottle

Our studies showed that a wide variety of odors have a positive effect on penile blood flow and women's responses tend to be more complex. Still, some odors stood out: pumpkin pie and lavender for men and cucumber and Good & Plenty for women.

Overall, the value of cologne for men and women remains in question, but colognes for men and perfumes for women that feature these food odors are now on the market. Called SA for Men and SA for Women, these colognes are formulated with pumpkin pie and lavender for men and cucumber and Good & Plenty for women. I expect to see additional products in the near future because we continue to study these and other odors. (See the "Resource" section for information about purchasing these colognes.)

Listening to Your Partner

Our research tells us that we should pay attention to our partners when they tell us they do or do not like a particular scent, even if we like it—it could make all the difference to our sex lives. If a woman says she doesn't like your cologne, believe her! If you don't listen, you may be interfering with her pleasure during a sexual encounter with you. And, the next time you decide to surprise your lover with a gift of candy, skip the chocolate bars and bring home a box of Good & Plenty, and better yet, mix up a cucumber salad!

Personality and Food Odors

Now that you have read about the link between odors and sexuality, answer the questions below to gain insight into your "sexual personality."

For Men:

Which do you prefer: Pick one group of foods, either 1 or 2.

1) Cranberries, chocolate, and pink grapefruit?

2) Pumpkin pie, donuts, and black licorice?

If you picked the first group, then you tend to think about sex much of the time. You're sexually expressive if you're in balance, but if you aren't, you tend to be sexually aggressive. You are a "people person," and you like close, intimate relationships. But, you could be considered domineering, too, unless you temper that side of your personality.

If you picked the second group, you tend to be sexually reserved and perhaps more interested in other parts of your life. You may be contemplative and thoughtful, but you enjoy group activities, too. You may be involved in some sports, and you value male friendships. You express your feelings to men easily, but fear of rejection tends to make you more reserved and even somewhat fearful around women.

For Women:

Which do you prefer: (Choose one from each group.)

1) Good & Plenty and banana nut bread?

2) Pumpkin pie and cherries?

If you prefer the candy and banana nut bread, you tend to escape into sexual and romantic fantasies. You enjoy physical contact and tend to be a sensitive person who enjoys self-discovery. You tend to be inquisitive.

If you prefer the second group, you tend to be more conservative, and you see things in terms of black and white—something is either wrong or right. You're a realist in your relationships.

As you can see, the results of our study show that we prefer what we need to complete ourselves on some level. So, if you preferred the most "sexy" foods, those foods that tended to increase arousal, then you tend to desire foods that increase your sexual feelings. On the other hand, if you already have sexual feelings, you do not desire the foods that increase your sexual desire or "sexual persona." Like the "vanilla personality," this might seem like the opposite of what you assumed to be true, but this is the way the results came out. We come back to the principle that we eat what we need, which is a way of eating that is different from eating who we are.

Ordering Ice Cream—a Sexual Experience?

Cosmopolitan magazine asked us to describe male behavior in romantic relationships based on ice cream preference. We haven't yet studied women's sexual behavior and preferred ice cream flavor, but our study results lead one to wonder if a cucumber/Good & Plenty ice cream flavor will appear one day. This is what we found:

Vanilla: He's seductive, flirtatious, easily bored, and craves novelty in his sexual activities. His desire for change means that he likes sexual experimentation with his partner, or if that's not available, he might be vulnerable to straying outside his primary relationship.

Strawberry: These men are generally more insecure than the vanilla-lovers, and this insecurity extends to the bedroom. This man likes to be dominated, but he is easily hurt and may feel inadequate by even minor criticism. Even neutral statements may be interpreted as criticism.

Chocolate: The chocolate lover tends to dominate, and he may be jealous if his partner mentions old boyfriends. Sexually, he may be on the selfish side, and when he's done, he thinks the act is over!

Butter Pecan: He is Mr. Routine—not very inventive, but he won't stray because he's loyal and true. Over time, his partner could become bored with him.

Combining Food and Sex

Our drives for food and sex are very powerful, and we often see them on the stage together. Many foods are considered romantic gifts and sharing a meal can be a romantic, even erotic event. In general, sharing food enhances communication, which is why many business transactions take place over lunch or dinner and explains the reasons why so much of dating involves going out for food.

If you have ever seen Dr. Alex Comfort's sex manual *The New Joy of Sex*, you will notice that he divides the book into sections that resemble a menu: "The Ingredients," "Appetizers," "Main Courses," and "Sauces." Sex and food is described in "Appetizers," which links food as a prelude to sex.

Our language also reflects the food/sex connection: "He's so handsome I could eat him up," or "I could just devour her." We talk about our sexual "appetites," and some people might say they're "hungry" for love. And you might look for ways to "spice" up your sex life. Perhaps a friend tells you she's enjoying her "juicy" love affair. "Juicy" gossip usually involves sex.

We use our mouths to eat and also to show affection and make love; the link couldn't be more clear given the many words and phrases we use to link food and sex. Pheromones and other scents may attract us, but as we begin to make love, we not only inhale these odors, we begin tasting each other, too.

Food as Aphrodisiacs

Aphrodisiac qualities have been linked with any number of foods either because they increase desire or improve performance. For example, alcohol is said to release inhibitions, but as you may know, too much of a good thing interferes

with performance. Based on surveys, wine is considered a sexy food, beer and hard liquor are not. One reason wine and champagne may be linked with romance and sex has to do with the glasses they're served in. The long stem and deep bowls containing the liquid may subconsciously remind us of male and female genitalia. Even the way we hold the glass can be suggestive of erotic caresses.

Data based on hard science have yet to show that any food is a true aphrodisiac, which does not eliminate the possibility of a placebo effect. If individuals believe they become more sexually powerful if they eat certain foods, then the mind could be influencing performance. In addition, these beliefs usually enter consciousness at a young age. If children learn that oysters are a sexy food, then they probably link oysters and sexuality as adults. Oysters are often eaten live and, therefore, are considered a life-giving food, which increases its value as an aphrodisiac. The same is true for caviar.

The word "aphrodisiac" comes from Aphrodite, the Greek goddess who was born from the sea. Many cultures have been influenced by Greek mythology, and hence, seafood in often associated with sexuality. Since female sexual odors are slightly salty, they may act as subconscious reminders of the sea. According to the folklore of aphrodisiacs, men are attracted to such foods as oysters and link them with sexual arousal and desire. In the last decade or so, many odorized household products have come on the market with names that are references to the ocean and sea breezes. The smells of the ocean are considered soothing, and some of the most romantic spots in the world (at least according to their reputation) are on the water.

Foods are sometimes invested with aphrodisiac qualities based on the way they look. For example, oysters, mussels, and bearded clams are said to resemble female genitalia; asparagus and ginseng resemble male genitalia. In some cultures, cinnamon and ginger are said to have aphrodisiac qualities, and this is especially interesting because they are spices traditionally used to flavor pumpkin pie. Also consistent with our study, licorice water is purported to be an aphrodisiac.

Although I discuss chocolate in detail in another chapter, the cocoa plant is a well-known proposed aphrodisiac. And the link between chocolate and love may be a chemical one. When we fall in love, our brain chemistry changes, and some popular psychologists have said this chemical change is what makes us feel so "intoxicated" by love. Chocolate contains phenylalanine, an amino acid that stimulates the production of endorphins, a chemical in the brain that dulls pain. People newly in love show elevated levels of phenylalanine, a state that is linked with the "heady" behavior of the newly in love. It is also associated with reduced appetite, which is why you may have the desire to eat less during the exhilarating infatuation period of a romance. Conversely, low levels of endorphins also are associated with depression, so craving chocolate may actually be a psychological craving for a way to lift one's mood, and in a sense, food becomes a substitute for love.

In popular folklore, animal substances such as the testicles of sheep and bulls are considered aphrodisiacs, along with other substances extracted from mammalian sexual organs. These substances are then made into sexual tonics and teas. Their effects are most likely related to a cultural belief that the substance has power as a sexual tonic. Ultimately, however, these substances may be found to contain components that increase blood flow to the genitals or, like chocolate, alter brain chemistry.

Beyond Sex

Sexual relationships are one thing; enduring romantic partnerships are another. In looking at food preferences in romantic relationships, we found that in stable partnerships, which we defined as marriage that have lasted three or more years, spouses tend to prefer the same foods. They may not start out with the same likes and dislikes, but over time they tend to accept and adopt each other's food choices. We found that in relationships that did not last a minimum of three years, the food preferences were different.

We cannot say for sure what these observations mean, except that on a primitive level, we tend to return to "love me, love my food" and "I love you, so I'll love your food" identification. Perhaps a growing stability within a relationship is reflected in the gradual blending of preferences in many areas, including food. I met my wife, Debra, almost twenty years ago. She was a vegetarian and I was

not. However, I changed my diet to match hers, which may have been my way of feeling close to her and perhaps of showing my acceptance of her through adopting her dietary preferences. So, on a symbolic level, blending food preferences may have a strong emotional component that includes forming a bond with another person. We know this happens in the short-term. Business etiquette almost demands that we order similar foods during business meals. A short-term bond is formed when we share food. Perhaps a long-term bond is strengthened when we develop matching or at least similar food preferences.

Chapter Ten

Can the Chef Taste the Soup?

"I feel a recipe is only a theme, which an intelligent cook can play each time with a variation."

—Madame Benoit

"The secret of good cooking is, first, having a love of it....If you're convinced cooking is drudgery, you're never going to be good at it, and you might as well warm up something frozen."

—James Beard

When you were in school or entering the military or applying for a job, you may have taken a battery of tests designed to assess your aptitudes. These tests may have helped you choose a career path, or they may have guided a potential employer about the best type of job to offer you. Career and employment assessment usually includes personality testing such as the Minnesota Multiphasic Personality Inventory (MMPI), which is one of the tests we have used in our food-personality studies. Although this isn't yet the case, one day it is likely that odor and food preference questions will become a standard part of personality assessment. As I've said, we're poised on the brink of a new world of information about smell and taste and their link to mood, behavior, and components of personality. It will probably not be long before psychotherapists, for example, will interview their patients to determine how their odor and taste preferences influence life decisions, as well as their mood states. Our study of olfactory-evoked recall suggests that therapists can use such information to learn more about sensory influences on their patients. For example, by suggesting unpleasant or pleasant odors and foods to patients, associations with the smells and foods may emerge. In addition, in the nostalgia study, one in fourteen individuals reported having an unhappy childhood and specific unpleasant odors were associated with their youth. These odors tended to be unpleasant, but it is possible that by talking with patients about the unpleasant odors details about the events and circumstances that contributed to the unhappy childhood would emerge.

As research continues, perhaps we will one day have the ability to link personality disorders with certain kinds of food preferences. For example, we know that potato chip lovers tend to be aggressive and are usually go-getters. Most people with aggressive tendencies become socialized and can modulate their behavior, but what about the pathologically aggressive? Eventually, we may be able to link excessive consumption of certain foods with expressions of aggression or hostility. The data to do this is lacking at this time, but food preference research may lead us in this direction.

Several years ago, I began to wonder if professional choices could be influenced by our olfactory acuity or perhaps even odor preferences. It seemed logical to start our research with a group of people for whom a sense of smell would be of paramount importance. We chose chefs for a variety of reasons that relate to olfactory ability.

Such a Good Sense of Smell

The medical term for an abnormally acute sense of smell is hyperosmia. Though relatively rare, it significantly affects those who live with this condition.

Hyperosmia is a symptom of a relatively rare illness, Addison's disease. In Addison's disease, the adrenal glands malfunction and are unable to produce sufficient amounts of hydrocortisone and aldosterone, hormones normally produced by the adrenals. This is always a serious disease, and treatment involves giving the patient corticosteroid drugs.

In the years that followed President Kennedy's assassination, we've learned he suffered from Addison's disease and was treated with corticosteroid medications, which were relatively new drugs at that time. Although his closest advisors knew about his illness, the general public was kept in the dark. Today, it would probably be impossible to maintain that level of secrecy about a serious disease affecting an important leader, especially an illness that may be exacerbated by stress. Hyperosmia itself can be an extremely disabling symptom of Addison's disease.

One of my patients at the Smell & Taste Treatment and Research Foundation suffered from this disease, and we evaluated her hyperacute sense of smell. After administering our standard smell and taste tests, we could indeed see why she said she was a prisoner of her nose. Her sense of smell was so good that she was unable to leave her house! She could smell a fire two miles away, and she was so overwhelmed by odors in stores that she had to leave. She used the word "flee" to describe the urgency with which she had to escape the assault of odors she faced in her day-to-day life.

Those who derive great pleasure from the smells around them might think that hyperosmia wouldn't be so bad—it could even be pleasant. However, our senses are moderated for a reason. What if you could hear every blade of grass being cut with a mower? Or, what if you could hear a baby crying a mile away, along with all the other sounds occurring in between? That's what my patient's sense of smell was like. She suffered even more because no one understood what she was talking about when she tried to describe the way both good smells and bad made her life hellish.

Her condition was ameliorated when her illness, Addison's disease, was diagnosed and treated. However, her condition led to speculation that having an increased sense of smell might lead individuals to professions where this ability

would be put to good use. In order to test this theory, we examined careers in which the sense of smell is critical.

Professional perfumers seemed like a logical and obvious choice, but it soon became clear that testing was impractical. Relatively speaking, an insufficient number of professional perfumers exist to form a pool big enough to draw from and adequately test.

Wine tasters also appeared to be a good choice, but on delving more deeply we learned that they lack consensus about what makes a good wine taster. Furthermore, studies already had established that wine tasters all described the same wine as different when the only factor that changed was the color. In other words, wine tasters who differentiate on the basis of the "bouquet" may be making their evaluations on how the wine looks, rather than on taste and smell.

We then decided to test high-caliber chefs (see Appendix 10). We chose chefs from ten restaurants that *Chicago Magazine* had rated as having superior culinary standards. We believed cooking in these upscale establishments demonstrated they had proven themselves in their profession. As would most people, we also assumed that these chefs were such accomplished cooks because their ability to detect odors was in the normal range, but that their ability to identify odors was probably superior and likely gave them an extra edge in their profession. We also believed that the chefs' ability to taste would be within the normal range. If chefs have a poor ability to taste, their tendency would be to overseason food as they prepared it, but if their taste acuity was above normal, they would underseason food and develop a reputation for preparing bland dishes.

The chefs from all ten restaurants agreed to participate in the study. Their average age was about 32.5 years, with the oldest being fifty and the youngest twenty-five. With the oldest at age fifty, our group of chefs would not have yet been affected by age-related olfactory impairment. We chose to design our study using male chefs. Women have a better sense of smell to begin with and would need to be tested differently because their olfactory acuity changes throughout the menstrual cycle, and this becomes an additional variable.

The protocol we used was very strict in order to eliminate possible contamination of the lab with odors introduced to it, but also to eliminate adaptation to odors. A person exposed to an odor will adapt to it, thereby losing the ability to perceive it. Most individuals cannot smell their perfume or aftershave lotion a short time after applying it. Adaptation to odors can persist in an individual, just as calluses may remain on a laborer's hands even after a vacation.

In order to eliminate possible adaptation and the effects of chemicals in foods and their byproducts, which may impair smell and taste, we asked the chefs to: 1) abstain from alcohol for four days, 2) give up caffeine and pastries for two days, and 3) not smoke, chew gum, eat and drink, or use scented soaps and shampoos and other cosmetic products, including deodorant and toothpaste, for eight hours. We then administered eleven standard smell and taste tests, such as the University of Pennsylvania Smell Inventory Test (UPSIT), which measures ability to identify forty scratch-and-sniff odorants and the Connecticut Olfactory Tests, which measures the ability to identify twenty odorants.

Other tests measured the ability to detect and/or identify odors in varying concentrations. Taste tests included one that measured the ability to detect the taste of sweet, sour, salt, and bitter at normally detectable concentrations; a second taste test measured the ability to distinguish among the four flavors and identify them.

Logic Does Not Always Rule

When looking at the results of the UPSIT, we found that the average score for the ten chefs was 97.5 percent correct (meaning they correctly identified the odors 97.5 percent of the time) on the forty scratch-and-sniff odor identification tests. The older chefs scored as high as the younger ones, which we expected. Relative to the thousands of normal individuals who have taken the UPSIT, the chefs ranked on a percentile basis from 29 at the lowest to 99 at the highest, with the average rank of 81. What this means is that among the male diners in restaurants where these men are chefs, almost 20 percent have a better sense of smell than the chef does. We can extrapolate that about 20 percent of these men will find the food not quite to their liking. One chef ranked at the 29 percentile, which is among the lowest third of the male population. So, this chef has a poorer sense of smell than about two-thirds of his male patrons. Before you wonder why he still

had his job, you should know that he is reputed to be one of the top chefs in the country!

On the Connecticut Olfactory Test, the average score was 32.5 percent, and three of the ten chefs scored so poorly that they met the clinical criteria for a diagnosis of hyposmia, or poor sense of smell. It is interesting to note that these three men were unaware of any difficulties with their sense of smell. In the general population, we know this is a typical response to diminished ability to smell. If you could not detect any odors (anosmic) you would probably report this failing to your doctor. You would certainly mention it to your spouse or friends. If you experienced phantosmias, that is, perceptions of odd smells, you would likely tell others, too.

Hyposmia is especially insidious because it often occurs gradually over many years, unless trauma or an acute infection brings it on. The affected individuals may unconsciously learn to compensate for the problem. Perhaps they begin ordering the spicier food on menus, which is an attempt to add taste by stimulating the trigeminal nerve (see chapter two). Perhaps they shake more salt on their food before they taste it, or if they prepare food, they may begin adding extra seasonings, which is what logic would lead us to expect from the chefs. Eventually, adaptation to a diminished ability to smell makes the situation seems normal—even to men who cook for a living.

On the taste tests, all the chefs easily detected the sweet, sour, and bitter tastes, but two chefs were unable to detect salt at normally detectable levels. Seven of the ten chefs (including the two who were unable to detect the salt taste) had difficulty when asked to distinguish between sour and bitter substances. These individuals rated poorer in overall ability to taste than is expected among the normal population. As odd as it appears, only three chefs rated normal on the taste tests.

The chefs had poorer ability to taste than expected, but six of the ten had excellent olfactory abilities. In addition, these six did not become insensitive to odors after repeated exposures, which presumably is an important skill for a chef who experienced daily exposure to the same group of smells. To summarize our results, we can state that between 30 and 40 percent of the chefs showed *reduced*

ability to smell, and 70 percent showed *reduced* ability to taste. And perhaps equally important, none of the others showed evidence of hyperosmia, the exceptional ability to smell. Despite the range of abilities demonstrated by these tests, none of the chefs felt at all deficient in ability to smell and taste, and each has distinguished himself as an excellent chef.

Explaining the Results

Needless to say, our venture into assessing chemosensory abilities and career choice did not turn out as we expected. Even considering the limitations inherent in the testing, we had to look for possible explanations. Tests for smell and taste tend to use simple chemical substances, where our chefs were accustomed to creating culinary feasts where the ability to perceive complex interactions among ingredients may be more critical to the success of the meal. Currently, neurological science cannot explain or analyze all the components that comprise the skills of a gourmet chef.

It is possible that the chefs had developed the olfactory equivalent of high-tone hearing loss. Factory workers who are continually exposed to loud noises eventually lose hearing for high frequencies. Since the chefs are continually exposed to odors, they may lose their sensitivity and be unable to detect certain categories of smells. This is unlikely, however, because we have no evidence that nontoxic odors can damage the olfactory apparatus. Nor do we have evidence that chefs tend to develop an "olfactory callus," similar to the callus we may develop when we write in longhand. Again, this change in ability would be related to continual use of a particular sense, but no evidence to date establishes this phenomenon for smell or taste.

The taste deficits may have a physiological explanation, in that taste receptors tend to change over time. The ability to detect a taste goes up and down depending on exposure. When tested, individuals who salt their food heavily are unable to detect small amounts of salt. Patients who start salt-free diets find their meals bland and dull for the first week or so, but then their taste receptors adapt and they enjoy other flavors. Once they adapt, these men and women are among the first to claim that the food is too salty, while others do not even notice it.

The Theory of Compensation

One explanation for the low scores on the chemosensory tests may be related to the theory of compensation. By that I mean that personality or physical characteristics or deficits can often drive people to over compensate, sometimes in dramatic ways. Entertainers may be very shy, but take to the stage to compensate for their difficulties. Michael Jackson is said to be extremely shy and is quite reclusive, yet he gives riveting performances to audiences of thousands. Wilma Rudolph suffered childhood polio and walked with her legs in braces, yet she went on to win Olympic medals in track and field events. James Earl Jones, an accomplished actor, has a speech impediment. Basketball players Mugsy Bogues and Spudd Webb were discouraged from going into the game because they are well below the height of the average male in this country, let alone the average professional player. Both became accomplished professionals.

It is not accidental that those whose lives have been troubled by a problem often go into medical and mental health fields where they work on that very issue—child abuse, addiction, phobia, fear of death, and so forth. In a way, each is compensating for something internal, although the motivation may not be conscious. So, we can't rule out the possibility that chefs are led to the profession because they are compensating for a problem they may not be aware of on a conscious level. Since we know that unconscious desires and drives stimulate many human behaviors, this isn't an illogical hypothesis.

When looking at careers and personalities, it may be that choices we make based on who we are involve a complex interaction, and draw upon conscious or unconscious deficits more than we realize. Striving to compensate for deficits often calls for great strength and determination. This is obvious when we look at public figures, celebrities, or actors whose personal barrier is apparent, but it may be subtler when we look at chefs, schoolteachers, or physicians.

We also noticed that the studied chefs were better at identifying odors than they were at detecting them. In other words, they had a high odor threshold, but once they knew an odor was present they accurately identified what it was. Detection and identification abilities are independent of each other. We believe an internal structure for odors exists, and that this structure is similar to that for

hue in color vision and for auditory pitch in hearing. This internal structure for smell and taste may well be the most significant attribute of a gourmet chef, and it is not dependent on sensitivity to odors. A hyposmic chef may be able to create a culinary masterpiece just as Beethoven could compose symphonies after he could no longer hear music.

Left-Brain/Right-Brain

In chapter two, I discussed the issue of handedness and the dominant nostril. In general, the dominant nostril correlates with the dominant hand, so a right-handed person smells better through the right nostril. However, among the ten chefs we tested, the opposite appears to be true. (Eight chefs were right-handed, one was left-handed, and one was ambidextrous.) The reason is not as mysterious as it may seem.

For most of us, odors are processed in the right brain, the emotional and creative control center. However, once odors and tastes become part of one's profession, they tend to be processed in the left brain, which controls intellectual skills. This "brain switch" is not restricted to chefs. Professional musicians perceive music in the left brain, while for the rest of us, music is a right brain or emotional and creative activity.

Once an activity becomes processed in a logical, rational way, then the theory of compensation for a deficit is likely at work, too. Beethoven composed when he was deaf, but he knew what the music should sound like. Similarly, chefs know intellectually how something should smell because they have such a wide knowledge of the subtleties of odors.

Choosing a Restaurant

It is likely that male chefs with a below average sense of smell season their dishes more heavily, which leads to the question: Who are the diners in these restaurants? We know that at least some of these upscale restaurants catered to older businessmen, who usually had at least one mixed drink before eating, and many were also smokers. Both alcohol and tobacco use diminish both smell and taste. Lightly seasoned food, which women tend to favor because their ability to

smell and taste is usually better anyway, would seem bland to these older male diners. A chef with a superior sense of smell and taste might be the opposite of what some of these restaurants need. The moral of the story is, if you own a restaurant, decide what population you're catering to and adjust your cooking to fit that group. Although not consciously aware of the link between their chef's and their customers' chemosensory abilities, these successful restaurants were catering to their niche market and satisfying their customers.

Salt and Pepper Please

Our study provides a clue about why so many men season their food with salt and pepper, sometimes before they taste it. Although sex roles continue to change, women in our culture still do most of the cooking at home and they season the food they prepare until it seems just right to their taste buds. However, the same plate of food may seem bland to their male partners, so over time, the men pour on the salt as a matter of habit.

If a woman is younger than her male partner, the problem is compounded because she most likely has a better sense of smell. Her partner's sense of smell is worse to begin with by virtue of being male, and if he's older, his sense of smell may be diminishing more quickly. She'll eventually catch up, but it may take decades! This disparity has led me to suggest that in a perfect "olfactory romance" the woman should be a few years older than the man.

This situation becomes complicated by the fact that in general women are more health conscious than men are. In recent years, women have tended to heed warnings about cutting down on salt. They also worry about their male partner's diets and urge them to use less salt, and they fail to understand why their partner stubbornly insists on adding salt. (Physicians hear these stories and complaints so often that I'm surprised there isn't more interest in smell and taste issues.) One solution to this problem is already in the works, however, as our population moves away from salt as a primary seasoning and toward harmless seasonings, such as parlsey, chives, garlic, cilantro, basil, thyme, and oregano.

In the next decade or two, I expect to see many studies that examine the way chemosensory abilities and preferences become integrated into our personality, and in some cases, influence important life choices. We may also find that certain careers may increase our risk of developing chemosensory disorders. Firefighters provided such an example.

Risk, Fighting Fires, and Pass the Spices

Some years ago, six City of Chicago firefighters scheduled appointments at our clinic because they believed they had impaired ability to smell, which they interpreted as an inability to taste food. After testing and evaluation, we found that all six firefighters had indeed lost their sense of smell. This led to a concern that these six represented the tip of the iceberg of a much larger problem. This could signal an "occupational epidemic" of chemosensory disorders resulting from exposure to toxic chemicals to which firefighters are repeatedly exposed. Based on our subsequent study, which we believe is the first study of olfactory ability among firefighters, it appears that firefighters are at high risk for impaired ability to smell (see Appendix 11). In the U.S. alone, there are one million men and women employed as firefighters, so this represents a signficant number of individuals.

Our study included 102 Chicago firefighters who volunteered to participate in the project. We tested these individuals using the UPSIT, the scratch-and-sniff test referred to earlier. After adjusting the results for age and sex, almost 48 percent showed diminished ability to smell. It is believed that about 2 percent of the population have impaired ability to smell, so this is a very significant finding. The degree of impairment was related to the number of years as a firefighter. We also found that 82 percent of the participants wore protective masks while fighting fires, and we speculated that those who wore masks throughout their years on the job would have experienced less damage to their sense of smell. However, we found that olfactory acuity did not correlate with the use of the protective masks. The number of years as a firefighter was a key factor in determining the degree of loss.

Our firefighter study revealed that among those who had impaired ability to smell, 87 percent believed their sense of smell was normal, which likely is

explained by the phenomenon of gradual loss. However, the ability to detect odors is important for fighting fires. For example, an odor is added to natural gas in order to make it detectable, and gas leaks are potentially dangerous as a cause of fire, but also as a byproduct of damage sustained during a fire. (Almost all the study participants had gas furnaces in their own homes.) In addition, firefighters use their sense of smell to distinguish between odors such as smoke and natural gas or burning wood and toxic chemicals. To date, though, no fire department we know of tests the ability to smell before hiring new firefighters, and as we observed, chemosensory testing is not routinely performed during medical examinations.

We also noted that the loss of the sense of smell potentially affected life outside the firehouse, too. Diminished sense of smell is linked with depression, reduced sex drive, and other quality of life concerns. But we also noted that 38 percent of the firefighters who showed olfactory impairment were the primary cooks in their households. Remember that most of these individuals believed their sense of smell was normal—just like the chefs in our other study—yet, 34 percent had experienced food poisoning one or more times. This isn't surprising. Our testing showed that some of the smell-impaired individuals could not distinguish between the odor of smoke and the odor of a dill pickle.

Most of us tend to think that the dangers associated with fighting fires largely involve the danger of smoke inhalation, heat, the potential for lethal explosions, and so forth. However, when we look more closely, we can see that firefighters are exposed to numerous synergistic toxins. A wood fire produces as many as two hundred toxic chemicals, and many of these are known olfactotoxins, meaning that they specifically adversely affect the sense of smell. The combination of extreme heat, toxic substances, and physical exertion, which increases respiration, heightens the potential for olfactory damage. In addition, some of the fire-fighting "habits" contribute to the problem. For example, most firefighters wore masks during the active stage of the fire, but removed them during what is known as "overhaul," the period after the flames are extinguished when the firefighters are looking for hot spots. Smoldering and charred wood, plastic, and fabric, for example, may still release fumes into the air, thereby causing damage to

olfactory neurons. Every year in the U.S., we have two million fires, so the extent of the olfactory damage may be greater than previously believed.

The Bland or Spicy Personality

The questions below provide insight into your tolerance for a potentially high-risk career and related issues.

Which do you prefer (choose one from each pair):

Chicken and pea pods or Szechwan chicken
Pot roast and carrots or ginger shrimp
Vegetable soup or minestrone
Tuna-noodle casserole or salsa and nachos
Broiled lamb chops or chili
Salmon and dill sauce or salmon teriyaki
Chicken salad or chicken curry
Cheese omelet or scrambled eggs with peppers and onions
Broiled pork chops or Southern barbecue
Hamburger or beef taco

In looking at the above quiz, the results break down as follows:

> If you chose seven or more of the second food in each pair, you are definitely a risk taker, and perhaps you'd be suited for a career as a firefighter, or perhaps an astronaut or a race car driver.

> If you chose seven or more of the first food in each pair, you are probably somewhat risk aversive, and you would probably pick a safer career—safe, as defined by lacking in physical danger. You may prefer the physical security of a job as an accountant or banker.

Perhaps you had mixed results, which probably indicates that you are a mix of personality characteristics. You may be a firefighter, but your hobby is collecting

stamps—or you are an accountant who races sailboats on the weekends. Chances are, though, you take more moderate risks both professionally and in your hobbies. Most of us probably fit a mixed profile.

They Fit Our Image

In the quiz above, you were offered a choice between a bland and a spicy dish in each pair. When we looked at firefighters and personality, we found that they were, as expected, risktakers, with a strong component of altruism. In other words, our society's image of firefighters is about right. They like the adrenaline rush associated with their profession, and they tend to accept, even enjoy, the sense of living on the edge. The altruistic component is probably what provides the sense of urgency and allows them to accept the enormous risks involved in rescuing people from burning buildings. When we view film clips on the news of firefighters at work, we see evidence of the adrenaline rush in their hurried movements and hyper-alert state. Later, when reporters ask about rescuing the small children or the even household pets from the blaze, they respond calmly, "I was just doing my job."

When we looked at personality and food preferences, we found that the firefighters liked spicy foods, and other studies have suggested that a preference for spicy food over bland indicates a risk-taking personality. However, research exists that suggests the opposite. We cannot be sure if the firefighters always preferred spicy foods or have developed this taste because of their olfactory impairment. If a person begins to add salt to food in later life, for example, he or she may be an *older* risk taker who now has olfactory impairment. Still, the risk taking personality is probably characterized by a preference for foods that pack a spicy punch.

Odors, often food smells, possess the power to influence our moods on a daily basis, and often hour by hour. In the next chapter, we'll discuss the way the foods you choose may reflect underlying moods and emotional tendencies.

Chapter Eleven
Personality and Mood

"He saw that there was no mood of the mind that had not its counterpart in the sensuous life, and set himself to discover their true relations, wondering what there was in frankincense that made one mystical, and in ambergris that stirred one's passions, and in violets that woke the memory of dead romances, and in musk that troubled the brain...."

—Oscar Wilde

Since olfaction is so closely linked with emotions, odors have both a direct and indirect influence on mood. In chapter two, I discussed the link between loss of olfactory ability and depression and other disorders, such as anxiety syndromes. Current research has suggested that certain odors have the ability to reduce anxiety. Some personality types tend to exhibit more anxiety than others, and anxious states tend to be self-reinforcing. If you experience mild anxiety, your awareness of your anxious state tends to make you more anxious. A public speaker, for example, may become afraid that others can observe the outward signs of his or her mood state (trembling hands, shaky voice, and so forth) and that fear will make the speaker even more concerned.

Anxiety in learning environments is so common that test-taking nervousness is considered a common malady among students and in some cases, a "condition" in a clinical sense. Using odors in classrooms, offices, public speaking situations, or even cocktail parties has the potential to reduce anxiety, thereby preventing the anxious state from escalating.

Using Odors to Alter Mood

Information about odors that may reduce anxiety and stress or lift mood comes from many sources, including those who study the science of perfumery and folklore. Some information about odors and mood can be found in medical texts dating back many centuries. In sixteenth century China, for example, the odor of rose oil was said to be an antidepressant; chamomile oil was used as a sedative, essentially as a way to relieve anxiety. Many people still drink chamomile tea to relax before sleep, and your grandparents may swear by its calming effects on both adults and children.

Four centuries ago, European medical thinking included the belief that peppermint strengthens the brain and preserves memory. Modern research shows that the odor of jasmine stimulates beta waves in the front of the brain and tends to make one feel awake and alert.

A shift in mood in response to certain odors is not necessarily a subjective phenomenon, but rather a physiological response to odors that act on the central nervous system in ways we can measure. In the 1970s, Paola Rovesti, a professor at the Milan University in Milan, Italy, investigated essential oils and came up with a list of potentially anxiety-reducing fragrances, including: lime, marjoram, violet leaf, rose, lavender, bergamot, and cypress. Lemon, orange, verbena, jasmine, ylang-ylang, and sandalwood were said to have antidepressive qualities.

Others have mentioned clary sage and grapefruit for their antidepressive qualities. In some cases, the scents are described as inducing mild euphoria, rather than working only to reverse depression.

Although I cannot recommend using any of these oils to treat clinical depression or chronic anxiety because consistent and effective treatments using odors are still in the future, research has documented that odors can bring about physiologic changes. Changes in brain wave patterns, heart rate, blood pressure, muscle tension, and skin temperature are among the documented responses.

In the 1980s, research showed that the odor of nutmeg oil may help reduce stress, as evidenced by reduced systolic blood pressure readings. Study participants also reported feeling less tension, anxiety, anger, and embarrassment, as well as feeling more calm, relaxed, and happy. Additional research demonstrated that a nutmeg-apple odor increased theta wave activity (associated with relaxation) in the brain, to a greater degree than either lavender or eucalyptus. Since all three odors were rated as pleasant, the difference in results may be attributable to the direct effect on the brain, or it may be that apple-nutmeg is a food odor, and as such, shows a greater ability to reduce stress.

Food odors are known to have a powerful influence on mood. Just imagining a favorite dessert resulted in EEG changes in study subjects that were similar to those that occurred when participants were given oral relaxation-inducing instructions and suggestions. In a similar way, the inability to detect an odor may serve as an indication of stress. For example, individuals who cannot detect the smell of a banana are probably under considerable stress.

The Meat Versus Apple Personality

Which do you prefer? Choose one.

Green Apples or Barbecued Meat

Based on your answer the following personality types can be defined.

If you prefer **green apples**, then you may be a more anxious, high-strung person with a tendency toward claustrophobia. You may tend to be a loner, and in social situations, you prefer a "safe" social distance between you and others. You do not like to have someone "in your face" while you interact, and it is easy for you to feel that your personal space has been invaded. You dislike being smothered in relationships and prefer to follow your own path. Some people would call you a nonconformist. You may be considered somewhat pessimistic and people would not necessarily call you fun-loving. No one will ever catch you dancing on a table with a lampshade on your head! You'd rather be home reading or surfing the Internet anyway. If a job opening comes up for a telecommuter, you would be a good candidate because you work well alone and unsupervised.

If you prefer **barbecued meat**, you are probably gregarious—a life of the party type, but not necessarily a born leader. You tend to depend on others for company, and you generally go along with what the crowd wants to do. You tend to conform to whatever standards are demanded on your job and you prefer to work with others, not alone. You like close, intimate relationships and tend not to be as exacting or demanding as the green apple personality. People call you eas going, and you tend to fit the popular image of a well-adjusted person. Because of your social nature, you would not be a good candidate for telecommuting. You may use the Internet for your work and you find it fascinating, but you prefer mingling with real people, not computer screens.

Anxiety and Spatial Perceptions

The meat versus green apple personality differentiation relates to mood and a sense of comfort in closed or open spaces. About 10 to 11 percent of the population suffer in varying degrees from claustrophobia, defined as fear in confined space. A smaller, but significant group (1 to 3.5 percent of the population) suffers from agoraphobia, which is fear of open spaces. Those with claustrophobia tend to be uncomfortable in elevators or trains; those with agoraphobia may be unable to tolerate the expansiveness of malls or even the open spaces of ordinary streets in their neighborhood.

Beyond the clinical issues of claustrophobia and agoraphobia, perceptions of room size influence a sense of comfort or discomfort within a space. Interior designers are trained in the "tricks of the trade" to expand perceptions of space in cramped offices or small rooms in homes, for example. They may be called upon to attempt to perceptually shrink space in certain circumstances, too, in order to create an intimate environment. We know those visual placements, such as mirrors and furniture, can help to expand or contract room size. Similarly, bare floors expand perceptions of space, and carpeting tends to contract perceptions. Room temperature influences perceptions as well. If you're confined in a hot car in a traffic jam, the space constricts, but a parking garage on a cold day in January may seem larger than it is.

Odors have not yet been extensively studied to determine their effect on spatial perceptions. In order to determine if odors could influence response to room size, we placed normal volunteers in a space-deprivation booth—a "coffin-like" tube is the best way to describe the booth, which measures 2.5 feet by 4.5 feet (see Appendix 8). By normal, I mean that these individuals were neither claustrophobic nor agoraphobic and they had a normal sense of smell. (The group included four women and four men, ages eighteen to sixty-four.)

While confined in this small space, we introduced the following odors: evergreen, barbecued smoke, Tranquility (an Elizabeth Arden perfume), vanilla, buttered popcorn, seashore, charcoal roasting meat, cucumber, coconut, and green apple. Each odor was introduced on a surgical mask worn for thirty-second intervals during which the individuals were asked if they experienced changes in their spatial perceptions. Between each odor, the subjects sat in the tube for an "odorless" two-minute interval.

Only two odors showed an effect on spatial perceptions: barbecue smoke caused the individuals to experience the space as smaller, whereas the odor of green apples caused the individuals to perceive the space as larger. We are not sure whether the responses resulted from conditioned responses to the odors or were perhaps associated with past experience. The barbecue smoke odor may have brought about an association with fire and hence, a mild feeling of entrapment. The green apple odor may have been associated with an orchard, which is an expansive outdoor environment. Both results have implications for the treatment of anxiety associated with certain phobias, but other anxiety disorders as well. A person with mild claustrophobia, for example, may want to sniff the odor of green apple to reduce potential anxiety before riding in an elevator. (I am not recommending this as a clinical treatment for claustrophobia, but only suggesting a potential connection between an odor and a shift in spatial perception. Eventually, such a treatment strategy may be developed, but we are still in the research phase of this work.)

The odor of heliotropin, which is a vanilla-like smell, reduced anxiety among individuals during a medical test called magnetic resonance imaging (MRI). An MRI is a painless test, but it can cause anxiety because it is noisy and confining. A claustrophobic response is not uncommon. Those exposed to the heliotropin at the time of testing reported 63 percent less anxiety than those in a non-odorized environment during the test. It is possible that the odor of green apple would produce the same effect.

In the food preference quiz presented earlier, the personality types described tend to conform to the idea that we seek what we need, and that our preferences reflect our needs. We may subconsciously desire the foods which help us self-medicate. For example, the gregarious person may need an odor—or a food—that shrinks the space around him or her and reins in expansiveness. On the other hand, a person who is anxious and feels confined may seek the odor or food that enlarges the world, both literally and symbolically. Even a mildly anxious loner will seek the company of others from time to time and will want to feel comfortable in a social setting; the gregarious sort may seek the foods he or she needs to be comfortable while alone and quiet in a more confined environment.

Preventing Migraine Headaches Using Odors

Almost forty million Americans suffer from migraine headaches, which are characterized by intense pain, associated with constriction and expansion of blood vessels. The pain of a migraine headache feels like expansion and swelling of the vessels. In a classic migraine, the pain is preceded by what is commonly called an "aura," which is a combination of visual disturbances such as flashing lights, blind spots in the field of vision, sensitivity to light, and so forth. The aura warns the individual that a migraine headache is starting. The "common" migraine does not include the aura, although it manifests itself with nausea and vomiting.

We also know that the sensation of an odor can be the aura to a migraine headache. Even in the nineteenth century, physicians reported that their patients talked about strange odors that they associated with the aura that warned them that a headache was on the way. These have been considered phantom or hallucinatory odors and included floral scents, decaying animals, gas, and burning material such as cookies or wood chips. In some cases, the odor seemed so real that the person began searching for the source of the smell.

The issue of phantom odors is separate from discovering odors that trigger migraine headaches. Cigarette smoke and certain perfumes are common olfactory triggers, and many who suffer with migraine headaches do their best to avoid these smells. A substance known as tyramine that occurs in common foods such as red wine, cheese, peanuts, and so forth may trigger a migraine, and susceptible people make it a practice to avoid those foods.

When we studied the relationship between migraine and odors at our center, we learned that about 14 percent of migraine sufferers have reduced ability to smell (see Appendix 13). Smell loss among migraine sufferers is difficult to explain, but we have speculated that the reason these people develop a headache may actually be the result of olfactory loss; the hyposmic or anosmic person can't detect an odor in the air that triggers their headaches. For example, they may feel fine, but they open the newspaper in the morning and chemicals in the newsprint trigger a headache. Or, there is cigarette smoke residue in the air, and while they can't detect the odor, it has the ability to trigger a headache. A particular perfume may be the culprit for some people. They can't smell the perfume, so they don't know to avoid it—and the headache.

In some cases, it may be possible to use odors to prevent a migraine headache or treat one in an early stage. For example, we've discovered that introducing a green apple smell may reduce the severity and the frequency of migraine headaches (see Appendix 12). Some correlation exists between the green apple

personality profile and migraineurs. In other words, the food odor preferred by individuals prone to migraine headaches is the same odor that may be able to prevent or stop a migraine headache. Some positive results have been shown with use of vanilla, which has been shown to reduce anxiety, so that it fits the profile of the food odor preference of migraineurs.

For many years, researchers have attempted to establish a migraine personality, and in general, the profiles are compatible with the "green apple" personality profiled above. Variation among the findings exists, of course, but most agree that these individuals tend to be ambitious and somewhat driven, and they have a greater reaction to stress, perhaps because they take situations they're presented with seriously. Historical figures such as Julius Caesar, Thomas Jefferson, Woodrow Wilson, Lewis Carroll, Edgar Allen Poe, and Sigmund Freud were all apparent migraineurs, so presumably they would have preferred green apple over barbecued meat. In addition, even though they were thrust in positions in which they had to lead or work with others, they had the ability to be self-starters, too, and they may have preferred working alone. Several researchers have noted that while the typical migraineur is socially courteous, he or she also prefers to remain distant from others.

In the future, we are likely to see research establishing that odors may go a long way in preventing a migraine headache or treating it in its early stages. I foresee a time that an individual who suffers from a migraine headache may be able to carry a device that looks like a tube of lipstick or a pen that contains an odor that will stop a debilitating headache before it starts. Perhaps they'll be able to leave their medications at home and the combination of drugs used today will seem rather primitive.

Finding Your Own Anxiety-Reducing Scents

Regardless of personality type, almost everyone experiences anxiety from time to time. For example, anxiety or apprehension prior to a test or a performance is both common and normal. In our society, testing is a traditional part of our educational system that very few of us escape. Admission into colleges and graduate

programs require testing as well. Even when school days are over, many companies perform batteries of tests on every job applicant.

A testing or performance setting is a good arena for you to test your own responses to individual odors. Finding the right scent can be challenging because a balance is needed. An aroused mood state before and during a test or performance may actually have a positive influence. A bit of anxiety may put us at the "top of our game," so to speak. However, extreme test and performance anxiety is debilitating and can interfere with a student's ability to reach educational goals or an adult's ability to fulfill professional ambitions.

Since we know that certain odors reduce anxiety, it makes sense to try them as a safe remedy for test and performance anxiety. Start with food odors, such as green apple, spiced apple, nutmeg, or vanilla. Research has shown that lavender, sometimes called the "student's herb," not only promotes relaxation, but may actually help students perform mathematical calculations. If, however, lavender makes you too relaxed, then try an odor that is more stimulating, such as lemon, which has been shown to help clerical workers make fewer errors. Both peppermint and jasmine influence beta wave activity in the brain, thereby promoting an awake and alert state, but they do not increase tension or anxiety.

Another strategy is to create a state-dependent learning environment that extends to the exams. For example, if you eat chocolate mints when you get a relaxing massage, you could sniff or eat chocolate mints prior to making a speech or interviewing for a job. The conditioned response to the odor may be sufficient to reduce anxiety in both settings.

It is probably no accident that an ocean beach is a favored vacation spot. For many people, a trip to the ocean can induce a profound sense of relaxation where cares and worries seem to fall away. Apparently, physical changes mirror the psychological response since sea odors have been found to reduce facial muscle contractions by 20 percent. You may have noticed that sea-scented colognes, shower gels, lotions, and soaps, as well as room deodorizing sprays are turning up on cosmetic counters. Some cosmetic companies have entire lines of these products, all marketed on the premise that the odor of the sea is by its nature relaxing. If we can't get away to the beach for a vacation, we can bring the beach home and relax in our bathroom "spa." And there is no harm in experimenting with these odors and monitoring how they make you feel.

Since everyone is different, there is no one odor that I can recommend that will work for everyone. Set up your own informal research project and test odors on yourself in settings where you want to increase relaxation and in settings and in testing and performance environments where you need to be alert and focused, but not too anxious to perform well. Use the scientific research results presented here as guidelines for your own experiments. In our laboratory, we found that mixed floral odor worked best to enhance learning (see Appendix 3).

Perfume and Mood

Sometimes we associate perfumes with sensuality and sexuality, which usually dominates the marketing efforts. Many millions of dollars are spent promoting the "scents of seduction." As previously mentioned, scents developed as a result of our sexuality studies use pumpkin pie and lavender for men and cucumber and Good & Plenty for women, in perfumes named SA, for Sexual Arousal. However, most of the time perfumes function as a type of accessory, particularly for women who may choose scents to "match" the occasion. On an unconscious level, both men and women probably choose scents that subtly alter their mood.

Types of scents used vary with time and place, but perfumes have been used for many centuries, probably from the earliest human societies. Evidence comes to us from eight-thousand-year-old Chinese writings that mention perfume, and anthropologists have established that perfumes were widely used by ancient Egyptian, Sumarian, Aztec, Greek, Roman, Indian, and Hebrew cultures. For a short period during the Puritan domination of England, it was against the law for women to wear any scented substances because of their potential to stimulate the senses.

The underlying reasons we use cosmetics, including scents, are complex and not completely understood. However, the motivation appears to come down to wanting to feel good about ourselves and simultaneously please others. Good smells are associated with positive value; conversely, bad smells are linked with negativity. Wearing pleasant fragrances on our bodies sends a subtle message that

we are good, just as the smell is good. This is one reason perfumes and colognes tend to be intimate gifts. We are telling another person that he or she fits the positive image of the scent, and in romantic situations a gift of perfume for women or cologne or after-shave lotion for men affirms their femininity and masculinity respectively.

In another chapter, I discussed the unconscious wish to take into our bodies a food that is associated with positive qualities, which is why a celebrity endorsement of a food product is a successful marketing strategy. Perfumes and colognes have a similar appeal, and scented products developed by celebrities such as Michael Jordan or Elizabeth Taylor have been quite successful. Both individuals have a larger than life image and both approach whatever they pursue with great passion. The scents developed by these celebrities carry an unconscious message that we can absorb their passionate attitude in our lives.

Perfumes, Gender, and Culture

Logically, commercial interests have driven research into odor preferences for perfumes and other scented cosmetics and products. Some research has attempted to establish odor preferences based on gender, culture, and personality. For example, while research has shown that both men and women enjoy floral odors, of those scents men specifically prefer phlox, orange, and heliotrope. Women are more likely than men to express strong reactions to odors generally considered unpleasant. In general, men like musky odors and women prefer nutty smells, such as almond.

In general, scented cosmetic products for men feature smells that appeal to women, such as the fresh, clean smells of the outdoors (or at least the idealized version of the outdoors!). The products are formulated this way because men wear colognes and after-shave lotions to please and attract women. On the other hand, women tend to wear fragrances they like because they use these products to please themselves, and indirectly, for the pleasure they derive from the positive responses from others.

Cross-cultural research indicates that in Japan and China perfumes are used less frequently than in the West, and when they are used, light, subtle fragrances

are preferred. The French enjoy warm, sensuous fragrances, such as jasmine, while Germans prefer the green, woodsy odor of pine.

Introvert or Extrovert/Moody or Stable

In a study conducted in Germany, female consumers were given personality tests, which were compared to their perfume choices. Researchers concluded that extroverted women tended to choose perfumes dominated by fresh fragrances, which include the clean, "green" scents that are quite popular today; introverted women preferred the spicy Oriental perfumes.

Most commercial baby powder is scented with fragrances from the Oriental spice family, and perfumes such as Tabu and Shalimar are dominated by the Oriental spice family of scents. Since most people have a positive association with baby powder, it is possible that the popularity of these perfumes is related to an unconscious nostalgic response. On the other hand, the Oriental spice family, particularly ginger (which is frequently used in pumpkin pie) is often used in fragrances designed to be haunting and mysterious. Perhaps on an unconscious level, a woman who uses this type of scent is challenging others to look beyond the label of introvert, and instead see subtlety and mystery.

Those labeled "emotionally ambivalent," which is defined as experiencing frequent shifts in mood and a tendency to be "dreamy" tended to choose the floral odors. Based on the personality testing, women who were labeled "emotionally stable" did not show significant preferences for any fragrance category.

One day, we may be able to correlate the preferences for certain scents with the ice cream, spice, or snack food personality, which would provide additional clues when we attempt to "read" other people. This type of information would certainly help us choose scents to give our lovers as gifts, and may also guide the scents we choose to wear that will be pleasant to our partner.

The Influence on Mood Is Always Present

When we discuss odors and mood, we should keep in mind that odors always influence mood in some way. Consumers spend more money in an odorized environment (see Appendix 4), and individuals may exhibit more aggressive behavior in the presence of a malodor, a bad smell (see Appendix 5). Questions remain about the effects of different types of odors on mood and behavior.

In general, lavender is linked with relaxation and peppermint is linked with an awake and alert state. Both mental states are necessary for focused concentration. Researchers tested both odors with sixty-seven volunteers (fifty-eight women, nine men) who were recruited to proofread pages of text that contained misspelled words. They performed the proofreading task in three sections, once in the presence of lavender, once with peppermint diffused in the environment, and once with no odor present. (The diffuser used, by the way, was similar to those you can buy for use in your home.) Each proofreading session was thirty minutes. While the men's sample was small, they generally performed better with the odor of peppermint in the room. Overwhelmingly, the women worked more efficiently and found a greater number of spelling errors when lavender was diffused through the room rather than in the presence of peppermint.

This research suggests that the same odors may influence men and women differently, or that perhaps the mood states of the sexes going into the proofreading settings were different. It is possible that the men required a more alert state to perform the proofreading tasks efficiently and the women required a greater degree of relaxation to do the job successfully. When you are experimenting in your home, keep in mind that even mild anxiety about a task may influence your degree of concentration. Likewise, an alert state is required to maintain motivation and concentration. These effects may be subtle, but as you notice your shift in mood, be aware of the odors in your environment.

In general, it is easier to remember information that is consistent with one's current mood. So, if you are already sad, unpleasant childhood memories, for example, are more likely to surface. When you are happy, you will remember happy childhood memories. Odors that are pleasant generally lift mood, which then results in recall of more pleasant memories.

Feeling Ambitious?

Research conducted with men and women in an office environment showed that, in the presence of a pleasant odor (five different odorized air fresheners were used), participants set higher work goals and were more likely to work more efficiently than they did when working in an unscented room. Researchers also found that in negotiation, a pleasant odor decreased confrontational behavior and subjects were more likely to make concessions, while at the same time setting higher monetary goals in the outcome of the negotiation.

In some situations, smells are associated with a pleasant experience, and the happy mood that is evoked may have little to do with a physiological response to a specific odor. For example, my daughter Marissa was always very happy when she went to Bright Beginnings preschool. The classroom at her school always had a strong odor of PlayDoh, and my daughter developed a conditioned response to this common childhood art and play material. It is possible that if the same odor were added to her other classroom environments, she would feel happy in response to the odor. A conditioned response to an odor is very powerful and has a lasting unconscious effect.

The first experience of an odor and the associated mood has a lasting effect, even if only on the unconscious level. For my daughter, the aroma of PlayDoh is associated with an emotionally charged event, her pleasant preschool experience. The odor of PlayDoh will be recognized when she detects it and the memory includes the emotional event. This is one of the reasons that your mood can shift and the content of your thought change so drastically in the presence of an odor with which you have emotional associations.

As you can see, adding specific odors to the office, classroom, or home environment may facilitate an alert or relaxed mood, relieve low-level anxiety, or simply lift your mood. Odors also may act indirectly to help you solve problems that interfere with performance and learning. Regardless of your personality type, the scents around you always exert an influence on your mood. How we feel may have much to do with the "odor soup" in which we live.

Chapter Twelve
Sacred Chocolate

"This is a place of opportunity, and I would suggest that you bring yourself and some of your chocolates up here. I have sold the 600 pounds that I brought and I feel there will be a great demand for it."

—James Lick, San Francisco, 1848
(from a letter sent to candy producer Domingo Ghirardelli)

"For some reason or another, a Hershey bar would save my soul right now...What I need, want, pray for, dying for, right now, is a Hershey bar...with nuts."

—Jack Kerouac, from *The Dharma Bums*

In ancient Greek and Roman myths that are such an integral part of Western culture, the food of the gods was called ambrosia, a term still used to describe a "heavenly" food. Today, chocolate is probably the food most likely to be considered the true ambrosia. The eighteenth century Swedish naturalist, Carolus Linneaus, whose system of plant classification is still in use, labeled the tree from which chocolate comes *Cacao theobroma*, which means "food of the gods." Today, the beans of the plant are called cocoa, probably as a result of an early misspelling that stuck. Chocolate was originally prepared as a beverage, and the word chocolate is a Mexican-Indian word, which literally means "foamy water."

Although our sexuality studies did not support the notion that chocolate has an aphrodisiatic effect, at least in terms of direct physiological response, the Spanish explorer, Hernando Cortez, observed that Montezuma drank chocolate drinks made with honey and vanilla before visiting one of his many wives. Thus, the link between romance and chocolate was born and brought back to Europe. While scarce at first and available only to the elite classes, chocolate developed an aura of mystery that remains to this day.

From the time chocolate was first introduced to Europe, heated debates went about the relative virtues or "sins" of chocolate. For example, a physician in the Spanish royal court believed chocolate drinks were beneficial as a treatment for fevers and others began to tout chocolate as good for the digestion and valuable in combating poisons. One authority claimed that chocolate, when correctly prepared, could make one strong and happy.

On the other hand, some authorities warned that chocolate could harm digestion and lead to melancholy. Because of its strong taste, chocolate developed a reputation as an effective disguise for poison, and according to a seventeenth story, that may have some truth in it. A prominent Spanish woman took revenge on a lover by luring him with a chocolate drink laced with poison. In my role as a neurologist, I once treated a patient who suffered from nerve damage, and further investigation revealed that he had arsenic poisoning. It turned out his wife was "hiding" the poison in his bonbons!

Moody Chocolate

Chocolate has a reputation as a mild mood-altering food. At various times, those concerned about pleasure and morals cast a suspicious eye toward chocolate, and the remnants of a Puritanical attitude toward chocolate exist today. Various dessert creations use terms like "sinful" or "decadent" in their names, which reflects the image of chocolate as an almost forbidden indulgence.

When we examine the chemical composition of chocolate we can see evidence of its power to alter mood and change how one feels. As you probably know, chocolate contains caffeine, which stimulates the central nervous system, and a chemical known as *theobromine*, which is found in other key plants, including the numerous varieties from which we derive coffee and tea. Coffee, tea, and chocolate share a chemistry that stimulates both desirable and undesirable effects. All three compounds are consumed routinely and in great amounts because of their physiological and psychological effects.

Chocolate also contains substances known as amines, which are a group of compounds that includes *tyramine* and *phenylethylamine*. Tyramine occurs in foods such as cheese and herring, both of which can trigger a migraine headache in susceptible individuals. Many migraineurs add chocolate to the list of foods they must avoid. Phenylethylamine and tyramine tend to be arousing chemicals and have the ability to raise blood pressure.

Chocolate is also high in magnesium, and it is possible that a craving for chocolate is actually a signal that the body is deficient in magnesium. The popular physician/author Andrew Weil has reported that supplementing the diet with magnesium relieved chocolate cravings. (Do not supplement magnesium or other nutrients on your own without seeking medical advice. Magnesium and other minerals must be in balance in the body. Elevated magnesium levels can be as detrimental as magnesium deficiencies.)

Many women report that chocolate cravings are more frequent and intense during the days prior to the onset of menstruation. In fact, some women know their periods are coming because they begin thinking about chocolate. To at least some extent, the craving is specific to chocolate, as opposed to a craving for sweets, which is common among women during the premenstrual phase of their cycle. A portion of the premenstrual craving may be related to dysphoria, a state of mild sadness or unhappiness experienced by some women prior to menstruation. This makes sense because chocolate cravings increase among those who are clinically depressed.

In terms of brain wave activity, a study conducted in England that included twenty-one students, ages seventeen to thirty-seven, showed a decrease in theta wave activity in the brain in the presence of the odor of chocolate. The twenty-one participants rated chocolate as more pleasant than other odors presented, which included strawberry, cumin, garlic, onions, various vegetables, and almond. Obviously, we do not expect some odors, such as garlic and onions, to be rated highly on an odor scale. For example, garlic tends to be pleasant only in the context of food and hunger, which were the conditions during our study of garlic bread and family interactions. However, almond and strawberry are both considered pleasant odors. Chocolate was also rated the most relaxing odor.

In terms of chemical structure, phenylethylamine is similar to amphetamine substances, which is probably the reason for its arousing effect. Chocolate and the phenomenon we call "falling in love" may be linked because the phenylethylamine is elevated in individuals during the early stages of infatuation and attraction. Since chocolate contains this chemical, which stimulates the production of natural painkillers, or endorphins, both chocolate and falling in love will produce similar changes in brain chemistry.

Although chocolate has a reputation as an aphrodisiac, our sexuality study showed no evidence that it significantly increases either penile or vaginal blood flow. It is far more likely that chocolate became associated with sexuality because of the chemical action of phenylethylamine, which produces the euphoria of love. If we offer our lover chocolate, we may be symbolically saying that he or she gives us the "heady" feeling that chocolate brings about.

An additional element is likely linked to the conditioned response. When food develops a romantic reputation, we tend to respond to it on an unconscious level. If we believe chocolate is a special romantic food, then it takes on romantic/sexual qualities. While it is linked to Valentine's Day, chocolate flavored body-paint and condoms give it a direct sexual connection.

Self-Medicating with Chocolate

Chocolate is an example of a food that is commonly used in attempts to self-medicate. By that I mean, cravings for chocolate tend to be greater among those who are depressed, which does not, by the way, mean that everyone who likes and craves chocolate is depressed. Cravings for sweets and carbohydrate foods tend to be higher among individuals with symptoms of depression, and when antidepressants are taken, the cravings tend to decrease. Neurotransmitters, such as dopamine and serotonin, are involved in regulating mood and perceived energy levels, and a craving for chocolate may represent a physiological "craving" to self-correct an imbalance in brain chemistry.

I do not believe that enjoying chocolate is necessarily a sign that one's brain chemistry is deficient in one of the key neurotransmitters, nor do I think that occasional cravings for chocolate means that one is addicted to it. After all, chocolate is enjoyed by about 97 percent of the population. However, chocolate is involved in problem eating, such as binges and eating in secret. Chocolate cravings can be powerful, and there is a sense of relief when the craving is satisfied; some individuals report withdrawal symptoms when they do not have chocolate. Because chocolate contains biologically active substances that are involved in mediating mood, energy, and even the perception of pain, it is not surprising that it is a potentially addictive substance. However, chocolate may seem addictive because it is so popular.

Because phenylethylamine is associated with endorphin production, it is possible that chocolate is involved in increasing tolerance to pain. In a Canadian study, forty women (ages sixteen to twenty-seven) were attached to a pressure algometer than applied pressure on four fingertips. The subjects were asked to monitor discomfort as the pressure on their fingertips increased. During the experiment, subjects were shown slides of foods, including chocolate chip cookies, which for purposes of the study was labeled a palatable food. The presence of a picture of chocolate chip cookies increased pain tolerance when compared with other non-sweet foods, such as rice cakes and blackolives. It may be that it was the sweetness of the cookies rather than the chocolate that triggered the response, which correlates with the experience of craving sweet "comfort foods" when we're under stress or in pain.

Everyone Loves Chocolate

Few foods can claim to be loved by so many. Reports place chocolate as the most craved substance in North America. Chocolate drinks and foods are linked to almost every holiday, and chocolate comes in so many varieties and prices that almost everyone can indulge in some form of chocolate. In 1991, writer Tom

Heyman reported that in an average lifetime, a person in the U.S would likely consume just over eight hundred pounds of chocolate. Considering that Americans eat about twenty-one pounds of candy a year, some of which is most certainly chocolate, it isn't difficult to see that most of us have at least occasional yearnings for chocolate.

Several years ago, the Smell & Taste Treatment and Research Foundation interviewed 3,193 overweight individuals for our odors and weight loss studies, and only 1 percent of these men and women did not have strong feelings for chocolate. (The results of the odor and weight loss study are discussed in detail in my book *Scentsational Weight Loss.*) Generally speaking, a sweet tooth exists, and overweight individuals tend to show greater preference for sweeter foods than individuals of normal weight. However, the normal weight population has its share of chocolate fans, too. Forty percent of women and 15 percent of men say they have actual *cravings* for chocolate, and within the chocolate-craving group, 77 percent of women and 75 percent of men claim that no other food is a satisfactory substitute for chocolate when a craving occurs.

Characteristics of Chocolate

Identical chocolate does not necessarily taste identical to everyone who eats it. The ability to taste chocolate is greatly controlled by one's ability to smell. If you hold your nose and take a bite of even the most expensive chocolate, it will taste like chalk. Those with a poor sense of smell do not enjoy chocolate as much as those whose sense of smell is normal. The odor of chocolate is considered hedonically positive apart from its taste. Even if you don't feel like eating chocolate, the odor of a candy counter is pleasant and inviting.

The perception of an odor changes after it is first detected, so your last bite of a chocolate bar will be different from your first bite. After you have consumed the whole bar, you will not find the chocolate quite as pleasant as you did when you rolled the first bite around in your mouth. This is part of a built-in satiety mechanism that inhibits the desire to keep on eating. The chocolate "addict" does not experience this inhibition and tends to desire more chocolate. (This phenomenon has been labeled "moreishness.")

It's been shown that eating chocolate has the ability to reduce the sensation of pain in those who are already experiencing discomfort, which means that it acts as an analgesic agent and probably tastes better to those in chronic pain. The way we perceive the taste of chocolate changes as we age, and a higher concentration of the taste is needed to gain the maximum amount of pleasure; hence, older individuals prefer a sweeter chocolate taste than younger people choose.

Chocolate Texture and Personality

Chocolate evokes different responses based on its texture and the sensory experience that comes from biting into it. The Smell & Taste Treatment and Research Foundation performed a study to look at personality characteristics and preference for either solid or hollow chocolate Easter eggs, using a product produced by Woolworths, a candy retailer in the U.K.

Overall, the quick burst of flavor experienced with the hollow egg was the dominant reason most people preferred the hollow eggs. Biting into the hollow chocolate afforded a more rapid sensory experience. So, this is how the "hollow versus solid" personality types break down.

If someone gave you a chocolate Easter egg, would you bite into it with the hope that it's *solid* or *hollow*? (Circle one.)

If you prefer the **hollow bar**, you like sudden thrills, and you are likely to enjoy adventure and seek experiences that challenge you—mountain climbers are probably "hollow egg" personalities. These individuals tend to be on the impatient side, at least in terms of everyday activities, and they might be dissatisfied with their current life.

If you prefer the **solid egg**, you tend to be risk-aversive—and you're willing to experience your pleasures more slowly. You are probably satisfied with your current life, and tend to like things to be predictable, and you're faithful and loyal to family and friends. However, you may settle for less in what you set out to accomplish.

Overall, our study found that most people prefer hollow to solid eggs for the following reasons:

- The solid eggs were perceived as too thick, and the chocolate didn't feel right, as if there was too much of it.
- The hollow eggs were preferred because they melted faster and were easier to bit into. Because the bite of chocolate melts faster, they don't require chewing and the melting temperature is lower, hence it feels better in the mouth. People also said that the solid eggs were a bit harder on their teeth.
- The sound of the hollow egg was preferred—it produced a "pop" sound in contrast to a crunchy sound with the solid egg.
- The hollow egg splits apart in the mouth and allows rapid olfactory stimuli, which brought about a quick burst of flavor—an immediate gratification. With solid chocolate, the taste is not as immediate because the smell is released more slowly, so gratification is delayed.
- The hollow eggs were perceived as sweeter, with a richer and stronger smell.
- The mouth feeling of the hollow egg was soft and velvety.

Milk Chocolate or Dark Semi-sweet?

Which do you prefer? (Choose one from each pair.)

Milk Chocolate or Dark Chocolate
Malted Milk Balls or Milk Duds
Grapes or Raisins
Plums or Prunes
Apple Pie or Rhubarb Pie

This quiz asks you to choose between two food items in a pair, and the first food tends to be sweeter than the second food. Here is what your food preferences mean:

If you prefer **four or more of the first item** (mild chocolate, milk balls, grapes, plums, or apple pie), you tend to be a contemplative, quiet person and probably consider yourself an introvert. You are more likely to pursue a solitary sport, such as running or cycling, and you enjoy working alone. You may enjoy spending time alone in nature. These individuals may be good computer programmers or they enjoy researching topics on the Internet.

If you prefer **four or more of the second item** (dark chocolate, Milk Duds, raisins, prunes, or rhubarb pie), you tend to an extrovert, an outgoing person who enjoys others and feels comfortable in social settings or working in large offices. You like to work on projects in a group, and if you pursue a sport, it is probably a group activity, such as bowling, volleyball, or softball. You may like to join others for a walking trip or tour abroad. These individuals may like working in a retail environment or as a team leader in an office.

Some of us may have more mixed results. Sometimes, we may feel contemplative at times, and at other times we reach out to others. Perhaps we play softball, but we go off to the woods alone. As with many of these tests, it is not unusual to find that we don't fit a pattern perfectly. But the next time you choose a chocolate bar or you bite into an Easter egg, think about the reasons you like what you like. Most of the time, we aren't conscious of the reasons behind our choices.

Chapter Thirteen

One Man's Meat

"My kitchen is a mystical place, a kind of temple for me. It is a place where the surfaces seem to have significance, where the sounds and odors carry meaning that transfers from the past and bridges to the future."

—Pearl Bailey

Each food that fills a space on your dinner table today has a history, which is usually shaped by at least one culture, but just as likely by many societies. Foods you serve carry a social status in some cases, and they have had an economic impact on our society, and perhaps on the economies of other societies as well. Today, you may eat cucumbers from Latin America or from south Florida. The orange you peel may be fresh picked from Texas or have just arrived from Israel.

Even with all the variety we're offered and the diversity of our food culture, we remain shaped by the conventions we're raised with. The television program *Survivor* illustrates the power of food conditioning. This program is one of the "gimmick" shows in the reality television genre that have become so popular in the last few years. *Survivor* takes men and women who want to win a million dollars to a remote island where they are faced with survival challenges, and the person who meets the challenges gets to stay on the island. (This is a little like *Who Wants to Be a Millionaire* meets *Gilligan's Island.*) In one episode, participants were presented with a plate of live worms, insect larvae, and if they wanted to maintain their status on the show, they had to eat one of these squirming little creatures.

In the Western world, most of us get shivers just thinking about eating a fat worm, and the aversion is so strong that many people would forgo the million dollars rather than consume an "unthinkable" food. In other parts of the world, a worm would be viewed as the makings of dinner. Although specialty stores carry products such as chocolate covered ants or bees, most Westerners do not find insects of any type appealing. However, insects, including ants and termites are consumed as a source of protein in Africa, and a variety of insects are collected and used for food in parts of South America and Asia. In rain forest regions, where mammals are not plentiful enough to be a reliable source of food and cannot be easily domesticated, the population uses insects. Many insects, especially in the larvae stage, are good sources of calories, protein, and fat.

Survivor shows us that although we may believe we are rational about food choices, our desire for certain foods and our acceptance of foods are largely conditioned. Cultural norms that dictate which animals are acceptable and which are not are related to relative scarcity and abundance of protein sources in general. For example, in China, a country that has for many centuries endured cycles of famine and social turmoil that affected food supplies, it is acceptable to eat dogs as a source of animal protein. Western cultures have strong taboos against eating dogs because we have used many breeds as protectors and as "workers" in raising more efficient sources of protein, such as sheep and cattle. Over time, dogs have become family pets, and even if we do not own a dog, the taboo against eating their flesh is strong. Once a food taboo is in place, it is difficult to remove.

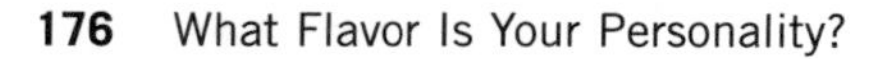

Politically Correct Food

Prohibitions tend to develop against certain foods for several reasons, including: it is unnecessary for the population to eat the foods to meet nutritional needs, the foods are not efficiently raised on the available land, or the animals in question are more useful to the population as "service" animals. We tend to think political correctness is a newer concept, but actually the history of a society and its religions can be viewed based on what kinds of foods they allowed, or equally important, forbid. Every society has had politically correct foods and those that, for various reasons, are outlawed foods, which, because of conditioning, may become repulsive.

Pork provides an example of a food forbidden in traditional Jewish and Moslem cultures, and because children raised in homes that follow the prohibition against pork learn from an early age that it is not an appropriate food, they may develop a revulsion to it. On the other hand, foods may become revered because populations are so dependent on them that the society is organized around them. In India, cows are a valuable source of milk and they are draft animals, too. In a sense, they are symbolic of Krishna, their protector, and of the mother, who provides nourishment. On a practical level, more people can be fed by using milk from cows and growing food on the land that would be consumed by cattle if they grazed and were killed for food. Dairy cattle convert feed into usable milk protein five times more efficiently than beef cattle convert feed into meat. Therefore, to eat cows would be a self-defeating practice in India, where arable land is scarce and must be reserved for vegetable foods. The sacred status of the cow is integral to Hindu religion, but its source is a practical consideration.

In Moslem and Jewish traditions, the pig is considered "filthy" because it eats dung. However, many animals eat dung when deprived of other food sources. At one time it was believed that the prohibition against pork had to do with trichinosis, which is infestation of a particular parasite that occurs in raw and undercooked pork. However, every society develops methods to safely handle food. No society would survive without passing on methods to preserve and properly cook foods. The Biblical instructions could have as easily stated that the flesh of pigs

should be cooked until it is no longer pink. The reasons behind the prohibition against pork are, like the Hindu prohibition against eating the cow, related to environment and the most efficient use of land.

In the ancient Middle East, the primary animals raised were sheep, goats, and cattle, all of which efficiently convert high-cellulose plant foods into protein. These animals do well on grass, hay, bushes, leaves, and other plant foods that humans do not eat. On the other hand, pigs are very efficient converters of plants into animal flesh, but they need low-cellulose plants such as wheat, potatoes, soybeans, and so forth. By prohibiting the use of pigs, the population did not need to share their food crops with their animals. In addition, pigs do not do well in the semi-arid climate of the Middle East, but thrive in humid climates with wooded land that provides shade. In short, the prohibition against pork is likely a prohibition against waste and the inefficient use of resources.

In the U.S., given the diversity of the population, it isn't surprising that we do not have one standard answer to what is allowed on our tables. In our culture, "politically correct" food may change from decade to decade, but some taboos have remained fairly constant. For the most part, we do not eat members of the family, which include our pets—cats, dogs, parakeets, and gerbils. We might start a boycott if we saw dolphin meat or whale rib steaks in the store, and any animal food is slow to gain acceptance in the U.S. Buffalo and ostrich are making their way into homes and restaurants in some places in the U.S., but these foods are not yet widely accepted.

At one time, vegetarians were considered odd, but in some circles, vegetarianism is viewed as the most politically correct way to eat, and animal protein consumers may feel apologetic for eating poultry or red meat. In a way, vegetarianism in the West is possible because of the year-round availability of such a vast variety of foods. We do not need to rely on dried meat and eggs from our chickens during long northern winters and short growing seasons, as many Europeans and North Americans have traditionally done in the past. In the West, some vegetarians abstain from meat for ethical reasons; they do not believe in killing any living creature. Others adopt a vegetarian lifestyle for ecological reasons; they do not believe the world's population can support the inefficient use of land to raise

livestock. Further, they support planting crops on land that is currently used for grazing. Some vegetarians believe that animal protein tends to be less healthful than plant protein, and this is another reason for leaving meat behind.

When the Values Are Unclear

U.S. society tends to be ambivalent about hunting, particularly deer. On the one hand, we know that hunting deer is not really so different from raising beef cattle, but once we've taken the kids to see *Bambi*, logic no longer prevails. Yet, we insist, if people want to hunt, they shouldn't let their kill go to waste—hunting for food is marginally acceptable, but hunting for the thrill of killing an animal is not, at least to most people in our society. In today's society, where the vast majority of people do not need to hunt for food, there is a strong bias against hunting. Obviously early European settlers in the U.S survived because they knew how to hunt. However, today there is a perception that we can raise and use certain animals, but species we have not domesticated are "wildlife" and are part of the landscape and the *ecology* of a region. For the most part, we believe they should be protected or at least left alone. Our ambivalence about hunting reflects both changing and conflicting social values.

Good Flesh/Bad Flesh

Today, despite changing trends, beef remains an important food in the U.S. per capita, Americans annually eat about 150 pounds of what we call "red meat." Sixty percent of that (by weight) is beef and veal, 39 percent is pork. Only about 1 percent is lamb or mutton. Each week, more than 90 percent of the households in the U.S. buy beef in some form. This emphasis on beef is fairly recent and does not date back to the colonial days, which were dominated by pork consumption, along with goats and fowl. Today, goat consumption is negligible, probably because goats are a source of milk. On small farms with limited grazing, goats are efficient milk producers. But as settlers pushed west, more land became available, and the cow began to take over. It takes four or five goats to produce the same amount of milk as one cow. It wasn't long before goat became a low-brow food, one associated with poverty and the inability to own enough land to keep a cow.

At one time, sheep were raised for meat, much like they are in Great Britain, as a byproduct of raising sheep for wool. In the U.S., raising sheep was not profitable because during colonial times, wool could not be exported to England because the English woolen merchants were protecting their own industry. Therefore, raising pigs became more profitable, and lamb and mutton fell out of favor. Pigs eventually became a steady protein source because they can convert grain to meat very efficiently and do not need extensive grazing land. Different varieties of domestic pigs were bred for heavy fat content for lard, and by the Civil War, the U.S. population consumed enormous amounts of pork, along with wheat, pork's sustaining grain.

In the Midwest, some farmers raised beef cattle and pigs, and when they drove them to the cities to sell, the pigs often followed behind the cattle and fed off the dung. Most of us missed this bit of historical trivia, and the picture of a pig drive does not mesh easily with the macho cattle drives of the old West. The gradual switch in preference to beef began when settlers moved to the Great Plains and in one of the most politically incorrect chapters in U.S. history, the buffalo were removed to make way for herds of cattle, which adversely affected the Native American population.

Beef took over as the most "American" of foods based on improved transportation and efficient breeds of cattle. When Americans started moving to suburbs and grilling in the backyard, the hamburger and the steak became mainstays of the "hunter husband" who "provided" the meat. Beef also cooks up fairly fast and relatively easy—quick dishes such as meatloaf and burgers and tacos are mainstays among working families. Some historians will link suburbia and the women's movement to the rise of beef as a favored main dish.

The American hamburger is said to have originated at a fair in Ohio in the 1890s, when a restaurant owner ran out of pork sausage and substituted beef. Or, it may have first appeared in 1904 at a fair in St. Louis as a novelty dish. Their origin aside, hamburgers swept the country. White Castle became the first chain, started in the 1920s. In 1955, Ray Kroc started McDonald's as a drive-in, adding chairs and tables in 1966, and ushering in a new institution, the fast-food restaurant. Legally, hamburger must contain only beef, a standard that had to be out-

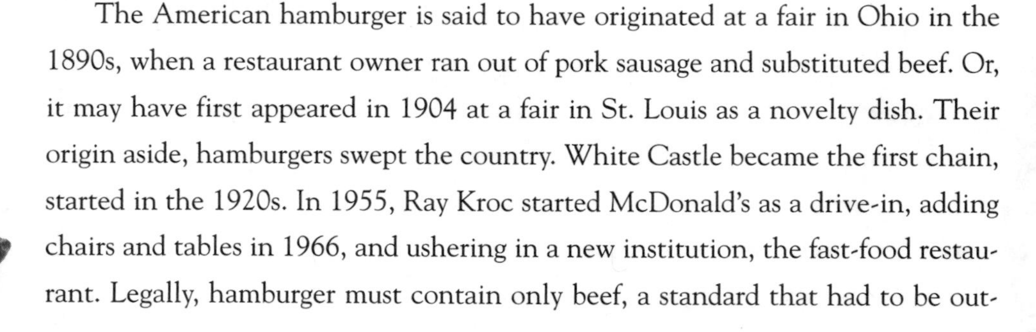

lined when horsemeat and pork were making their way into dishes called hamburgers. The fast-food concept originated in the U.S., but by 2000, major fast-food chains could be found across the globe. Beyond the burger craze, beef is still among the prominent foods in restaurants in every region, and in the U.S., a sixteen-ounce steak on the menu is not an unusual item. To many people, beef remains the king of animal foods.

Red meat has lost a bit of its "glow" primarily because of health concerns, particularly the link between its saturated fat and elevated cholesterol levels. Because of both health and ecological concerns, poultry and fish have tended to take over as the most "proper" foods, but that does not stop most Americans from eating beef. Over the next few years, we will probably see more varieties of red meat, such as buffalo, which ironically is making its way back into U.S. culture as a grazing animal raised for its meat. We also may see the trend toward vegetable protein such as soy continue, both for health and economic reasons.

Have You Ever Seen a Chicken?

We have removed ourselves from the source of food, so we tend not to think of a chicken as a bird that pecks on the ground, or at least they did at one time. Now they are mass-produced in indoor coops. We might not link the chicken parts that appear in plastic trays in see-through wrap with a living bird; whole chickens take up less space in the meat counter than ever before. It's likely that many children in cities and even suburbs have never seen a live chicken, except perhaps at a farm "display" in a museum or in a zoo.

At one time, chicken had status as a special food slowly roasted and served on Sunday or on some other special day. Eggs were everyday food, but roast chicken was special because it was more expensive protein and killed the source of useful eggs. Fried chicken was a favorite finger food among Americans, and has the distinction of being just about the only animal food one could eat with one's hands. Even etiquette expert Emily Post said so.

Today, fried chicken has lost its status, and is considered a "low-brow" food, probably because we don't talk about fried foods except as something to avoid. The space in a meat counter is taken up with chicken pieces, and the most acceptable chicken is served "lite." By current standards, chicken breast is the most "politically correct" part of the chicken because of its low-fat content, and the fact that it can be grilled, broiled, or stir-fried chicken, with the skin and bones and fat carefully removed. The less it resembles a chicken, the more desired it is. It may be wise to eat "leaned down" chicken for health reasons, but as you can see, it doesn't take long for social status issues and other judgements to make their way to the dinner table. It shouldn't surprise us because this is the way humans always have structured food. Foods that are familiar and available are considered good, and foods the affluent classes eat the not-so-affluent groups soon want on their tables, too.

Throughout the world, eggs have been considered symbols of fertility and also evidence of the "unseen" force. An egg will indeed turn into a chicken in ways ancient people did not understand. Among some of the ancient seafaring cultures, chickens were brought along to lay eggs and provide a steady source of food. However, not all cultures embrace eating the birds. In some parts of Africa the fact that hens lay their eggs in various spots is a sign that they are "promiscuous" and furthermore, they eat worms and insects off the ground. Other cultures also have deemed chickens as dirty because they eat from the dirt. Since the adage "we eat who and what we are" is true in every culture, then eating chickens would by extension lead one to promiscuity and eating dirty things. Ironically, in the U.S., the most desirable and "politically correct" chickens are those that are called "free-range" chickens, which means they are allowed to roam and peck grain that is scattered on the ground, as opposed to being raised in a cage-like chicken houses.

High-cast Indian Hindus generally do not eat chicken because they consider them unclean, but Moslems in India do consume them, which is one of the dietary distinctions among these two major religious groups in India. In countries that are traditionally Buddhist, such as Tibet, fowl is repulsive because of the claws; vultures pick at carcasses with their claws, and since chickens have claws, chickens are too closely related to be appealing.

Most of us call the male chicken a rooster, but that is because in the Victorian era, calling him by his old name, "cock," was just too vulgar. The cock represents male sexual organs in many cultures, and in general the cock is associated with lust. The strutting nature of the cock has also made its way into the language in form of "cocky" and "cocksure," which are terms generally applied to young men who believe they "know it all." In some cultures, the rooster's combs and testicles have been considered aphrodisiacs.

Cockfighting may be one of the oldest "sports" that still survives, and it may be the reason behind the domestication of chickens. It always had a theatrical quality, which may date to the early Greeks whose cockfighting festivals were staged in the Athenian theater, which honors Dionysus, a god whose costumes resembles the cock in all his finery. Cockfighting remains a symbol of a readiness to do battle, even if only with words.

We Aren't Likely to Eat Each Other For Dinner

Cannibalism, which is humans eating humans, seems unthinkable to most of us. Yet, evidence of human flesh eating can be traced back to the Paleolithic period. Excavation sites show evidence of bones that were split in order to extract the bone marrow. Anthropologists believe the appearance of the split bones indicates that humans, not gnawing or chewing animals, opened the bones. While cannibalism is no longer practiced, it is part of our cultural past and is still discussed, probably because of the fascination with a practice that seems macabre.

Two primary motivations for cannibalism existed. The first, peaceful cannibalism, is related to ingesting the essence of a person. As mentioned earlier, we eat what we want to *become* as well as what we are. So, eating the body, or the cremated ashes of a loved one, has been used in mourning rituals in a few societies. This type of human flesh eating has a supernatural or magical quality associated with it.

The second type of cannibalism generally results from war or perceived threats and invasion of enemies. In general, small village societies were more likely than large, state societies to consume their prisoners because they represented a source of food, particularly protein. As societies grew larger and more complex, prisoners of war were more efficiently used as labor and eventually, the idea of eating human flesh, even the flesh of one's enemies, became one of the most serious taboos ever developed in human culture.

On occasion, the taboo is broken in efforts to survive in situations in which no other food source is available. However, the morality of eating dead human flesh is not universally accepted, even under extreme conditions. The famous case of the Donner Party is still debated. Two men and five women survived thirty days in the snow by eating the flesh of their companions that died in the ordeal. Did they have the moral right to do this or didn't they? This question has been debated for more than one hundred years.

Mind Your Manners

Once individual cultures decided what was appropriate to eat, they also developed ways to eat their food. The most common eating utensils are your fingers, and all the other eating implements are merely the extensions of the hand. Liquids are among the only foods that cannot be managed by either using the fingers, although soaking up broth with bread tends to make a utensil out of food itself.

While eating with one's fingers is simple, societies develop ways to differentiate social classes and privilege by the way they eat. The blurring of social classes can be seen by the similarities in not only what we eat but also how we eat. In the U.S. and other Western countries, most of our dinner tables look much the same in terms of the kinds of eating utensils. Some may use silver and others stainless steel, and our dishes range from plastic to artistic pottery, but the implements we use are much alike.

No matter where we're raised, many of us sit down to a formal dinner and take an inventory of the forks and spoons, mentally trying to match them with the food to come. From the time we're children, learning to use the correct fork was one of the small tasks of socialization. However, the fork is a relatively recent eating tool, and didn't become widely used in the U.S. until the late eighteenth century. Prior to that, most people balanced food on a knife, so spearing food with a fork was a simplification late in coming. Once the fork arrived, it was considered proper to eat almost everything with it, except beverages and soup, and

eating ice cream with a spoon was considered a sign of bad manners. Thankfully, practicality eventually won out.

Knives always have been common eating tools, but in most Asian cultures, chopsticks were developed early, probably close to five thousand years ago. According to a legend about their origin, the philosopher Confucius believed that knives were instruments of violence and war and should not be brought to the table, and chopsticks were developed as a substitute. The nonviolent association endured through the development of Buddhism to the present day. After the fingers, chopsticks are the second most common eating utensil. Like silverware, chopsticks are part of the art of presentation, and they can be mass-produced in plain wooden varieties or designed and produced by artisans that give them distinct artistic patterns. The kinds of chopsticks and individual or family use reflect who they are, just as silver patterns offer clues to a family's status.

Religion and Food

Evidence exists that the earliest societies used food symbolically in the rituals of religion. Food and religion have remained linked throughout human history, with no sign that the link is weakening, even as the globe becomes smaller and we import and export religious traditions, along with the foods that symbolize the belief system.

Most early religious traditions recognized, and, indeed, organized themselves around the connection between the "fat of the land" and the power of unseen forces. Many believed that if the God or gods were pleased, food would be plentiful. Hunter-gatherer cultures employed special rituals invoking the divine through music, dance, and sacrifice to ensure a successful hunt to feed their clan. Agricultural societies have no shortage of ceremonies intended to call forth blessings of fertility to help bring about an abundant crop in order to survive another year. The Aztecs went to the extreme and made human sacrifices to the Sun god as a prayer for abundant harvests, quality tobacco, and good health. In a more gentle tradition, the Japanese invoked the rice goddess in their planting ceremonies, and in many societies, harvest time inspired a host of religious ceremonies to thank the divine powers for the bounty provided.

Christians in England carried loaves of bread baked with the first grain of the harvest to church services. Ancient Jewish worshippers expressed thanks to their God by carrying the first fruits of the season to the temple. Although not as widely observed as other Jewish holidays, Shavuoth occurs seven weeks after Passover and marks the beginning of the wheat harvest. Traditionally, it's a time to eat cheese-filled pancakes known as blintzes and to decorate the synagogue with flowers. It is also customary to eat the first seven fruits (which we may not label as fruits today) mentioned in the Torah: wheat, barley, grapes, figs, pomegranates, olives, and dates.

Mother Earth—and Sea

The Incas, a group that thrived in the sixteenth century and maintained a sophisticated empire of six million people, practiced a paganistic religion, in that they believed gods existed everywhere in the world around them. Religious feasts centered on the meat of the llama, accompanied by a type of corn beer called "chicha." In everyday spiritual practices, when the women sowed seeds they poured chicha on the ground as they prayed to the Pacha Mama, the earth goddess. Incan miners sacrificed llamas to Pacha Mama so that she would make the earth give up its riches to them. The idea that the earth is our symbolic mother runs deep in human culture and religion. Planting, tending crops, and reaping the final harvest are like the trimesters of pregnancy that ends in the "harvest" of birth. Fertility rites and food rituals often are closely related.

Like the Incas, the Eskimo peoples of North America honored the tangible gods of the natural world, just as they honored unseen powers. They believed that animals, like humans, had souls that must be honored—if an animal's soul was disrespected, it would not allow itself to be killed. If a hunter offered a dying seal a drink of water before the hunter slit its throat, then it would recognize the hunter's respect and would release its "yua," or its soul. According to the belief, the dead seal's yua withdrew to the bladder. The Eskimos saved the bladders of their kills in order to honor the soul of the animal later at religious festivals, during which they slipped the bladders through a hole in the ice so that the yua could be reincarnated in the body of another seal.

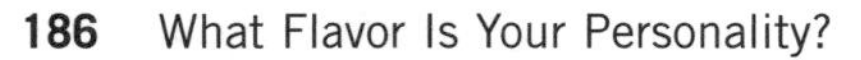

Greek and Roman mythologies are filled with food references and symbolism, some of which made their way into Christian symbolism. The Greek word *Delphos* meant both fish and womb. Aphrodite, born of the sea, was also known as the "fish goddess," Aphrodite Salacia. Her sacred day was Friday, which eventually became the "meatless day" in the Catholic Church. Today, restaurants may advertise a Friday "fish fry" or "shrimp boil," which may have its original roots to ancient Athens. Friday was also the Day of Venus in Roman culture, and in Northern Europe, Friday was also the Goddess Freya's sacred day and considered the best day for weddings and lovemaking. The Chinese Great Mother often appeared as a fish goddess, and other cultures have used the symbol of fish for sexuality and fertility.

Food and Western Religion

The special and symbolic foods eaten during certain ceremonies show us the intimate link between food and faith. In some cases, the defining symbol of the religion is used in food. Both the English and North Americans enjoy hot cross buns in conjunction with Lent and Easter—the raisin-filled sweet rolls are topped with frosting in the shape of a cross, symbolizing the crucifixion, and were once prepared especially for Good Friday. Around Easter, it is common to see cakes baked in the shape of a cross. During the Christian festivals of southern Greece, traditional bread is adorned with a cross, and walnuts embedded in the breads represent the Virgin Mary.

Kreplach, or meat-filled pancakes, is traditional fare on the day before the Jewish holiday, Yom Kippur, the Day of Atonement, which is a fasting day. The meat came to symbolize judgment, which is then wrapped in the pancake, which symbolizes mercy. For Jewish New Year—Rosh Hashana—celebrations, bread and apple slices are dipped in honey as wishes for a sweet year ahead, and other sweet foods such as dried fruit and cakes made with fruit and honey are also served. Rosh Hashanah observations do not resemble the more celebratory "Times Square" events, but rather are quieter celebrations during which one evaluates the past year and looks ahead with hope. The sweet foods served are associated with hope. Some of the dishes served depend on the traditions of spe-

cific Jewish populations. For example, Jews from Central Europe might celebrate Chanukah with latkes, which are potato pancakes, but Greek Jews might eat loukamades, fried dumplings that are rich with honey. In Israel, one might find holiday foods from all regions in which Jewish populations have lived.

The Passover *seder* (seder means order) uses foods in virtually every phase of the highly ordered event, which celebrates release of Israelites from the bondage of slavery in Egypt. Although many foods are used, the unleavened bread, the matzoh, is central to the holiday, because, according to the traditional beliefs, God ordered the Israelites to leave Egypt so quickly there was no time for dough to rise.

Other food is consumed in a particular order that matches the story upon which the holiday is based. For example, a vegetable, usually parsley, is used to symbolize spring and rebirth, and by dipping it in saltwater, it reminds participants of the tears shed during slavery. Bitter herbs, often horseradish, symbolize the bitterness of slavery, are dipped in a mixture of chopped apples, nuts, and wine that symbolize the mortar slaves used to make bricks in Egypt. Recipes for this mixture, which is called *haroset* or *charoset* vary from region to region, but they follow the same pattern of providing a mixture of sweet foods in which to dip the bitter herbs.

An egg and a lamb shank also are used as sacrificial symbols. The flat bread, or matzoh, itself is a symbol of affliction, and part of the ongoing ritual is prearranging for a child to steal the bread and hide it. The meal isn't over until those gathered search for it and eat it together. In addition to the food, wine is also a symbolic part of the dinner, usually taken to remind participants of blood that has been shed.

When we look at traditions across the religious spectrum, it is not so surprising that they exist, but that they have endured for so many centuries. The Passover seder remains essentially unchanged after several thousand years. The Christian world observes the event of Passover, in the form of the Last Supper, a Passover seder that is said to have occurred with Jesus and his disciples before the crucifixion. The ritual of communion derives from the Passover rituals, and in the Christian world, the bread and wine is transformed into the body and blood

of the Christ. With minor variations, communion is another ritual that has remained the same for about two thousand years during which dozens of Christian sects have formed.

Long-standing traditions endure for many reasons and among them the power of nostalgia, and specifically olfactory-evoked recall, form important mechanisms through which we struggle to keep familiar customs and traditions. Religious customs help to maintain stability and strong bonds within groups, but also among geographic regions and families. The food becomes part of what is anticipated year after year in each commemoration or celebration of religious concept. When we eat the special foods, we take in a sense of sacredness about the tradition irrespective of our belief in the dogma that underlies the rituals. These special foods usually carry the additional feature of being "blessed" by the aura around their preparation and symbolism. As a result, when you join with others and eat these foods you are encouraged to feel special, too.

Mixing Old and New

Christmas and Easter are two holidays that obviously are religious, but whose nonreligious rituals have spilled over into other cultures. Christmas trees have made their way into homes in such places as Japan, which has a very small Christian population. Although religious individuals sometimes object the secularization of what are, at least to many, sacred days, frankly, economic incentives usually prevail and some rituals and traditions have gone mainstream.

As attached as we may become to certain holiday customs, many of the rituals and traditions were borrowed from even older holidays. Many of the rituals associated with Easter, the most prominent holiday of the Christian calendar, evolved from the pagan Anglo-Saxon holidays that celebrated the new life or "birth" of spring after the long, cold, barren winter. The symbols associated with Easter, such as eggs, which are ancient female fertility symbols and lamb, a food newly available each spring, were incorporated in Christian traditions and transformed into death and resurrection symbols.

Christian Easter celebrations mark the end of a forty-day period known as Lent, which represents a period of fasting and repentance modeled on the forty

days Jesus is said to have spent in the wilderness, a time during which Christians believe he was confronted with and overcame temptation. The symbolic significance of foods associated with Easter actually begins forty days prior to the festival, when some Christians, particularly those following a Catholic faith, choose to refrain from a particular food or a behavior.

The practice of giving up a food for Lent was supposed to afford a period of contemplation about religious life and symbolize a sacrifice meant to strengthen faith. For many people, abstaining from such foods as chocolate or pastries during Lent is a sacrifice that serves as a reminder of the religious significance of the holiday. In religions that call for fasting or abstaining from food—or sex—the sacrifices are linked with cleansing and purification. Denying the body the pleasure of food or sex then allows greater concentration on spiritual values. Early Christians abstained from meat, cheese, fat, and eggs, the absence of which simplified their food and made their meals considerably more austere during Lent.

Early Christians in Europe used eggs in pre-Lenten rituals. The Saturday before Ash Wednesday, which is the first day of Lent, was called Egg Saturday, because children went door to door in villages begging for eggs that had to be eaten prior to the start of Lent. Many of these eggs were used to make the staple of Shrove Tuesday, which fell the day before Ash Wednesday. Also known as Pancake Tuesday, this was the last day that households could use up their stores of eggs and fat before Lent, when they would give them up until Easter, so pancakes became a traditional dish. In France and French-speaking countries, the same day goes by the name of Mardi Gras, or Fat Tuesday, again indicating the need to exhaust the cooking fat supply before Lent, the period of sacrifice.

Many European countries called the day before Lent "carnival," which literally means "farewell to meat." It's interesting that carnival or Mardi Gras evolved as cultural celebrations that are now secular in nature. Many people are almost completely ignorant of the original purpose behind Pancake Tuesday, for example, and instead, think of Mardi Gras as a tourist celebration in New Orleans.

In Islam, a month of fasting is called for during Ramadan, during which one is expected to abstain from food and other sensual pleasures from sunrise to sunset. This period is analogous in theme to the Jewish High Holy Day of Yom

Kippur, in which one is supposed to examine one's life and ask for forgiveness for wrong doing, as well as resolve to improve one's relationship with God in the coming year. Ritualistic fasting is generally undertaken as a form of spiritual discipline, and the theme usually centers on the idea that these disciplines improve character and symbolically "cleanse" the person on all levels.

The symbolism of Easter involves rebirth and triumph over death, which appears in some form in almost every spiritual system in the world. The egg, long a symbol of fertility and new life, plays a central role in the holiday's rituals and in spring festivals throughout the world. In some of the earliest Easter rituals, men and women danced around a pile of snakes eggs to express their joy in seasonal rebirth. Eventually, European Christians decorated hens' and other birds' eggs as a way to display their happiness about Easter and the resurrection, which to them literally meant new life. Known as pysanki, or "written eggs," the elegant Easter creations of Eastern and Central Europe involved elaborate dying techniques. The Russian artist Carl Faberge created some of the world's most precious eggs from gold, silver, and jewels to be given as Easter gifts by the Russian Czar.

Even today, children dunk hard-boiled chicken eggs in colored dyes that represent spring life: the pale blue of robins' eggs, the green of spring grasses, the yellow of baby chicks, or the light purple of spring violets. In some traditions, the children hang the painted eggs from tree branches, a tradition started by the Pennsylvania Dutch, who decorated the first egg trees for Easter. Legend has it that a German duchess started the tradition of hiding Easter eggs, but most historians agree that First Lady Dolley Madison started the annual Easter Egg Roll, which is now an annual event that takes place on the White House lawn.

The Symbols in Our Dreams

Dreams speak to us in a language even psychiatrists find challenging. In fact, no one, neither Sigmund Freud or Carl Jung, has definitively unlocked the mysteries of dream symbols, so everyone's system for interpreting dreams is speculative. However, it is likely that what occurs in your dreams reflects both cultural and individual significance, and food may occupy a prominent place in the messages from the unconscious mind.

In general, food in dreams may mean that you are involved in chewing over an issue or trying to digest information or issues. The specific foods may then lead you to the kind of issue you may be dealing with. For example, if your dream includes bread, it may be a symbol of everyday life and to an extent it is a universal symbol. If you baked bread earlier that day, the bread might represent a creative act or a desire to express creativity, but if you have no bread in your house, the bread may be a reminder of your busy schedule and the fact that your forgot to go to the store. If you're eating bread with others, you may be thinking about sharing your life or you may have mundane family concerns on your mind. Eating bread in church or temple may be a symbol of spiritual growth or conflict.

Perhaps in your dream, a woman is serving desserts and is urging you to eat. The atmosphere in the dream is fun, as if you were at a banquet or in an up-scale restaurant. Perhaps you desire more sweetness in your life, or your life is already sweet and your needs are met. If particular individuals appear in the dream they may represent emotional nourishment. If you are eating alone, perhaps you seek emotional nourishment.

In the Freudian system of dream analysis, foods and other items often have obvious sexual meaning, so if you're dreaming about bananas and figs, an issue of maleness or male sexuality may have emerged in your life. Dreaming of pears or apples or moist fruits may indicate issues involving feminine sexuality. In the Jungian system, these same images may not be sexual, but may relate to the traits we associate with the masculine or feminine, or left- or right-brain issues. For example, fruit may not be a specifically sexual symbol, but may be more closely related to a project coming to fruition or a sign of personal growth. Fruit also may represent feminine wisdom and intuition.

In general, try to note food appearances in your dreams and note any patterns. If you dream about crunchy foods, think about your food cravings in waking life. Do you have the urge to bite down hard on a raw carrot or a handful of nuts? If so, you may be frustrated or feeling aggressive. If you dream about bland, soft foods, perhaps you feel passive or calm. In Freudian terms, the desire for crunchy or soft foods correlate to aggressiveness or passivity, and your dreams may reflect your current moods.

The food that appears in dreams reflects universal symbols within the larger culture. But symbols, like societies, change. Modern dreams might include burgers and shakes and multicolored popcorn. Tomorrow's dreams will have new images too, which brings us to my predictions about the foods of the future.

From the Old to the New

Food has long represented our link to the past, and regardless of what is ahead, it is difficult to imagine the demise of cultural traditions. However, what we eat on a daily basis will continue to change in the future even more rapidly than in the past. During the twentieth century, food-processing technology galloped ahead, and a discussion of "future foods" sounded more like "future shock." To an extent, one prediction that has come to pass is the use of "food cubes." These cubes are a mixture of protein, carbohydrate, fat, some fiber, and the correct balance of vitamins and minerals, perhaps even designed to meet your individual need for calcium or vitamin C. Choose your flavor—butter pecan if you like an ordered life and generally follow the rules, or if you're a daring personality, you might choose vanilla. Either way, you have your meal in a cube. This type of food probably will be widely available.

Food cubes are available now. Look at the increasing number of meal-replacement shakes and bars. However, with the exception of those designed for weight loss, most people do not plan their diets around these "food cubes," which usually come in the size and shape of typical candy bars. The growing market for meal bars and "meals-in-a-can" speaks loudly about our "on the go" culture that centers around work and being busy. We're so busy, we grab meal bars on the run—why waste time sitting at a table? No wonder the "food cube" concept does not appear so far-fetched. Besides, if the astronauts eat a meal-in-a-cube, then it must be good.

Future foods likely will fit into a new category of foods called "designer foods." At the tame end of the spectrum, the relatively new genetically engineered foods, such as soybeans with increased vitamin E content, are quite common. Hardy tomato strains that will grow rapidly in cold climates with short growing seasons represent another example. This kind of genetic manipulation

has been going on for a long time. Hybrid fruits, such as the uglifruit, the result of a grapefruit crossbred with an orange or a tangerine, are available in typical supermarkets. Crossbreeding also has produced a light green vegetable that is a cross between broccoli and cauliflower.

As a result of even greater cross-cultural cuisine, we also are likely to see greater use of sea vegetables, such as wakame and kombu, which are commonly used in Asian countries such as Japan and Korea. We already have adopted many tropical fruits and vegetables such as plantain and mango into a typical U.S. diet.

The kind of designer foods we will see in the future will tend to be more individualized. For example, you may want your nutritionally fortified "food cube" to be shaped like a turkey—and taste like a drumstick, too. Maybe you prefer raspberries that taste like pizza, but your children want grape-flavored spinach. If this sounds far-fetched, consider that supermarkets are filled with foods that are essentially chemical mixtures that come from the lab, not a plant or an animal. Whipped topping made without butter fat and cheese foods that contain no milk are only the beginning of the chemical food revolution. Many of our most popular beverages contain sweeteners, either a form of sugar or an artificial sweetener, mixed with an artificial flavor. To many of us, the idea of drinking a glass of lemonade made with real lemons seems like a quaint idea! Market research has confirmed that many people prefer artificial odors to natural smells. Candy, such as jellybeans, are all made with the same basic flavor, but the added manufactured odors makes gives them their different tastes. Many children believe that strawberries smell like a box of strawberry Jello dessert, and the odor of real strawberries may seem inferior or even odd.

In the future, the generations may eat differently from one another because foods can be designed to accommodate varying ability to smell and taste. For example, many older people eat meals that younger people prepare. The foods are seasoned for a younger palate—a young nose—and may be quite bland to a person with diminished sense of smell. Many older people lose interest in food because they can't taste it. Weight loss among the elderly population is a serious public health concern. Like the younger population, however, older individuals tend to eat more in a group, so senior centers that offer a hot meal at noon are a

good idea if for no other reason than the social contact they offer. The food served in these centers will increasingly reflect individual chemosensory abilities where the cook adds flavor-enhancing products. Rather than spicing the roast chicken with sage or salt, a person will add the level of *chicken flavoring* he or she prefers. To a young palate, the taste may seem odd, but to the older palate, the chicken will taste like chicken.

A variety of flavor-enhancing substances—perhaps in the form of sprays or liquid seasoning—will soon find their way to supermarkets in the near future. Imagine genetically engineered apples or pears grown with a "super apple" or a "super pear" taste designed to appeal to older people. As the population ages, we will see an increase in the types of food products marketed to older groups. However, don't look for labels that shout "Elderly Pasta Sauce" or "Senior Citizen Apple." Adding flavors to breakfast cereal that could stimulate the trigeminal nerve and add taste and enjoyment seemed like a good idea. However, the "over sixty cereal" idea was a big flop—in our youth-oriented culture, men and women over fifty-five, sixty, or even seventy do not think of themselves as old. When we see "super apple" in the produce section, it will carry a subtler message.

Some Things Do Not Change

I do not believe we will be parted easily from the foods that give us pleasure, particularly social pleasure. So far, people are not sitting down together for an intimate dinner and unwrapping food bars. The rituals involved in eating meals in groups remains as important today as it was when we roamed the forests looking for food supplies, and when we gathered to share a kill and probably to select our mates. Eating likely will remain a social activity, and most people consume more food when they eat with other people, a phenomenon known as a "herd effect." The social and cultural meaning of various foods remains important, whether we meet at the cafeteria in the local mall or we gather around our dining room table.

Food cubes, artificial flavorings, and manufactured foods are part of the future, but so is greater sophistication about why we choose certain foods over others. I envision a day when our favorite television sitcoms, dramas, or movies use information about food preferences to help describe characters. Over time, as viewers gain more knowledge about the ways food choices reflect personality, they will begin to understand the significance of a character who orders a double scoop of butter pecan ice cream over vanilla, or one who needs the stimulation of a steady diet of spicy foods.

One day, we will use this type of information routinely as we assess other individuals. When we say we want to understand what makes another person "tick," we will note their food choices as one of the tools we use. Obviously, based on current knowledge, I cannot provide definitive information about a potential mate or employee based on snack food preference—or any other single factor, for that matter. However, we can begin now to understand that our food preferences have the potential to reveal the essence of who we are just as our clothing styles provide insight into our personality and our fluctuating moods. We live in a society whose economy is driven by consumption, and those who sell products and services to us amass data banks filled with facts and figures about who we are and what we buy.

I predict that one day our food-buying habits are going to be even more fine-tuned, and marketing efforts will be targeted to groups of consumers based on individual food preferences and the personality types that match them. Remember, too, that the foods we choose reflect not only who we are but also who we *want to become*. Those who urge us to buy certain types and brands of food know this just as surely as those who attempt to sell us cars and vacations do.

This book represents one step in a long journey to understanding human behavior. It is a journey that transports us into the realm of our five senses, which together bring us information about the world and the people around us. About twenty years ago, I described the sense of smell as a new universe to explore, an invisible universe at the tip of our noses. Over the last two decades, our understanding of the sense of smell and its partner, taste, has increased dramatically. We stand at a similar threshold in our understanding the new universe of food preferences and personality. As we've seen, our increasing knowledge of smell and taste has led us to expanded insight into numerous areas of human life, including sexuality, consumer behavior, occupational safety, malodors, mood, psychiatric disorders, headaches, memory, and learning. Our ability to correlate

personality traits with food preferences provides a new pathway to explore the mysteries of behavior. I hope this book will continue to help you gain greater insight into yourself and those around you.

Chapter Fourteen

The Food Attitude Survey

This is the final quiz in this book, and as you can see, it isn't actually a quiz at all. It is designed as an inventory of your food likes and dislikes. The Food Attitude Survey (FAS) was developed by Dr. Bryan Raudenbush at Wheeling Jesuit University in Wheeling, West Virginia. With permission, we have adapted it for use in this book. For each specific food listed, and considering your own food preferences, you are asked to respond using the following categories:

1. I really like this food. I think it tastes good.
2. I can take or leave this food. It tastes OK.
3. I dislike this food. It tastes awful.
4. I've never tried this food, but I would taste it if I had the opportunity.
5. I've never tried this food, and I never intend to try it.

As you consider each food, think of the best possible preparation of that food. For example, if you think Grandma's spaghetti is the best, then keep Grandma's spaghetti in mind when you come to spaghetti on the food list. Place a check mark in the numbered column that best describes your like or dislike of that food, or your willingness to try it if you never have. Please be sure that you do check one column for each food, without skipping any foods.

FOOD	1	2	3	4	5
1 Hot Potato Salad					
2 French Fried Cauliflower					
3 Pears (canned)					
4 Deviled Eggs					
5 Veal Parmesan					
6 Jalapeno Peppers					
7 Peach Shortcake					
8 Stuffed Green Peppers					
9 Polish Sausage					
10 Whole Wheat Bread					
11 Peach Pie					
12 Sugar Cookies					
13 Martini					
14 Fried Chicken					
15 Tomato Vegetable Noodle Soup					

FOOD	1	2	3	4	5
16 Fruit Cup					
17 Pickle Loaf					
18 Sweet Potatoes					
19 English Muffins					
20 Carrot, Raisin, & Celery Salad					
21 Fried Parsnips					
22 Roquefort Cheese					
23 Vanilla Wafers					
24 Stuffed Cabbage					
25 Sauerbraten					
26 Pumpernickel					
27 Enchiladas					
28 Butterscotch Sundae					
29 Sour Cream Dressing					
30 Vegetable Juice					
31 Peaches (fresh)					
32 Frijole Salad					
33 Banana Cream Pudding					
34 French Fried Scallops					
35 Buttered Succotash					

FOOD	1	2	3	4	5
36 Chocolate Covered Ants					
37 Mustard Greens					
38 Strawberry Chiffon Pie					
39 Stewed Tomatoes					
40 Doughnuts					
41 Baked Bean Sandwich					
42 Cashew Chicken					
43 Fried Cabbage					
44 Lobster Newburgh					
45 Hot & Sour Soup					
46 Fried Okra					
47 Limburger Cheese					
48 Bean Soup					
49 Banana Cream Pie					
50 Peanutbutter Pie					
51 Vegetable Soup					
52 Sweet Potato Pie					
53 Waldorf Salad					
54 Venison					
55 Pickled Beet and Onion Salad					

FOOD	1	2	3	4	5
56 Buttered Carrots					
57 Boiled Navy Beans					
58 Apples (fresh)					
59 Grilled Snake					
60 Buttered Mixed Vegetables					
61 Spaetzle					
62 Cream of Potato Soup					
63 Meat Loaf					
64 Ham					
65 Mushrooms					
66 Pears (fresh)					
67 Mixed Fruit Salad					
68 Creamed Onions					
69 Black Olives					
70 Freeze-dried Coffee					
71 Coconut Raisin Cookies					
72 Chocolate Pudding					
73 Cantaloupe					
74 Salami Sandwich					
75 Malaysian Dog Stew					

FOOD	1	2	3	4	5
76 Omelet					
77 Corn Chowder					
78 Butterscotch Cream Pie					
79 Green Pepper					
80 Creamed Ground Beef					
81 Turkey Rice Soup					
82 Milk					
83 Buttered Wax Beans					
84 Shrimp Tempura					
85 Spice Cake					
86 Asparagus					
87 Potato Skins					
88 Zucchini Bread					
89 Coffee Cake					
90 Gin & Tonic					
91 Stir Fried Beef w/Pea Pods					
92 Caramels					
93 Iced Tea					
94 Hot Pastrama Sandwich					
95 Vealburger					

FOOD	1	2	3	4	5
96 Banana Cake					
97 Cabbage					
98 Baked Fish					
99 Cream of Mushroom Soup					
100 Feta Cheese					
101 Beer					
102 Relish					
103 Chitterlings					
104 Caviar					
105 Turnip Greens					
106 Pad Thai					
107 Baked Yellow Squash					
108 Boiled Pig's Feet					
109 Blackened Grouper					
110 Hot Reuben Sandwich					
111 Sliced Tomato Salad					
112 Tofu (Bean Curd)					
113 Braised Liver with Onions					
114 Fish Chowder					
115 Mashed Rutabagas (Turnip)					

FOOD	1	2	3	4	5
116 Rabbit Stew (Hasenpfeffer)					
117 French Fried Potatoes					
118 Breaded Veal Steaks					
119 French Fried Carrots					
120 Egg Drop Soup					
121 Sausage Stuffing					
122 Apricot Pie					
123 Seaweed					
124 Gingerbread					
125 Egg Salad Sandwich					
126 Fishwich					
127 Bacon					
128 Plums (canned)					
129 Muktuk (Whale Fat)					
130 Bologna Sandwich					
131 Grape Soda					
132 Vinegar & Oil Dressing					
133 Coconut Cream Pudding					
134 Cole Slaw					
135 Nachos					

FOOD	1	2	3	4	5
136 Frankfurters					
137 Grape Lemonade					
138 Cottage Cheese & Fruit Salad					
139 Braunsweiger					
140 Buttered Whole Kernel Corn					
141 Western Sandwich					
142 Broccoli					
143 Pineapple Juice					
144 Coconut Custard Pie					
145 Fried Fish					
146 Cold Cereal					
147 Beef Rice Soup					
148 Stewed Prunes (canned)					
149 Possum					
150 Corn-on-the-Cob					
151 Blueberry Pie					
152 Cranberry Juice					
153 Sweet Cherries (canned)					
154 Baked Chicken					
155 Garden Cottage Cheese Salad					

FOOD	1	2	3	4	5
156 Milkshake					
157 Onion Soup					
158 Humus (chick peas)					
159 Russian Dressing					
160 Lox (smoked salmon)					
161 Sushi					
162 Lemon Chiffon Pie					
163 Figs (canned)					
164 Blackberry Pie					
165 Sliced Orange Salad					
166 Apricots (canned)					
167 Stuffed Grape Leaves					
168 Hominy Grits					
169 Harvard Beets					
170 Barbecued Spareribs					
171 Cucumber & Onion Salad					
172 Cherry Upside Down Cake					
173 Giblet Stuffing					
174 Pineapple Cheese Salad					
175 Buttered Asparagus					

FOOD	1	2	3	4	5
176 Brie					
177 Tomato Soup					
178 Potato Chips					
179 Pineapple Cream Pie					
180 Kidney Bean Salad					
181 Scrapple					
182 Pineapple Upside Down Cake					
183 Ham Loaf					
184 Pickled Pig's Feet					
185 Sukiyaki					
186 Collard Greens					
187 Squid (Calamari)					
188 Raisin Pie					
189 Fruit Punch					
190 Peanut Butter & Jelly Sandwich					
191 Mashed Potatoes					
192 Spicy Chinese Stir Fry					
193 Creole Soup					
194 Soft Serve Ice Cream					
195 Cherry Cake Pudding					

FOOD	1	2	3	4	5
196 Spanish Rice					
197 Smoked Eel					
198 Tomato Juice					
199 Buttered Zucchini Squash					
200 Spareribs w/ Sauerkraut					
201 Watermelon					
202 Creamed Chipped Beef					
203 Frankfurter w/Cheese & Bacon					
204 Root Beer					
205 Turkey Pot Pie					
206 Grilled Steak					
207 Baked Macaroni & Cheese					
208 Pineapple Pie					
209 Minestrone Soup					
210 Banana Salad					
211 Fruit Cocktail (canned)					
212 Swordfish					
213 Hot Whole Wheat Cereal					
214 Buttered Cauliflower					
215 Clam Chowder					

FOOD	1	2	3	4	5
216 Jellied Vegetable Salad					
217 Bread Pudding					
Total (# boxes checked in each column)					

Evaluating Your Responses:

If you responded to 144 or more questions with #2 or #3 ("I can take or leave this food" or "I dislike this food"), then you probably are among the majority of people who are about average risk takers. You aren't likely to become a firefighter or an astronaut, but you will take risks in your career in order to advance. You consider yourself moderately ambitious, and you enjoy careers that involve working with others. In terms of hobbies, you'll take moderate risks, but you probably prefer hiking for fun rather than turning your attention to becoming a racing sailor. You're more likely to choose a partner who has similar food preferences and you try new restaurants if others suggest it. No extremes for you!

If you responded to 144 or more questions with #5 ("I've never tried this food and I never intend to try it"), you may need to ask yourself why you are so timid about food choices. We'll call you an accountant, a person who plays by the rules and can give your attention to detail work for hours at a time. Others may call you a problem solver. Your steady, calm nature is admirable and you are a loyal lover and friend. But you are not likely to apply for a trip on the space shuttle, and it's possible that if you won't try new and unfamiliar foods, then you may not be willing to try new professions or hobbies. You may choose a partner who is lively and social and his or her gregarious nature may coax you to more parties. You don't like what you don't like and you don't want to experiment with new foods. You take comfort in the familiar.

If you responded to 144 or more questions with #1 or #4 ("I really like this food" or "I've never tried this food, but I would taste it if I had the opportunity"), then you are an astronaut personality, willing to take risks and try new things. In fact, some people may think your willingness to take risks borders on reckless. You will probably choose a steady, level-headed partner, a person who is comfortable staying home now and again, but he or

she supports you when you decide to take up river rafting or mountain climbing. You are probably ambitious, but you have trouble sticking to projects and you may need help from your "accountant" personality friends to stay focused on your goals.

Appendices

J Neurol Orthop Med Surg (1996) 17:25-30
Editorial Office: 3601 W. Sahara Ave., Suite 201, Las Vegas, NV 89102-5821, USA

Chemosensory Disorders and Psychiatric Diagnoses

Alan R. Hirsch, M.D., F.A.C.P.[1] and Thomas J. Trannel, M.D.[2]

[1]Assistant Professor, Departments of Neurology and Psychiatry, Rush-Presbyterian–St. Luke's Medical Center, Chicago, Illinois
[2]Department of Psychiatry, University of Hawaii at Manoa, Honolulu, Hawaii

Abstract. To explore the neuroanatomic link between olfaction and emotion noted by Freud and MacLean, we tested 46 consecutive patients presenting with smell and taste problems using the Minnesota Multiphasic Personality Inventory–2 (MMPI-2), Millon Clinical Multiaxial Inventory II (MCMI-II), and Beck Depression Inventory as well as odor and taste threshold tests and the University of Pennsylvania Smell Inventory Test (UPSIT). Based upon their scores, 15 patients (33%) met criteria for 30 DSM III-R Axis I diagnoses and 44 patients (96%) met criteria for 74 DSM III-R Axis II diagnoses. Nine patients (20%) met criteria for dysthymia. Only two patients (4%) did not meet criteria for any psychiatric diagnosis. Certain chemosensory deficits correlated with certain psychiatric diagnoses at better than 95% confidence. A low olfactory threshold for a standard odorant, para-ethyl phenol (PE phenol), correlated with dysthymia ($p<0.016$). Apparently, patients with chemosensory disorders often suffer from mood disorders as well. The feasibility of a PE phenol-odor-threshold test as a marker for depression deserves study.

Key Words: Smell and taste disorders, psychiatric assessment.

Introduction

A neuroanatomic link exists between chemosensory dysfunction and psychiatric illness. Freud noted the integral relation between olfaction and emotion [1], and MacLean's original description of the limbic system includes the olfactory lobe as a neuroanatomically integrated constituent [2].

Clinical experiences of various authors reflect this linkage. Subjective evidence includes complaints of decreased olfactory sensitivity in patients with diagnoses of melancholia [3]. Two studies have shown impaired ability to detect and identify odors among patients with depression [4,5] and a further study has shown impaired ability to identify odors but no change in ability to detect them [6]. Deems et al. [7] found a 35% incidence of depression among subjects with dysosmia and dysgeusia and a 24% incidence among subjects with hyposmia and hypogeusia. Studies of olfactory bulbectomy as a model of depression in animals also support the association between chemosensory dysfunction and mood disorder [8].

On the other hand, other investigators have found no such linkage. Amsterdam et al. [9] found no impairment in odor-identification abilities among 51 depressed patients. Ackerman et al. [10] noted normal odor-detection abilities among a group of melancholic patients.

To help explore the relation between chemosensory disorder and mood disorder, we studied 46 patients who sought medical advice for chemosensory problems, namely anosmia, hyposmia, dysosmia, phantosmia (imaginary odors) and their taste analogs: ageusia, hypogeusia, dysgeusia and phantogeusia.

Methods

Subjects

Forty-six consecutive patients, 28 men and 18 women who presented with chemosensory problems at the Smell & Taste Treatment and Research Foundation in Chicago during 1989 and 1990 comprised the study group. Their ages ranged from 18 to 70 years with a mean age of 40 years, median 39.

The Human Investigational Review Board-approved experimental protocol was fully explained and written informed consent obtained..

Measures

Olfactory tests included: the University of Pennsylvania Smell Inventory Test (UPSIT), a series of 40 scratch-and-sniff odor identification tests [11]; and Unilateral Threshold Odor Detection Tests of sensitivity of one nostril at a time to various concentrations of the following standard odorants: phenylethyl methylethyl carbinol (PM carbinol), W-hydroxy-pentadecanoic acid lactone (PD lactone), cineole, -chloroacetophenone (CA phenone), para-ethyl phenol (PE phenol), pyridine and thiophane [12].

Gustation was assessed according to the Accusens T Taste Test which measures threshold taste detection of salt (NaCl), sweet (sucrose), sour (HCl) and bitter (urea and propyl thiocarbinol [PTC]) [13].

Written psychological tests included the Minnesota

Statistical information not included. If any interest in this information please contact the author.

Offprint requests to: Alan R. Hirsch, M.D., Smell & Taste Treatment and Research Foundation, Water Tower Place, Suite 990W, 845 North Michigan Avenue, Chicago, IL 60611, USA.

ISSN 0890-6599 © 1996 AANOS, Inc. Las Vegas, Nevada

Multiphasic Personality Inventory 2 (MMPI-2) [14,15] Millon Clinical Multiaxial Inventory II (MCMI-II) [16] and Beck Depression Inventory [17]. Psychiatric and neurologic histories also were taken and examinations performed..

Statistical Analysis

Data were analyzed using univariate methods to obtain simple summary statistics. Statistical relationships among variables were examined by applying correlation methods [18]. Since multiple tests were involved, all significance levels were adjusted to Bonferroni correction [19]. Correlations significant with Bonferroni at 0.05 level were reported as alpha less-than-or-equal-to 0.008. Since Bonferroni corrections tend to be conservative with large numbers of comparisons, we included variables that exhibited a strong degree of correlation so as not to lose sight of any clinical significance they may have. This seems appropriate for an exploratory, hypothesis-generating study..

Results

The subjects' chemosensory problems had diverse origins and had persisted for varying lengths of time ranging from 0.2 years to over 40 years; with a mean duration of 5.7 years and median of 2 years. Eighty percent had their complaints less than 7 years (Table 1).

Presenting complaints, most frequently hyposmia/anosmia (98%), hypogeusia/ageusia (96%), and the patients' subjective evaluations of their problems are shown on Table 2.

Patients' psychological complaints, self-reported during psychiatric examination, are shown on Table 3. Most had problems with well-being and memory. Sleep disturbances, fatigability and emotions problems were common.

Results of taste tests are shown on Table 4 and smell tests on Tables 5 and 6.

Four male patients complained of smell loss but had normal scores on all olfactory tests. They did not have normal scores on taste tests, however. Based upon their written psychological tests, these four patients with subjective hyposmia were found to have multiple psychiatric disorders as shown on Table 7. Seven patients demonstrated normal thresholds for odor detection on all tests and 13 patients were within the normal range on the UPSIT. Six patients rated normal on both but they nevertheless had at least mild to moderate gustatory deficits.

Psychiatric diagnoses based upon results of the written psychological tests are shown on Table 7. Based upon computerized analysis of the psychological tests MMPI-2 and MCMI-II, 15 patients (33%) met criteria for DMS III-R Axis I diagnoses and 44 patients (96%) met criteria for DSM III-R Axis diagnoses [20]. The numbers of patients with various DSM III-R diagnoses are shown on Table 8.

Of the 2 patients who did not meet criteria for any psychiatric diagnoses, one was only slightly hyposmic (for PM carbinol only); but the other had severe deficits.

The longer the duration of the patients' chemosensory complaints, the more likely they were to have fulfilled criteria for DSM III-R diagnoses based upon their MCMI-II and MMPI-2 scores and the worse were their reported mood states and subjective complaints (Table 9). Longer histories of chemosensory problems were associated with depression as indicated by increasing values on the Beck Depression Inventory ($p<0.001$).

The more severe the patients' subjective perception of olfactory problems, the more likely they were to have a DSM III-R Axis II diagnosis of obsessive compulsive-personality disorder based on their MCMI-II test ($p<0.018$).

Eight subjects experienced a diminished sex drive; phantosmia was diagnosed in five of them.

Sic of the 17 patients with phantogeusia (the taste analog of phantosmia) had coexisting anxiety disorders [21].

The 13 patients who had allergic rhinitis as the origin of their olfactory loss all had low Beck Depression scores. Six of the 13 had diagnoses of narcissistic personality disorder ($p<0.006$) based on their MCMI-II tests.

Seventeen patients described olfactory windows, transient flashes of restored olfactory ability. These phenomena showed no positive correlation with any psychiatric diagnoses, but did correlate negatively in the cases of the women, with a DSM III-R Axis II diagnosis of obsessive-compulsive personality disorder ($p<0.001$) based on MCMI-II tests.

Nine patients described gustatory windows, the taste analog to olfactory windows. Four of the nine experienced a lowering of sex drive ($p<0.05$).

Certain measured chemosensory deficits correlate with certain psychiatric diagnoses at better than 95% confidence (Table 10).

Discussion

Our data show significant associations between chemosensory problems and psychological ones. Indeed, 44 of our 46 patients with chemosensory problems met criteria for 30 DSM III-R Axis I diagnoses and 74 Axis II diagnoses based upon their written tests. And as the duration of their chemosensory problems increased, so did the probability that they fulfilled criteria for psychiatric diagnoses.

Long-standing chemosensory complaints seemingly may produce or exacerbate psychiatric problems in various ways: As chemosensory problems persist over time, patients may become pessimistic about an eventual recovery and this may lead to depression. Prolonged sensory deprivation in auditory and visual spheres has been shown to produce depression [22,23] and hearing loss has been postulated to play a role in the development of schizophrenia as well as depression [24]. Thus, chemosensory deprivation may play a similar role in the development of psychiatric problems. Moreover, the narcissistic insult, the lack of public understanding, physician apathy and subsequent social isolation suffered because of chemosensory loss may combine to induce depression [25].

Conversely, psychiatric disturbances may predispose patients to complain and seek medical intervention for their chemosensory problems, real or imagined. Just as pain, dizziness and headache are commonly seen in depressed patients [26], chemosensory complaints may be somatic manifestations of emotional problems [27]. In our study, the more severe the patients' ratings of their olfactory problems, the more likely they were to meet criteria for a diagnosis of obsessive compulsive-personality disorder, which may not be surprising since it is in the nature of patients with this disorder to amplify somatic complaints. Fliess's model of the phallic nose adds credence to the theory of a primary psychiatric disorder [28]; the displacement of attention from the genitals to the nose allows the "safe" manifestation of the sexual.

Cortical representation of chemosensation and of emotion both are localized in the frontal lobe/limbic systems [2], thus, the common anatomic substrate of the emotional and olfactory systems must be considered. A single pathogen, whether a virus [29], toxin [30], degenerative disease [31] or trauma [32] might involve both systems.

The common link may be biochemical. Degenerative diseases that deplete neurotransmitters could cause dysfunctions in both olfactory ad emotional systems, as for example, in Parkinson's disease, which depletes dopamine and in senile demential of the Alzheimer's type, which depletes acetylcholine [33,34]. Serotonin, known to mediate olfaction [35,35,37,38], has been postulated also as a neurotransmitter that regulates affective states [39]. Similarly, legal and illegal drugs can adversely affect biochemical pathways in both systems [40].

Autoimmune similarities in the olfactory and limbic lobes may produce dysfunction in both systems in a phenomenon analogous to basal ganglia dysfunction in response to anticardiac antibodies in Sydenham's chorea [41].

Disease may affect one system before the other. A pathogen may invade the blood-brain barrier, cross the olfactory lobe, cause damage there, then secondarily spread through the limbic system. This sequence has been postulated in senile dementia of the Alzheimer's type and is seen in some infectious processes [22,23].

Olfactory loss may more directly produce psychiatric disease by preventing exogenous axiolytic agents that may be present in the environment from acting upon the limbic system via the olfactory lobe. Such natural external agents can regulate mood as evidenced by the action of pheromones [42].

Inability to detect interpersonal olfactory cues and associated misperception and apprehension in social situations may lead to chronic maladaptive behavior and predispose to depression. Twenty-nine of our patients (63%) admitted being functionally disabled by their chemosensory loses, i.e., were fearful of being unable to detect smoke, natural gas, spoiled food or body odor (Table 2). Older patients were less likely than younger ones to complain of functional disability ($p<0.003$), but this may be due to their experiences with deterioration in other sensory areas (hearing, vision and peripheral neuropathy), and consequent lower expectations.

On the other hand, psychiatric dysfunction may precede or induce chemosensory dysfunction. Hallucinations, misperceptions and distortions of reality are inherent in many psychiatric diseases such as schizophrenia, bipolar disorder and major depression with psychotic features [15]. Such distortions may extend to chemosensation as well. Often psychiatric illness involves withdrawal, apathy, and internalization of focus so that external stimuli, including chemosensations are reduced or excluded [42,43]. Affected individuals may ignore odors and flavors, then perceive a reduction or distortion in their sensations.

The medical treatment of psychiatric disorders also may cause secondary physiologic chemosensory dysfunction. Many psychiatric drugs reportedly have affected chemosensation; for example, amitriptyline [44].

The particular chemosensory complaint may provide insight into the underlying psychiatric illness. The following comments, while speculative, may be worth consideration in future investigations:

Like chemosensation, sex drive is localized within the limbic system [45]. Hence, it may not be surprising that 8 of our subjects admitted to diminished sexual function. In our study, impaired abilities to taste PTC ($p<.003$) and hydrochloric acid ($p<0.03$) accompanied a diminished sex drive. Since both taste and sex drive are mediated through the rhinencephalon, and since ability to taste PTC is genetically determined [46], sex drive also may be inherited.

The complaint of hyperosmia accompanied a diminished sex drive ($p<0.008$). Perhaps detection of a competing pheromone may result in limbic system inhibition [47]. Or hyperosmia may lead to olfactory reference syndrome with a contrite reaction and anxiety regarding bodily odors, triggering social isolation as a paranoid avoidance reaction [48].

Diminished sex drive has been associated with affective disorders [49]. Phantosmic women in our study manifested diminished sex drive ($p<0.017$) and other signs of depression including energy loss ($p<0.002$) and increased Beck Depression Inventory scores ($p<0.016$). Phantosmia may be a somatic manifestation of a psychiatric disorder, but it is also possible that the travails of living with persistent phantosmia may induce depression and other psychiatric disorders in a phenomenon analogous to that seen with other somatic disease states including chronic pain, cancer, and heart disease [50]. Phantosmia and subjective hyposmia in patients with a diminished sex drive may reflect underlying psychiatric dysfunction rather than chemosensory loss.

Of our 17 patients with phantogeusia, six had anxiety disorders. Hallucinated smells, lacking validation in reality, may cause self-doubt and result in anxiety. Or a common pathogenic mechanism may induce both the anxiety and the chemosensory disturbance as is the case in temporal lobe epilepsy that can cause fear and anxiety as well as insular hallucinations. Illegal drugs (hallucinogens) also can cause generalized anxiety and gustatory hallucinations [51,52,53,54].

Our 13 patients with allergic rhinitis met criteria for fewer psychiatric diagnoses than did patients whose chemosensory complaints had other origins. All 13 had low Beck Depression Inventory scores and were less likely to have Axis I psychiatric diagnoses (p<0.007). Six of them, however, had Axis II diagnoses of narcissistic personality disorder (p<0.006) based upon their MCMI-II scores. The relative paucity of Axis I psychiatric diagnoses among this group may be due to the widespread public familiarity and empathy with problems of allergic rhinitis and with the relative ease of its medical detection. Social acceptance and validation of these patients' complaints reinforces their sense of well-being and self-assurance, minimizing the psychic stress factors. Whether patients with other allergic conditions also meet criteria for narcissistic personality disorder would be interesting to know.

Estrem [55] has linked olfactory windows to postviral hyposmia but in our study, windows occurred independently of the origin of the olfactory loss. Olfactory windows may signal the return of true olfactory ability or they may be illusions, i.e. contextually appropriate hallucinations. Deja vu, the transient activation of a memory engram is possible. Or, an active mind may fill the void where a sensory deficit exists, such as when a blind person "sees" (phantom vision) [56]. (Walt Disney successfully used this phenomenon in his animated cartoons; viewers' minds fill in the gaps between picture frames, creating the illusion of smoothly continuous action.)

Olfactory windows, reported by 17 patients (37%), correlated with diagnoses of DSM III-R Axis II histrionic personality disorder based upon MCMI-II tests (p<0.007). Histrionic individuals are, by nature, excessively emotional. Their easy access to their imaginations, evidenced by dramatic exaggeration and flights of fantasy, and their impressionability [57] suggest a receptivity to illusory smells in the context of environmental cues.

At the opposite extreme of the psychiatric spectrum, patients with obsessive compulsive-personality disorder may be reluctant to report vague perceptions as real; such patients would not be likely to describe olfactory windows. This was the case among the 9 women diagnosed with DSM III-R Axis II obsessive compulsive-personality disorder in our study; none reported olfactory windows (p<0.001). Of the seven men so diagnosed, three reported olfactory windows.

Gustatory windows, like olfactory windows, may be a somatic hallucination rather than a true sensation. Misperceived as true taste, the hallucination is not reported as phantogeusia. Thus, reports of gustatory windows may mask phantogeusic episodes, and this may account for their high comorbidity with psychiatric diagnoses since chemosensory hallucinations are common manifestations of psychiatric disorders, including schizophrenia [58].

Among our patient population, higher Beck Depression Inventory scores correlate with increased ability to detect PE phenol (left nostril p<0.007, right nostril p<0.02); the correlation is more pronounced among male patients (left nostril p<0.018, right nostril p<0.016).

Conclusion

Apparently a high incidence of mood disorders exists among patients seeking medical advice for chemosensory problems. It is imperative that clinicians be aware of this in order properly to evaluate and treat such patients.

In our study, patients' objective chemosensory test results strikingly correlate with certain DSM diagnoses based upon their written psychological tests. Thus the possibility of using chemosensory tests as aids in diagnosing psychiatric disorders is a possibility worth exploring. In particular, the threshold for detecting the odor of PE phenol may be an indicator for depression. Further studies using such formalized psychiatric assessment procedures as Structured Clinical Interview for DSM-III-R (S.C.I.C.) [59] would ensure more diagnostic accuracy than obtained with procedures used in our study which, though sensitive, are nonspecific. To eliminate selection bias, future studies might focus on patients who present with unrelated problems or at a tertiary referral center. Longitudinal surveys may be useful.

References

1. Freud S: Bemerkungen über einen Fall von Zwangs Neurosa. Ges Schr VIII:350, 1908
2. MacLean PD: Triune Concept of the Brain and Behavior. Toronto, University of Toronto Press, 1973
3. King LD, Lohr N: Chemosense disturbance in melancholia: preliminary results of a questionnaire study. Presented at the Fourth Annual Meeting of the Association for Chemoreception Sciences, Sarasota, FL, April 14-18,1982 quoted in Settle RG, Amsterdam JD: Depression and the chemical senses. In Getchell T, Doty R, Bartoshuk L, Snow J (eds), Smell and Taste in Health and Disease. New York, Raven Press, 1991, 854
4. Moberg PJ, Pearlson GD, Speedie LJ, Lipsey JR, DePaulo Jr: Olfactory recognition and mood in major depression. Presented at American Psychiatric Association Annual Meeting, Washington, DC, May, 1986 quoted in Serby MJ, Larson PM, Kalkstein D: Olfaction and neuropsychiatry. In Serby MJ, Chobor KL (eds),Science of Olfaction. New York, Springer-Verlag, 1992, 576
5. Suffin SC, Giltin M: Olfaction in depression and recovery: a new marker. Presented at American Psychiatric Association Annual Meeting, Washington, DC, May, 1986 quoted in Serby MJ, Larson PM, Kalkstein D: Olfaction and neuropsychiatry. In Serby MJ, Chobor KL (eds), Science of Olfaction. New York, Springer-Verlag, 1992, 576
6. Serby MJ, Chobor KL (eds): Science of Olfaction. New York, Springer-Verlag, 1992
7. Deems D, Doty R, Settle G, Snow J: Chemosensory dysfunction: analysis of 750 Patients from the University of Pennsylvania Smell and Taste Center [Abstract], Tenth Annual Meeting of the Association for Chemoreception

Sciences, April 27, 1988

8. Jesberger JA, Richardson JS: Brain output dysregulation induced by olfactory bulbectomy: approximation in the rat of major depressive disorder in humans. Intern J Neurosci 38:241-265, 1988
9. Amsterdam JD, Settle RG, Doty RL, Ableman E, Winokur A: Taste and smell perception in depression. Biol Psychiatr 22:1481, 1987
10. Ackerman SH, Mattis S, Schzer JA, Russ M, Burton L, Henriques JB: Gustatory and olfactory changes associated with depression. Neurosci Abst 12:1359, 1986
11. Doty RL, Newhouse MG, Azzaslina JD: Internal consistency and short-term test-retest reliability of the University of Pennsylvania Smell Identification Test. Chem Senses 10:297-300, 1985
12. Amoore J, Ollman B: Practical test kits for quantitatively evaluating the sense of smell. Rhinology 21:49-54, 1983
13. Accusen T Taste Function Kit Instruction Manual. Westport, CT, Westport Pharmaceuticals, 1982
14. Friedman AF, Webb JT, Kewak R: Psychological Assessment with MMPI. Hillsdale, NJ, Lawrence Earlbaum Associates, 1989
15. Hathaway SR, McKinley JC: Minnesota Multiphasic Personality Inventory-2. Regents of the University of Minnesota, 1989
16. Millon T: Manual for the MCMI-II 2nd ed. Minneapolis, MN, National Computer Systems, 1987
17. Beck AT, Beamesderfer A: Assessment of depression: depression inventory: psychological measurements in psychopharmacology. In Pinchot (ed), Modern Problems in Psychopharmacology, 9th ed. Basel, S. Karger, 1974
18. Colton T: Statistics in Medicine. Boston, Little Brown and Co., 1974
19. Kleinbaum DG, Kupper LL, Muller KE: Applied Regression Analysis and Other Multivariate Methods. Boston, PWS-Kent Publishing Co., 1988
20. American Psychiatric Association: Diagnostic and Statistical Manual of Mental Disorders III-R. Washington, DC, American Psychiatric Association, 1987
21. Hirsch AR, Trannel T: Salty and bitter taste. JAMA 266:1360, 1991
22. Berrios GE, Brook P: Visual hallucinations and sensory delusions in the elderly. Br J Psychiatry 144:662-664, 1984
23. Guensberger E, Fleischer J: Depresia a poruchy vnimania. Klinicke sdeleni. Ceskoslovenska Psychiatrie 70:369, 1974
24. Cooper AF, Curry AR: Pathology of deafness in the paranoid and affective psychoses of later life. J Psychosom Res 20:97-105, 1976
25. Tennen H, Affleck G, Mendola R: Coping with smell and taste disorders. In Getchell T, Doty R, Baroshuk L, Snow J (eds), Smell and Taste in Health and Disease. New York, Raven Press, 1991, 787-804
26. Diamond S: Mask of depression. Clin Med 72:1629, 1965
27. American Psychiatric Association: Diagnostic and Statistical Manual of Mental Disorders III-R. Washington, DC, American Psychiatric Association, 1987, 257
28. Freud S: Report on my studies in Paris and Berlin 1886. Extracts from the Fliess papers. Standard Edition 1892-99;1:173-280
29. Monath T, Cropp B, Harrison A: Mode of entry of a neurotropic arbovirus into the central nervous system. Laboratory Investigation 48:399, 1983
30. Roberts A: Alzheimer's disease may begin in the nose and may be caused by aluminosilicates. Neurobiol Aging 7:561-567, 1986
31. Serby M, Corwin J, Novatt A, Conrad P, Rotrosen J: Olfaction in dementia. J Neurol Neurosurg Psychiatry 48:849, 1985
32. Levin HS, High WM, Eisenberg HM: Impairment of olfactory recognition after closed head injury. Brain 108:579-591, 1985
33. Ward CD, Hess WA, Calne DB: Olfaction impairment in Parkinson's disease. Neurology 33:943-946. 1983
34. Serby M, Larson P, Kalkstein D: Nature and course of olfactory deficits in Alzheimer's disease. Am J Psychiatry 148:357, 1991
35. Halasz N, Shepherd GM: Neurochemistry of the vertebrate olfactory bulb. Neurosci 10:579-619, 1983
36. Haberly LB, Price JL: Association and commissural fiber systems of the olfactory cortex in the rat. II-Systems originating in the olfactory peduncle. J Comp Neurol 178:781-808, 1978
37. Macrides F, Davis BJ: Olfactory bulb. In Emson PC (ed), Chemical Neuroanatomy. New York, Raven Press, 1983, 391.
38. Mair RG, Harrison LM: Influence of drugs on smell function. In Laing DG, Doty RL, Breiphol W (eds), Human Sense of Smell. Berlin, Springer-Verlag, 1991- 336-355
39. Davis JM, Glassman AH: Antidepressant drugs. In Kaplan HI, Sadock BJ (eds), comprehensive Textbook of Psychiatry Vol 2, 5th ed. Baltimore, Williams & Wilkins, 1989, 1643-1644
40. Schiffman SS: Taste and smell in disease. N Eng J Med 308:1275-1279, 1983
41. Nausieda PA: Sydenham's chorea: Update. Neurology 30:331-334, 1980
42. Diagnostic and Statistical Manual of Mental Disorders III-R. Washington, DC, American Psychiatric Association, 1987, 194, 224
43. Hurwitz T, Kopala L, Clark C, Jones B: Olfactory deficits in schizophrenia. Biol Psychiatry 23:123-128, 1988
44. Schiffman SS: Drugs influencing taste and smell perception. In Getchell TV, Doty RL, Bartoshuk LM, Snow JB (eds), Smell and taste in Health and Disease. New York, Raven Press, 1991, 847 Table 2
45. Adams RD, Victor M: Principles of Neurology, 4th ed, New York, McGraw-Hill, Inc, 1989, 441
46. Snyder LH: Inherited taste deficiency. Science 74:151-152, 1931

47. Lee CT: Agonistic behavior, sexual attraction, and olfaction in mice. In Doty RL (ed), Mammalian Olfaction, Reproductive Processes, and Behavior. New York, Academic Press, 1976, 161-180
48. Hirsch AR: The nose knows. Chicago Medicine 93:17-31, 1990
49. Diagnostic and Statistical Manual of Mental Disorders III-R. Washington, DC, American Psychiatric Association, 1987, 293
50. Kaplan HI, Sadock, BJ: Synopsis of Psychiatry. Behavioral Sciences and Clinical Psychiatry. Baltimore, Williams & Wilkins, 1988, 299-301
51. Walker JT: Anxious patient. J Fam Prac 12: 733-738, 1981
52. Herman BP: Interictal psychopathology in patients with ictal fear: quantitative investigation. Neurology 32:7-11, 1982
53. Adams RD, Victor M: Principles of Neurology, 4th ed. New York, McGraw-Hill, Inc, 1989, 252-253
54. Grinspoon L, Bakalar JB: Drug dependence: non-narcotic agents. In Kaplan HI, Sadock BJ (eds), Comprehensive Textbook of Psychiatry, 4th ed. Baltimore, Williams & Wilkins, 1985, 1003-1015
55. Estrem S, Renner G: Disorders of smell and taste. Otolaryngol Clin of N Am 20:135, 1987
56. Cytowic RE: Synesthesia: Union of the Senses. New York, Springer-Verlag, 1989, 300-305
57. Diagnostic and Statistical Manual of Mental Disorders III-R. Washington, DC, American Psychiatric Association. 1987, 348
58. Ndetei DM, Vadher A: Comparative cross-cultural study of the frequencies of hallucination in schizophrenia. Acta Psychiatr Scan 70:545-549, 1984
59. Spitzer RL, Williams JBW, Gibbon M, First MB: User's Guide for the Structured Clinical Interview for DSM-III-R (SCID). Washington, DC, American Psychiatric Association, 1990

TABLE 1

Characteristics of 22 Subjects

Subject No.	Sex	Age	Smoker	Floral Odor Hedonics	Olfactory Test of Amoore Pyridine Threshold (decismels)*
1.	M	23	N	positive	25
2.	F	43	Y	negative	25
3.	M	43	N	positive	25
4.	M	32	N	negative	25
5.	M	15	N	negative	25
6.	F	37	Y	positive	25
7.	F	26	N	positive	25
8.	F	35	N	positive	25
9.	M	26	N	positive	25
10.	F	31	N	indifferent	25
11.	F	35	Y	positive	25
12.	F	55	Y	indifferent	25
13.	F	25	Y	positive	25
14.	M	39	Y	indifferent	25
15.	M	25	N	indifferent	25
16.	M	23	N	positive	55
17.	M	26	N	positive	25
18.	M	33	Y	negative	25
19.	M	62	N	negative	25
20.	F	54	Y	positive	25
21.	F	38	N	negative	25
22.	M	65	N	negative	25

*Normal range is -25 to +25 decismels.

TABLE 2

Odors and Learning Experiment

	Unscented Trials							Scented Trials						
Subject No.	Order of Presen-tation	trial 1 seconds	trial 2 seconds	trial 3 seconds	% delta trial 1-2	% delta trial 2-3	% delta trial 1-3	Order of Presen-tation	trial 1 seconds	trial 2 seconds	trial 3 seconds	% delta trial 1-2	% delta trial 2-3	% delta trial 1-3
1.	first	38.4	27.7	25.7	- 27.9%	- 7.2%	- 33.1%	second	53.1	30.6	30.2	- 42.4%	- 1.3%	- 43.1%
2.	second	46.2	57.2	41.9	+ 23.8%	- 26.7%	- 9.3%	first	54.7	43.3	56.7	- 20.8%	+ 30.9%	+ 3.7%
3.	first	72.5	57.9	51.9	- 20.1%	- 10.5%	- 28.4%	second	74.2	53.4	42.4	- 28.0%	- 20.6%	- 42.9%
4.	second	38.0	38.0	32.2	0%	- 15.3%	- 15.3%	first	49.6	37.4	34.4	- 24.6%	- 8.0%	- 30.6%
5.	first	82.8	57.9	64.7	- 30.1%	+ 11.7%	- 21.9%	second	53.6	48.6	44.8	- 9.3%	- 7.8%	- 16.4%
6.	second	33.9	32.0	31.4	- 5.6%	- 1.9%	- 7.4%	first	51.3	35.3	42.9	- 31.2%	+ 21.5%	- 16.4%
7.	first	50.4	40.6	40.1	- 19.4%	- 1.2%	- 20.4%	second	44.1	46.9	42.7	+ 6.3%	- 9.0%	- 3.2%
8.	second	35.0	33.1	43.2	- 5.4%	+ 30.5%	+ 23.4%	first	34.0	26.4	24.8	- 22.4%	- 6.1%	- 27.1%
9.	first	32.8	26.8	33.9	- 18.3%	+ 26.5%	+ 3.4%	second	34.5	25.1	25.1	- 27.2%	0%	- 27.2%
10.	second	60.1	53.2	40.4	- 11.5%	- 24.1%	- 32.8%	first	59.1	87.1	59.2	+ 47.4%	- 32.0%	+ 0.2%
11.	first	75.1	63.1	58.0	- 16.0%	- 8.1%	- 22.8%	second	67.3	43.8	42.2	- 34.9%	- 3.7%	- 37.3%
12.	second	57.6	57.7	61.5	- 0.2%	+ 6.6%	+ 6.8%	first	75.5	126.6	48.4	+ 67.7%	- 61.8%	- 35.9%
13.	first	55.5	63.3	44.6	+ 14.1%	- 29.5%	- 19.6%	second	41.1	41.8	32.0	+ 1.7%	- 23.4%	- 22.1%
14.	second	49.5	45.8	35.3	- 7.5%	- 22.9%	- 28.7%	first	52.2	53.8	48.1	+ 3.1%	- 10.6%	- 7.9%
15.	first	40.9	35.7	37.2	- 12.7%	+ 4.2%	- 9.0%	second	28.3	26.0	33.7	- 8.1%	+ 29.6%	+ 19.1%
16.	second	37.5	38.9	25.3	+ 3.7%	- 35.0%	- 32.5%	first	49.3	31.5	38.6	- 36.1%	+ 22.5%	- 21.7%
17.	second	44.3	46.8	39.4	+ 5.6%	- 15.8%	- 11.1%	first	74.9	45.3	42.6	- 39.5%	- 6.0%	- 43.1%
18.	first	93.8	91.9	77.4	- 2.0%	- 15.9%	- 17.5%	second	77.5	55.8	54.9	- 28.0%	- 1.6%	- 29.2%
19.	second	47.9	59.9	52.8	+ 25.1%	- 11.9%	+ 10.2%	first	50.9	58.6	64.5	+ 15.1%	- 10.1%	+ 26.7%
20.	first	75.2	54.1	63.6	- 28.1%	+ 17.6%	- 15.4%	second	70.1	44.0	43.1	- 37.2%	- 2.0%	- 38.5%
21.	second	46.2	39.3	56.6	- 14.9%	+ 44.0%	+ 22.5%	first	60.3	47.8	52.8	- 20.7%	+ 10.5%	- 12.4%
22.	first	56.3	45.8	58.9	- 18.7%	+ 28.6%	+ 4.6%	second	59.9	36.8	44.3	- 38.6%	+ 20.4%	- 26.0%

TABLE 3

10 Normosmic Volunteers with Positive Hedonics

	Unscented Trials							Scented Trials						
Subject No.	Order of Presen-tation	trial 1 seconds	trial 2 seconds	trial 3 seconds	% delta trial 1-2	% delta trial 2-3	% delta trial 1-3	Order of Presen-tation	trial 1 seconds	trial 2 seconds	trial 3 seconds	% delta trial 1-2	% delta trial 2-3	% delta trial 1-3
1.	first	38.4	27.7	25.7	- 27.9%	- 7.2%	- 33.1%	second	53.1	30.6	30.2	- 42.4%	- 1.3%	- 43.1%
3.	first	72.5	57.9	51.9	- 20.1%	- 10.5%	- 28.4%	second	74.2	53.4	42.4	- 28.0%	- 20.6%	- 42.9%
6.	second	33.9	32.0	31.4	- 5.6%	- 1.9%	- 7.4%	first	51.3	35.3	42.9	- 31.2%	+ 21.5%	- 16.4%
7.	first	50.4	40.6	40.1	- 19.4%	- 1.2%	- 20.4%	second	44.1	46.9	42.7	+ 6.3%	- 9.0%	- 3.2%
8.	second	35.0	33.1	43.2	- 5.4%	+ 30.5%	+ 23.4%	first	34.0	26.4	24.8	- 22.4%	- 6.1%	- 27.1%
9.	first	32.8	26.8	33.9	- 18.3%	+ 26.5%	+ 3.4%	second	34.5	25.1	25.1	- 27.2%	0%	- 27.2%
11.	first	75.1	63.1	58.0	- 16.0%	- 8.1%	- 22.8%	second	67.3	43.8	42.2	- 34.9%	- 3.7%	- 37.3%
13.	first	55.5	63.3	44.6	+ 14.1%	- 29.5%	- 19.6%	second	41.1	41.8	32.0	+ 1.7%	- 23.4%	- 22.1%
17.	second	44.3	46.8	39.4	+ 5.6%	- 15.8%	- 11.1%	first	74.9	45.3	42.6	- 39.5%	- 6.0%	- 43.1%
20.	first	75.2	54.1	63.6	- 28.1%	+ 17.6%	- 15.4%	second	70.1	44.0	43.1	- 37.2%	- 2.0%	- 38.5%
	Average	51.3	44.5	43.2	- 12.1%	+ 0.4%	- 13.1%		54.5	39.3	36.8	- 25.5%	- 5.1%	- 30.1%

J Neurol Orthop Med Surg (1996) 17:119-126
Editorial Office: 3601 W. Sahara Ave., Suite 201, Las Vegas, NV 89102-5821, USA

119

ORIGINAL ARTICLES

Odors and Learning

A.R. Hirsch, M.D.,[1] and L.H. Johnston, M.D.[2]

[1]Smell & Taste Treatment and Research Foundation, Ltd.,
Water Tower Place, Suite 990W, 845 North Michigan Avenue, Chicago, Illinois, USA
[2]Department of Neurology, Emory University Hospital, Atlanta, Georgia, USA

Abstract: Various studies have demonstrated effects of ambient odors on behavior, but none has systematically assessed the effects of odors specifically on performance of cognitive tasks. The present study examined the ability of twenty-two subjects to complete the trail-making subtest of the Halsted-Reitan Test Battery both in the presence and in the absence of a specific floral odor. Results indicate that normally achieving, normosmic subjects who considered the floral odor hedonically positive learned, on average, to complete the paradigm 17% faster on subsequent trials when the odor was present. The number of possible reasons for the results are detailed. Further studies are needed to validate the use of odors as adjuvants in the rehabilitation of individuals with pathologically-induced learning disabilities and in general education.

Key Words: Emotions, Learning, Odors

Introduction

Increasingly sophisticated understanding of the impact of emotions on behavior has prompted various studies of the effects of sensory stimuli on the emotions. The baseline emotional state of the organism, however, is a function of the limbic system and by definition, the limbic system includes within it only one sensory system, namely the olfactory system[1]. Theoretically, therefore, odors directly impact on emotion and behavior through limbic functioning.

A number of experimenters have studied effects of odors on anxiety and memory. Two studies present effects of odors on normal anxiety: Reportedly, anxiolytic effects occur with nutmeg-apple, mace, valerian, neroli (orange flowers)[2] and lavender[3]. Pathologic anxiety has not been investigated, but loss of olfactory ability has been associated with generalized anxiety disorder, a fact consonant with the possible existence of an endogenous antianxiety aroma in the environment[4].

Little research has been conducted into the effects of odors on learning behavior. In a 1989 study, Ludvigson and Rottman[5] evaluated the odors of lavender and cloves for their possible impact on learning, using as paradigms the group-embedded figure, word recall, multiple-choice vocabulary, analogies and arithmetic tasks. They found that these odors did not affect memory or cognition; the odor of lavender actually impaired performance of arithmetic tasks.

On the other hand, odors of peppermint and muguet (lily of the valley) improved the performance of stressful visual tasks[6]. Among subjects who found them hedonically positive, odors improved creativity scores on the remote associates test[7] and increased efficiency in work situations[8].

The purpose of the present study was to assess the effect of a pleasant floral odor on learning in subjects with normal olfactory ability.

Method

Subjects

Twenty-two volunteers, twelve men and ten women ranging in age from 15 to 65 years (mean 36, median 34) were recruited from the shopping mall at Water Tower Place in Chicago and paid a nominal sum to participate in this study which was conducted in the offices of The Smell & Taste Treatment and Research Foundation also located at Water Tower Place. Subjects were told we wished to test their ability to complete the maze test while wearing masks. All subjects rated them selves as normally achieving. All were given the pyridin odor threshold test of Amoore[9] to establish that they were nc mosmic.

Instruments

Two trail-making (maze) tests modified from the trail making subtest of the Halsted-Reitan Neuropsychological Test Battery[10] which is used to detect neurological problems were used.

Address Correspondence and offprint requests to: Dr. Alan R. Hirsch, Smell & Taste Treatment and Research Foundation, Ltd., Water Tower Place, Suite 990W, 845 North Michigan Avenue, Chicago, IL 60611, USA.
ISSN 0890-6599

Procedure

Prior to testing, subjects accustomed themselves to the masks by wearing unscented masks for one minute. They then underwent testing in randomized, single-blinded fashion. Each subject performed the trials twice: once wearing an unscented mask and once wearing a floral-scented mask. The scented masks had one drop of a mixed floral odorant applied, resulting in a suprathreshold level of scent.

The order of presentation of scented versus unscented masks was random, but the order of maze presentation was constant. Each subject completed the set of two mazes a total of three times sequentially with each mask. The time required to carry out each of the trials was measured.

Statistical Analysis

The percent change in the time required to complete the second and third trials compared to the first trial was analyzed using Man-Whitney-U, Spearman-rank correlation, and Wilcoxon rank-sum tests for nonparametric data.

Results

Characteristics of the twenty-two volunteers are shown on Table 1. One subject, number 16 failed the pyridine odor-threshold test of Amoore and was therefore considered impaired in olfactory ability. Of the twenty-one normosmic subjects, ten considered the mixed-floral scent hedonically positive. The other eleven considered it either neutral or hedonically negative.

Table 2 shows the amount of time in seconds each subject took to complete each of the three trials, both with the scented and with the unscented masks.

As shown on Table 3, normosmics who found the odor hedonically positive (n=10) displayed a significant improvement in learning due to its presence. While wearing scented masks, they learned to complete the tasks in an average of 30.1% less time in the subsequent trials. While wearing unscented masks, they learned to complete the tasks in an average of only 13.1% less time in the subsequent trials. In other words, they learned to complete the tasks in an average of 17% less time in the presence of the odorant.

Normosmics who found the odor hedonically negative (n=7) also displayed a slight, but statistically nonsignificant improvement in learning in the presence of the odor. An average of 9.9% less time was needed by this group to complete the trial in the presence of the odorant versus 8.2% less time without the odorant ($p=0.45$).

For the twenty-one normosmic subjects, the results were not significantly affected by the order of presentation of scented versus unscented masks ($p>0.05$), the subjects' sex ($p>0.05$), their smoking status ($p>0.05$), or their ages ($p=0.06$).

For those subjects who found them hedonically positive, the odors had a greater impact on learning from the first to second trial than from the second to third trial. The average improvement with the scented masks was 25.5% less time for the second trial compared to the first, and with the unscented masks only 12.1% less time ($t = 9$, critical value = 8,   = 0.05, 2 - tail). From the second to the third trial, average time required was 5.1% less with the scent while the performance with unscented masks actually worsened, requiring slightly more time for the third trial than for the second ($t = 19$, critical value = 8,   = 0.05, 2 - tail). Hence the presence of the odor continued substantially to improve relative performance from the second to third trial, while in the absence of odor, performance slightly worsened.

Discussion

Subjects with subjectively normal learning ability and a normal olfactory sense learned to complete the trail making subtest of the Halsted-Reitan Test Battery 17% faster on subsequent trials in the presence of the mixed floral odor which they perceived as hedonically positive. The improvement was greater from the first to the second trial than from the second to the third.

It was originally hypothesized that the presence of any hedonically positive odor would improve learning performance, but early pilot tests at various times with various groups of subjects did not support this. Odors of oriental spice, baked goods, lavender, citrus, parsley and spearmint tested in a manner similar to the current study, showed no effect on learning time in the trail-making test even though subjects considered them hedonically positive. Thus positive hedonics alone appear to be insufficient to improve learning. Only one odor, the mixed floral scent used in the present study, caused a significant improvement in learning. Hence, specific characteristics of that odor are apparently essential.

Learning, due to its complex nature, involves a multitude of integrated neurologic functions. The neurophysiological mechanism by which the floral odor mediated the improvement cannot be localized. The odor may have facilitated deposition of short term memory, the processing of newly learned material, or the access of these memories for subsequent tasks. Or, it could have facilitated the creation of new strategies for solution of problems.

Learning depends upon multiple variables: attention, interest, underlying neurologic substrate, task difficulty and competing environmental distractions. Learning may be impacted by changes in attention/wakefulness, distraction, motivation and mood. Since a degree of alertness is necessary for learning, the mixed floral odor may have acted by stimulating the reticular activating system, which has been shown to be affected by other odors, for example, jasmine and smelling salts[11,12].

On the other hand, odors can act as competing stimuli, thereby reducing concentration on the task. In that case, the distraction must be overcome before learning can occur[13]. Plainly, this was not the case in our study with the mixed floral scent.

The level of motivation affects learning ability. An odor may possibly increase motivation in a classical Pavlovian conditioned response: A stimulus, in this case the odor, induces recall of a past behavior. For example, the smell of chalk on a chalkboard may induce recall of past learning situations and thus enhance the learning state in an individual who had positive learning experiences as a child. Similarly, the same smell of chalk could hinder learning in one who had negative learning experiences associated with that smell.

Odors may have a direct physiologic impact upon the brain[14]. A knowledge of the anatomy and neurophysiology of olfaction and learning is basic to an understanding of how such direct action on the brain may affect learning.

The anatomy of learning involves multiple structures. Two that are essential are the hippocampus and cortex. Interestingly, the same areas are directly influenced by anatomic projections from the olfactory system. The primary olfactory cortex, the area on the cortex where olfaction is localized, includes the prepiriform area, the periamygdaloid area, and the entorhinal cortex. Efferent fibers from the cortex project via the uncinate fasciculus to the hippocampus, the anterior insular cortex (next to the gustatory cortical area), and the frontal cortex[15]. This anatomic overlap is best demonstrated by the fact that electrical stimulation of the cortex of the hippocampal gyrus induces uncinate fits[16].

Pathology of these structures that is known to impair learning also affects olfactory ability: Korsakoff's syndrome[17], temporal-lobe epilepsy[18], and schizophrenia (prefrontal cortex)[19]. Other more diffuse neurologic diseases that impair both learning and olfaction include senile dementia of the Alzheimer's type[20], and head injury[21].

Many of the same neurotransmitters are involved in the process of learning and in the process of olfaction; modulation of these may explain our findings. These neurotransmitters include the classic norepinephrine, dopamine, serotonin, acetylcholine, and GABA[22,23,24], as well as the hypophyseal neuropeptides and nonhypophyseal hormones. Examples of the hypophyseal hormones include methionine-enkephalin and beta endorphin and examples of the nonhypophyseal hormones include substance P, neurotensin and cholecystokinin[22,25].

Whether odors could influence neurotransmitters, and hence learning, by a multitude of diverse mechanisms, is speculative. No studies have yet demonstrated an effect of odors on cerebral neurotransmitters. Norepinephrine is an example of such a construct: Inhalation of odorants may increase norepinephrine discharged from the locus ceruleus. Norepinephrine could thus act directly as a neurotransmitter to increase learning[24]. Or norepinephrine could stimulate the reticular activating system, making the individual more alert, and in that way improve learning[12]. Or norepinephrine may act indirectly by causing an increase in attention (i.e., stress), secondarily causing an increase in vasopressin level.

This introduces a second construct, namely vasopressin, which in addition to being released secondary to stress (alertness), may also be released from the olfactory bulb by the direct action of odorants. This may further enhance alertness and memory both of which can improve learning[25].

A third construct is that of ACTH. When norepinephrine stimulates the reticular activating system, as in response to stress[26], it causes release of ACTH[27] which increases attention-enhanced learning[25]. ACTH also causes release of cortisol which acts on those structures of the brain that are jointly involved in learning and olfaction. These include the amygdala, piriform cortex, and entorhinal cortex[28].

Similar constructs may also be hypothesized for the other neurotransmitters that are common to both learning and olfaction.

In the present study, the odor may have improved learning through the following mechanisms, which were not assessed.

1. The odor may have induced a positive feeling which secondarily enhanced cognition. Exposure to odors experienced as hedonically positive produces a positive affective state and exposure to odors experienced as hedonically negative produces a negative affective state[8]. And positive mood states may directly improve learning.

2. The odor may have decreased anxiety, which inhibits learning. On the other hand, too much relaxation may impair performance[5] and a less relaxing odor may possibly have a greater positive effect on learning.

3. The odor may impact upon the limbic system itself, as has been shown to occur with other odors, for instance jasmine or lavender[11]. Substantial evidence exists that odor affects mood. As early as 1908, Freud[29] noted this, stressing the importance of olfaction on emotion in his description of a patient with an obsessional neurosis:

> "By his own account, when a child, he recognized every one by their smell, like a dog, and even when he was grown up he was more susceptible to sensations of smell than other people... and I have come to recognize that a tendency toward osphresiolagnia which has become extinct since childhood may play a part in the genesis of neuroses.
>
> In a general way I should like to raise the question whether the inevitable shunting of the sense of smell as a result of man's turning away from the earth and the organic repression of smell pleasure produced by it does not largely share in his predisposition to nervous diseases. It would thus furnish an explanation for the fact that with the advance of civilization it is precisely the sexual life which must become the victim of repression. For we have long known what an intimate relation exists in the animal organization between the sexual impulse and the function of the olfactory organs."

Of all sensations, olfaction is the one most intertwined with limbic system functioning[1]. The profuse anatomic and physiologic interconnections through the olfactory bulb, stria, and nuclei to the olfactory tubercle and from there to the prepiriform cortex to the amygdala and numerous other limbic system structures support this[15].

The way smells are commonly described adds credence to their connection to emotion. They are described differently than are other sensory modalities. They are described first of all affectively: one says "I like," or "I dislike" the odor. But all other sensory modalities are described first of all cognitively. A picture, for instance, is identified as being of a ship, a woman, or a house and only secondarily is it described affectively: "I like," or "I dislike it"[30].

The same olfactory/limbic/hippocampal connections help to explain olfactory-evoked nostalgia, the phenomena whereby an odor induces a vivid recall of a scene from the distant past[31]. In 86% of people, certain odors may trigger vivid associations analogous to a flashbulb memory. Classically, an event that induces strong emotions is required for deposition of such memories[32,33]. By directly stimulating the limbic system, odors likewise can act as the inducing agent. This phenomena was vividly described by Proust[34]: the aroma of madeleine dipped in tea evoked his flood of memories and nostalgic feelings. Olfactory evoked recall is usually a positive experience but it can sometimes be negative, as in the olfactory flashbacks of posttraumatic stress disorders[35]. Hence, it seems possible that olfactory evoked nostalgia may also cause a change in learning when a strong affective tone is associated with these memories.

Beyond these known variables, results of animal studies suggest that drugs used to improve olfaction may also improve learning[36]. Norepinephrine, as mentioned, is a common neurotransmitter to both systems[22,23,32]. Amphetamine, a norepinephrine agonist, has been shown to improve learning as well as olfaction in rats[37,38].

Similar effects may occur in human pathology. Acetylcholine is a neurotransmitter common to both the learning and olfactory systems[22,23,32], and phosphatidylcholine is known to increase central nervous-system acetylcholine levels[39]. Thus, treatment with phosphatidylcholine may possibly improve both functions in patients deficient in acetylcholine (i.e., those with senile dementia of the Alzheimer's type)[40]. Phosphatidylcholine has been used to treat olfactory deficiencies in those with hyposmia or anosmia and to improve functional ability in those with learning impairments due to senile dementia of the Alzheimer's type[41,42,43].

Likewise, dopamine is a neurotransmitter of both systems[22,23,32]. A dopamine agonist, amantadine,[44] may both improve olfactory ability in those with olfactory loss and improve overall cognitive ability in those with Parkinson"s disease[45,46]. Another overlapping neurotransmitter is serotonin[22,23,32], dysregulation of which may cause depression[47]. Amitriptyline, a 5HT agonist, improves both learning ability in those with depression and may also improve olfactory ability in those who are hyposmic[45,48]. Theoretically, milacemide (proglycine), a learning enhancing drug, should be investigated as an olfactory enhancing agent[49].

The trail-making test is a paradigm for the learning tasks of spatial analyses, motor control, attention shifting, alertness, concentration, and number sense[50]. Brain damage at various locations can impair trail-making, so it is logical that intervention at these locations could improve performance. The floral odor in our experiment may have acted at any of these sites to improve learning.

While the odor may have affected any of these tasks, its effect on improved spatial analysis/orientation is of particular interest. This cognitive process is localized in the nondominant right hemisphere[51]. Likewise, olfaction is predominantly processed in the right nondominant hemisphere[52]. This anatomic overlap may be of such significance that our results are not generalizable to learning paradigms not involving the right hemisphere. This requires further exploration.

In our study, the odor's diminished effect from the second trial to the third may have occurred because: 1. The subjects adapted to the odor and its impaired perception possibly reduced its efficacy; 2. The odor-induced change in mood or its effect on learning may be transient; and 3. The ease of the task may have precluded further improvement. Had the task been harder, the effects of the odor may have been more pronounced. A ceiling effect of noncognitive variables such as hand-eye coordination, motor skills, etc. may have hampered further improvement. Even so, the effect of the odor remained statistically significant from the second trial to the third.

The ease of the task may also explain why the order of presentation of scented and unscented masks had no effect on results. We had anticipated, based on a learning curve, that the second trail-making test would be completed faster even without any effect due to odor. But no substantially significant improvement occurred when subjects wore the unscented masks. With a harder task, practice may have had more effect and the odor may have had a greater impact.

The subjects' sex and their smoking status did not significantly affect their performance in the study. It might be anticipated that the odor would have more impact on women and nonsmokers than on males and smokers since: 1. Women and nonsmokers have better olfactory ability than have males and smokers[53,54] and 2. An earlier study of the effect of odor on perception of a consumer product, showed that another pleasant floral odor had a greater effect on women and nonsmokers than upon men and smokers[55].

Possible reasons that no significant differences appeared in this study due to sex or smoking status are: 1. The cognitive task was not sex dependent; and 2. The level of odorant was sufficiently suprathreshold that ability to detect it was not a factor.

Is it possible that the floral odor did not directly affect learning but acted on noncognitive variables mentioned above to improve hand-eye coordination, cerebellar and basal-ganglia function for coordination of movements, or pyramidal-system function for motor integration of fine movements? This appears doubtful since odors have not previously been demonstrated to affect motor function.

Conceivably, the subjects could have experienced a placebo effect based on preconceived notions that the odor would affect their learning. The subjects were not queried on this, but placebo effects have been postulated with odors in other, nonlearning, circumstances[56]. This seems doubtful in the present study, however, since no similar effects occurred in the pilot tests with other odors.

This study was conducted in a relatively isolate environment. Real-life learning situations, however, have many distractions. Normal classrooms present a cacophony of sensory stimuli which may be so great as to lessen the positive effects of odors on learning.

Nevertheless, the present study provides evidence that a potential exists for improving learning in subpopulations with primary learning disabilities and certain pathology, e.g., stroke, head trauma, and senile dementia of the Alzheimer's type in addition to the possibility of improving learning in general education.

If other studies validate the use of odors as adjuvants to teaching, the universal childhood memory of chalk on the chalkboard may eventually be replaced by the memory of a pleasant floral aroma in the classroom.

References

1. MacLean PD: Triune concept of the brain and behavior. Toronto: University of Toronto Press, 1973
2. Warren CB, Munteanu MA, Schwartz GE, et al: Method of causing the reduction of physiological and/or subjective reactivity to stress in humans being subjected to stress conditions. U.S. Patent Number 4,671,959, 1987
3. Torri A, Fukuda H, Kanemoto H, et al: Contingent negative variation (CNV) and the psychological effects of odour. In: Van Toller S, Dodd GH (eds). Perfumery: Psychology and biology of fragrance. New York: Chapman and Hall, 1988, 107-120
4. Hirsch AR: Olfaction and anxiety. Clin Psychiatr Quarterly 1993; 16:4
5. Ludvigson HW, Rottman TR: Effects of ambient odors of lavender and cloves on cognition, memory, affect and mood. Chem Senses 1989; 14:525-536
6. Ehrlichman H, Bastone L: Olfaction and emotion. In: Serby MJ, Chobor KL (eds). Science of olfaction. New York: Springer-Verlag, 1992, 410-417
7. Ehrlichman H, Bastone L: Odor experience as an affective state: Effects of odor pleasantness on cognition. Perfumer & Flavorist 1991; 16:11-12
8. Baron RA: Environmentally-induced positive affect: Its impact on self-efficacy, task performance, negotiation, and conflict. J Appl Soc Psychol 1990; 20:368-384
9. Amoore JE, Ollman BG: Practical test kits for quantitatively evaluating sense of smell. Rhinology 1983; 21:49-54
10. Reitan RM: Halstead-Reitan Neuropsychological Test Battery. Tucson, AZ: Neuropsychology Laboratory, University of Arizona, 1979
11. Sugano H: Effects of odors on mental function (abstract). Japanese Association for the Study of Taste and Smell 1988; XXII:8
12. Arnold MB: Memory and the brain. Hillsdale, New Jersey: Lawrence Erlbaum Associates, 1984, 13
13. Piaget J: Contributions of the psychosocial sciences to human behavior. In: Kaplan HI, Sadock BJ (eds). Synopsis of psychiatry, behavioral sciences, clinical psychiatry. 5th ed. Williams and Wilkins, Baltimore, 81-89
14. Long TS, Huffman E, Demartino AB, et al: EEG and behavioral responses to low-level galaxolide administration [Abstract 98]. Association of Chemoreception Science Annual Meeting, Sarasota, FL, 1989
15. Brodal A: Neurological anatomy in relation to clinical medicine. 3rd ed. New York: Oxford University Press, 1981, 640-697, 839-840
16. Penfield W, Kirstiansen K: Epileptic seizure patterns. Springfield, IL: C.C. Thomas, 1951
17. Mair RG, Doty RL, Kelly KM, et al: Multimodal sensory deficits in Korsakoff's psychosis. Neuropsychologia 1986; 24:831-839
18. Eskenazi B, Cain W, Novelly R, et al: Odor perception in temporal lobe epilepsy patients with and without temporal lobectomy. Neuropsychologia 1986; 24:553-562
19. Hurwitz T, Kopala L, Clark C, et al: Olfactory deficits in schizophrenia. Biological Psychiatry 1988; 23:123-128
20. Doty R, Reyes P, Gregor T: Presence of both odor identification and detection in Alzheimer's disease. Barin Res Bull 1987; 18:598
21. Hirsch AR, Wyse JP: Posttraumatic dysosmia: central versus peripheral. Southern Med J 1990; 83:28-34
22. Halasz N, Shepherd GM: Neurochemistry of the vertebrate olfactory bulb. Neurosci 1983; 10:579-619
23. Macrides F, Davis BJ: Olfactory bulb. In: Emson PC, (ed). Chemical Neuroanatomy. New York: Raven Press, 1983, 391
24. Squire LR: Memory and brain. New York: Oxford University Press, 1987, 40-49
25. Koob GF: Neuropeptides and memory. In: Iversen LL, Iversen SD, Snyder SH, (eds). Handbook of psychopharmacology. New York: Plenum Press, 1987, 532-561
26. Adams RB, Victor M: Principles of Neurology. New York: McGraw-Hill, 1989, 307
27. Guyton AC: Textbook of medical physiology. 7th ed. Philadelphia: W.B. Saunders Company, 1986, 919
28. Meyer JS: Biochemical effects of corticosteroids on neural tissue. Physiological Review 1985; 65:946-1020
29. Freud S: Bemerkungen über einen Fall von Zwangs Neurosa. Ges Schr 1908; VIII:350
30. Ehrlichman H, Halpern JN: Affect and memory: Effects of pleasant and unpleasant odors on retrieval of happy and unhappy memories. Journal of Personality and Social Psychology 1988; 55:769-779
31. Hirsch AR: Nostalgia: Neuropsychiatric understanding. Advances in Consumer Research 1992; 19:390-5

32. Squire LR: Memory and brain. New York: Oxford University Press, 1987, 53-54
33. Brown R, Kulik J: Flashbulb memories. Cognition 1977; 5:73-99
34. Proust M: Remembrance of things past. Vol. 1 Swann's way. Translated by CK Scott Moncrieff. New York: Random House, 1934, 36
35. Kline N, Rausch J: Olfactory precipitants of flashbacks in post traumatic stress disorders: Case reports. J Clin Psychiatr 1985; 46:383-384
36. Mair RG, Harrison LM: Influence of drugs on smell function. In: Laing DG, Doty RL, Preipohl W, (eds). Human sense of smell. Berlin: Springer-Verlag, 1991, 354
37. McGaugh JL: Drug facilitation of learning and memory. Annual Rev Pharmacol Toxicol 1973; 13:229-241
38. Doty R, Ferguson-Segall M: Odor detection performance in rats following d-amphetamine treatment: signal detection analysis. Psychopharmacol 1987; 93:87-93
39. Wurtman RJ, Hefti F, Melamed E: Precursor control of neurotransmitter synthesis. Pharmacological Reviews 1980; 32:315-335
40. Adams RB, Victor M: Principles of neurology. New York: McGraw-Hill, 1989, 927
41. Hirsch AR: Open label trial of phosphatidylcholine for olfactory and gustatory problems. Chem Senses 1990; 15:591-592
42. Hirsch AR, Daugherty DD: Phosphatidylcholine for olfactory problems. Chem Senses 1992; 17:643
43. Little A, Levy R, Chuaqui-Kidd P, et al: Double blind placebo controlled trial of high dose lecithin in Alzheimer's disease. J Neurol Neurosurg Psychiatr 1985; 48:736-742
44. Physicians Desk Reference: 46th ed. Oradell, NJ: Edward R. Barnhart, 1992, 936-937
45. Benson DF: Treatable dementias, in: Benson DF, Blumer D, (eds). Psychiatric aspects of neurologic disease. Vol. II. New York: Grune & Stratton, 1982, 139-141
46. Hirsch AR, Aranda JG: Treatment of olfactory loss with amantadine-open label trial. Chem Senses 1992; 17:642
47. Physicians Desk Reference. Ibid. p. 2170
48. Hirsch AR, Vanderbilt JG: Treatment of olfactory loss with amitriptyline. Chem Senses 1992; 17:643-644
49. Schwartz BL, Hashtroudi S, Herting RL, et al: Glycine prodrug facilitates memory retrieval in humans. Neurol 1991; 41:1341-1343
50. Lishman WA: Organic psychiatry. Psychological consequences of cerebral disorder. Oxford: Blackwell Scientific Publications, 1978, 141
51. Smith ML, Milner B: Role of the right hippocampus in the recall of spatial location. Neuropsychologia 1981; 19:781-793
52. Hirsch AR: Demography of olfaction. Pro Inst Med Chicago 1992; 45:6
53. Doty RL, Applebaum S, Zusho H, et al: Sex differences in odor identification ability: a cross-cultural analysis. Neuropsychologia 1985; 23: 667-672
54. Frye R, Schwartz B, Doty R: Dose-related effects of cigarette smoking on olfactory function. JAMA 1990; 263-1233
55. Hirsch AR, Gay SE: Effect of ambient olfactory stimuli on the evaluation of a common consumer product. Chem Senses 1991; 5:535
56. Knasko SC, Gilbert AN, Sabini J: Emotional state, physical well-being, and performance in the presence of feigned ambient odor. J Appl Soc Psychol 1990; 20:1345-1357

5 — Sensory Marketing

ALAN R. HIRSCH MD, FACP

Dr Hirsch is Neurologic Director of the Smell & Taste Treatment & Research Foundation Ltd in Chicago and is also now a member of the IJA Editorial Advisory Board.

That aromas often affect our general emotional state is well known. For example, the enticing odours of favourite foods cooking arouse our appetites and the refreshing scent of a garden after a summer shower invigorates us. On the other hand some odours have a negative impact among 1,000 people questioned the most disliked was that of fish - bad odours usually prompt us to want to flee.

Of all the human senses, the olfactory sense has the greatest impact on the emotions because the olfactory sensory apparatus is intertwined with the limbic system - the part of the brain associated with emotions.

Profuse and intricate anatomic imbrications run through the olfactory bulb, stria, and nuclei to the olfactory tubercle and from there to the prepyriform cortex to the amygdala and numerous other limbic system structures. Through these pathways the common experience of a "first impression" may arise whereby a strong emotional judgment is made about a person or a place based upon preconscious or unconscious perceptions of their odours.

Conscious use of this knowledge is relatively new. In the US business managers have been among the first to make use of this knowledge, by perfuming their products or sales areas, they hope to enhance the desirability of products to potential customers. It may seem ironic that amid the myriad appeals to the senses of sight, sound and touch, particularly in retail marketing, the sense of smell has heretofore been utilised only to a minor extent.

In today's intensely competitive retail market, companies do not expect consumers to beat a path to their door just because they offer an excellent product. Business managers realise they need something more to lure the customers. Since liking or not liking a product is, first of all, an emotional choice, direct appeals to the senses are common strategies used to influence consumers' moods and buying behaviour.

Music wafts through the air in stores and elevators. Special yellow-white lights enhance the visual appeal of gems on their plush velvet backgrounds at the jewellery counter.

> *"Direct appeals to the senses are common strategies used to influence consumers' moods and buying behaviour."*

Luxurious carpeting on automobile showroom floors lures potential customers and induces a positive mental state conducive to buying.

Scents Appeal

It is well known that the aroma of freshly baked goods conjures up warm childhood memories. When an odour of baked bread was released in a US supermarket, sales in the bakery section increased threefold. Movie-theatre managers infuse the air in their lobbies with the aroma of popcorn to entice patrons to buy. The smell of chocolate-chip cookies released into the air in front of cookie stands induces people to salivate and buy cookies.

The unique leathery "new-car scent" is an exciting enticement to most customers and a positive inducement to make a purchase. Victoria's Secret, a successful women's under clothing chain, uses a special floral potpourri throughout its stores. Many of their customers say that the aroma lifts their spirits.

Scientific Studies

As part of a pilot study, the Monell Chemical Senses Center in Philadelphia, Pennsylvania released perfumes into the air at a local jewellery store and studied the effects on customers (1).

Shoppers lingered longer than usual without knowing why. When a spicy fragrance filled the air, more men were inclined to linger. When a floral fragrance was released, more of both men and women lingered. No increase in sales was recorded during the experiments, however, perhaps because customers need more than one visit before deciding to buy high-priced items.

We know that some floral scents are exciting while others are calming. To assess these effects of floral perfumes scientifically, we made electroencephalograms (EEGs - graphs of currents emanating from the brain) of six medical students at the Smell & Taste Treatment and Research Foundation in Chicago, Illinois.

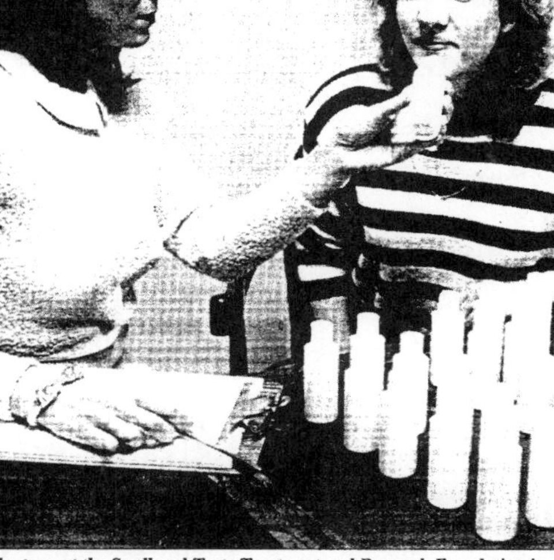

A volunteer at the Smell and Taste Treatment and Research Foundation is tested for olfactory response.

At the same time students were exposed to various scents by having them breathe through special oxygen masks through which we infused measured amounts of odorant.

Our analyses of the EEG frequencies revealed activity in the form of an increased amplitude of slow waves in the frontal lobes (the area of the brain where emotions are conceived) in response to aroma. We also had the students answer a questionnaire on their feeling states throughout the experiment; their answers demonstrated that their changes in subjective moods corresponded with observed changes in EEG activity.

Other studies of EEGs indicate that the fragrance of jasmine tends to increase beta waves frontally, said to be associated with stimulation or activity (2).

These data further indicate that the fragrance of lavender tends to increase alpha waves posteriorly, said to be associated with relaxation.

We wished to study the effect of adding a mood-enhancing perfume to a normal marketing environment without having the encumbrance of electrodes hooked up to the customers' heads or having them breathe through masks.

We selected Nike Shoes as an ordinary, effectively neutral product (3). Then we recruited 31 shoppers to act as volunteers, 26 women and five men, but did not tell them that our experiment involved olfaction. Each person was asked to examine two identical pairs of Nike shoes which were placed in two separate rooms which were identical except for one variable: the air. One room contained clean, odour-free, filtered air; the other room was perfumed with a mixed floral scent that our prior studies showed to have a positive hedonic impact, particularly on women.

Immediately after each examination and before leaving the room, each subject filled out a questionnaire discussing the hedonics, likelihood of purchase, and estimated monetary value of the shoes just examined. Out of the 31 volunteers, 26 (84%) indicated a greater likelihood of buying the shoes in the room with the mixed floral scent.

Smokers

Several of them estimated the price of the shoes in the perfumed room to be more than ten dollars higher than the price of the same shoes in the room with clean air. Even so, they were more likely to buy them at this higher price.

The scent had the overall effect of enhancing the perceptions of all of our subjects except the smokers. Smokers were negatively affected, reporting that they were less likely to buy the shoes in the room with the fragrance.

In performing this experiment, we attempted to maintain the perfume at suprathreshold levels, that is at concentrations that most people can detect, but as the study progressed, we found that many of our subjects

> *"The fragrance of jasmine tends to increase beta waves frontally, which is said to be associated with stimulation or activity."*

could not detect the mixed floral scent.

Whether they could detect it or not was immaterial, however. Those who reported that they detected no odour still said they were more inclined to buy the shoes in the scented room. The perfume had an impact even at a subliminal level, which is not surprising and supports those studies of EEGs which suggest that brain waves are affected by odours so weak as to be completely undetectable.

Whether the volunteers liked the mixed floral scent or not also was immaterial. Some reported they hated the smell, but still they were more inclined to buy the shoes in the scented room.

We chose Nike Shoes for our study feeling that they were an effectively neutral product. However during the course of our study, an African-American civil rights group, Operation PUSh, initiated a boycott of Nike Shoes as part of their economic programme to force companies to expand their African-American representation in management.

Boycott

This boycott transformed our emotionally neutral consumer item into one highly charged with emotions. What we found was that before the boycott, people rated the shoes in the middle of a scale from positive through neutral to negative, and in the presence of the perfume these ratings went up.

Once the boycott was underway, people rated the shoes either very high or very low on the same emotional scale. Interestingly, even when the shoes were rated extremely low in the clean-air room, in the presence of the mixed floral odour the ratings were not as low, despite the apparent wish on the part of some subjects to honour the boycott. The odour clearly affected their perceptions.

Towards the Future

Thus we see that certain scents, even in fairly low concentrations, can affect our moods. And further, when concentrations are so weak they are below the threshold of consciousness, they still affect our moods subconsciously.

By virtue of advanced technological expertise, it is now possible to release odorants in accurately measured, standardised concentrations at predetermined intervals, thus opening the way to strategies undreamed of in the past.

It is probable that by the year 2000 managers will use perfumes in department stores the world over as commonly as the US housewives of today use them in their bathrooms, because odorants are potentially more efficacious than any other modality in increasing saleability.

> "*When concentrations are so weak they are below the threshold of consciousness, they still affect our moods subconsciously.*"

This is true regardless of whether or not the odour is actually related to the product. In sensory marketing, particular scents will become associated with individual products that traditionally have no odours associated with them. In Japan, a clockmaker sells an alarm clock that arouses the sleeper by scenting the room with a formula to stimulate alertness. It makes sense!

References

1. Knasko, S.C. **AChemS-XI. 1989; Abstract 143.** *Ambient odor and shopping behavior.*
2. Van Toller, S. and Dodd, G.H. (eds.) **Perfumery: The Psychology and Biology of Fragrance. London: Chapman & Hall, 1988.**
3. Hirsch, A.R. and Gay, S.E. **AChem S-XIII. 19C Abstract 88.** *Effect of ambient olfactory stimuli the evaluation of a common consumer product.*

J Neurol Orthop Med Surg (1998) 18:43-45
Editorial Office: 2300 S. Rancho Dr., Suite 202, Las Vegas, NV 89102-4508, USA
43

ORIGINAL ARTICLES

Negative Health Effects of Malodors in the Environment — A Brief Review —

A.R. Hirsch, M.D., F.A.C.P.

[1]Smell & Taste Treatment and Research Foundation, Ltd.,
Water Tower Place, Suite 990W, 845 North Michigan Avenue, Chicago, Illinois, USA

Abstract: Malodors impact upon human health directly through neurotoxic effects and indirectly through stress. Depression, insomnia, impaired appetite, nausea, vomiting, headaches, coughing, exacerbation of asthma, permanent olfactory loss, cardiovascular effects and immune function compromise are some consequences. Chronic exposure to intermittent malodors near a U.S. Navy landfill was associated with encephalopathy, limbic encephalopathy and cephalgia. Persons under stress or suffering chronic diseases may be particularly vulnerable to psychological effects of malodors as demonstrated by motor vehicle accidents, family disturbances, and psychiatric hospital admissions. Children at a school southeast of Chicago demonstrated more behavioral problems on days that malodors wafted to the school from a mulching site across the street. In communities exposed to unpleasant odors, individuals report increased feelings of helplessness and frustration, impairing their job performance, learning ability, familial harmony and their motivation and capacity to cope with other stressors. These ills threaten the stability of communities and families and undermine the health and well-being of their children.

Key Words: Air pollution, Malodors, Neurotoxic effects, Psychologic effects, Stress

Introduction

My studies over the past ten years show that ambient malodors produce various negative effects on human emotions, behavior, and physical health. Odorants can directly impact on neuromechanisms or they can indirectly affect the physical health of the individual through their psychological consequences.[1] In either case, the individual's health before the exposure is a factor. Chronic disease states or emotionally stressful conditions render persons especially vulnerable to the toxic effects of environmental malodors, and persons on medications may, as a side effect, perceive odors in a distorted manner.

Negative Health Effects

Exposure to mephitic chemical emanations, besides being irksome, induce various negative physical effects according to a number of studies. In 1980, Miner[2] described results of exposure to the odor of livestock waste, including annoyance, depression, nausea, vomiting, headache, shallow breathing, coughing, insomnia and impaired appetite.

Among other pollutants that have been studied, trichloroethylene, a universally present air pollutant, can cause cephalgia.[3] Acute exposure to nitrogen tetroxide can cause cephalgia[4] and chronic neurotoxicity.[5] Acute exposure to chlorine gas can cause neurotoxicity.[6] In 1991, Neutra[7] reported that people living around hazardous waste sites reported more physical symptoms at times when they detected malodors than at times when they were unaware of them. Shusterman[8] demonstrated that even at levels considered non-toxic, chemical effluviums can cause physical symptoms.

Health effects of malodors can be divided into six categories: respiratory, chemosensory, cardiovascular, immune, neurologic and psychologic.

Respiratory effects occur most notably among asthmatics. Any strong odor may induce an attack in persons with unstable asthma.

Chemosensory. Chronic exposure to malodors from pulp mills can cause permanent olfactory loss.[9]

Cardiovascular. Certain malodors can induce an adrenocortical and adrenomedullary response leading to elevation of blood pressure and subsequent increase in stroke and heart disease.[1]

Immune. Immune function may be compromised either directly, as a result of olfactory/neural projections to lymphoid tissue,[1] or indirectly, as a result of malodor induced depression or other negative mood states.[10]

Neurologic. In a recent study, chronic exposure to intermittent malodors from a U.S. Navy dump site in Port Orchard, Washington induced cortical and subcortical dysfunction manifested by encephalopathy, limbic encephalopathy and cephalgia.[11]

Psychologic effects of odors, recognized for centuries and noted by Freud and others, vary widely among individu-

Address Correspondence and offprint requests to: Dr. Alan R. Hirsch, Smell & Taste Treatment and Research Foundation, Ltd., Water Tower Place, Suite 990W, 845 North Michigan Avenue, Chicago, IL 60611, Phone 312-649-5829

ISSN 0890-6599

als. Persons under major stress are particularly vulnerable to the psychological effects of ambient malodors.[1] And those with a distorted or impaired olfactory sense may often be annoyed by odors that other persons usually consider pleasant.[1]

It is logical that odors influence moods and emotions because the olfactory lobe, which is the part of the brain believed to account for smell, anatomically belongs to the limbic system, the seat of the emotions.[12] Thus, the olfactory sense is the sensory system that, more than any other, has the potential to affect brain functioning.

Psychophysiologically, odors may impact upon human emotions through any of three mechanisms: 1. by inducing a Pavlovian conditioned response, 2. through olfactory evoked recall or nostalgia,[13] and 3. by direct action upon the brain, in a manner similar to that of a drug.[14] This last mechanism is demonstrated by measurements of subjects' EEGs, or brain wave frequencies.[15]

Certain bad odors irritate nasal passages and resultant trigeminal stimulation releases adrenalin, leading to a tense and angry state. Thus bad odors can trigger aggression which may then be covertly expressed. For example, subjects of one experiment, college men, were instructed to apply electric shocks of varying intensity to their colleagues, supposedly for the purpose of training them. These subjects chose to inflict greater degrees of pain upon their colleagues when bad odors were present.[16] As another example, on days when malodorous air pollution is high, the numbers of motor vehicle accidents also is high, indicating that people drive more aggressively in a polluted environment.[17]

Various studies show how mood and well-being suffer in the presence of malodors. Residents exposed to the effluvium from nearby commercial swine operations reported that they suffered increased tension, fatigue, confusion, depression and anger, and that their vigor decreased.[18] According to one study,[19] ambient pollutants decreased personal attraction. And in a German urban area, the moods of young adults fluctuated in synchrony with the daily fluctuations in quality of environmental air, a pattern especially marked among more emotionally unstable individuals.[20] Further, daily diary entries of women in Bavaria showed that variations in their psychological well-being coincided with variations in ambient air quality; the correlation was particularly marked among women suffering from chronic diseases such as diabetes.[21,22] Similarly in Israel, negative health effects were significantly associated with levels of urban pollution.[23]

The numbers of family disturbances and the numbers of 911 emergency psychiatric calls also were linked to malodors in the environment, as determined by ozone levels.[24] And in several cities, the numbers of psychiatric admissions paralleled the quality of environmental air.[25]

In our study of the malodorous emanations from a mulching site southeast of Chicago undertaken for the Illinois Environmental Protection Agency, Illinois Attorney General's Office, we found that on days when the miasma wafted from the site to the school across the street, children at the school demonstrated an increase in behavioral problems.

Community and Social Effects

The fatigue and annoyance caused by ambient malodors undoubtedly reduce individuals' capacities to function normally. Their abilities to tolerate frustration, to learn, and to cope with other stressors are impaired. These effects may combine to increase familial and community disharmonies[1] to the detriment of the nurturance, growth and well-being of individuals and society.

Unfortunately, human awareness of these conditions and concern and motivation to change them are problematic. Migrants from rural areas are apt to notice the poor quality of urban air and to judge odor pollution as serious.[26] However, after prolonged exposure they become pessimistic about improving the situation. In a laboratory study, subjects exposed to unpleasant odors experienced increased feelings of helplessness and their motivation to remedy the problem was reduced.[27] Furthermore, the longer people live in a polluted atmosphere, the less they notice it.[28] Many long-time city dwellers no longer even bother to take precautions in response to air pollution advisories.[29] The future looks hazy indeed.

References

1. Evans GW: Psychological costs of chronic exposure to ambient air pollution. In: Isaacson Rl, Jensen KF (eds). The vulnerable brain and environmental risks, Vol. 3: Toxins in air and water. New York: Plenum Press, 1994, 168-172
2. Miner JR: Controlling odors from livestock production facilities: State-of-the-art. In: Livestock waste: renewable resource. St. Joseph, MO: American Society of Agricultural Engineers, 1980, 297-301
3. Hirsch AR, Rankin KM: Trichloroethylene exposure and headache. Headache 1993; 33:275
4. Hirsch AR: Cephalgia as a result of acute nitrogen tetroxide exposure. Headache 1995; 35:310
5. Hirsch AR: Neurotoxicity as a result of acute nitrogen tetroxide exposure. International Congress on Hazardous Waste: Impact on human and ecological health. Atlanta, Georgia: U.S. Department of Health and Human Services, Public Health Agency for Toxic Substances and Disease Registry, 1995, 177
6. Hirsch AR: Chronic neurotoxicity of acute chlorine gas exposure. Proceedings of the 13th International Neurotoxicology Conference. Development and neurotoxicity of endocrine disrupters, 1995, 13
7. Neutra R, Liescomb J, Sitin K, Shusterman D: Hypotheses to explain the higher symptom rates observed around hazardous waste sites. Environ Health Perspect 1991; 94:31-38
8. Shusterman D: Critical review: Health significance of environmental odor pollution. Arch Environ Health 1992; 47:76-87
9. Maruniak JA: Deprivation and the olfactory system. In:

Doty RL (ed). Handbook of olfaction and gustation. New York: Marcel Dekker, 1995, 463

10. Weisse CS: Depression and immunocompetence: Review of the literature. Psychol Bull 1992; 111:475-489
11. Hirsch AR: Chronic neurotoxicity as a result of landfill exposure in Port Orchard, Washington. International Congress on Hazardous Waste: Impact on human and ecological health. Atlanta, Georgia: U.S. Department of Health and Human Services, Public Health Agency for Toxic Substances and Disease Registry, 1995, 126
12. MacLean PD: Triune concept of the brain and behavior. Toronto: University of Toronto Press, 1973
13. Hirsch AR: Nostalgia: Neuropsychiatric understanding. Advances in Consumer Research 1992; 19:390-395
14. Sugano H: Effects of odors on mental function [Abstract]. JASTS 1988; XXII, 8
15. Allison DJ and Powis DA: Early and late hindlimb vascular responses to stimulation of receptors in the nose of the rabbit. J Physiol (Long.) 1976; 262:301-317
16. Rotton J, Frey J, Barry T, et al: Air pollution experience and physical aggression. J Appl Soc Psychol 1979; 9:347-412
17. Ury HK, Perkins MA, Goldsmith JR: Motor vehicle accidents and vehicular pollution in Los Angeles. Arch Environmental Health 1972; 25:314-322
18. Shiffman SS, Sattely Miller EA, Suggs MS, Graham BG: Effects of environmental odors emanating from commercial swine operations on the mood of nearby residents. Brain Res Bull 1995; 37:369-373
19. Rotton J, Barry T, Frey J, Soler E: Air pollution and interpersonal attraction. J Appl Soc Psychol 1978; 8:57-71
20. Brandstatter H, Furhwirth M, Kirchler E: Effects of weather and air pollution on mood: Individual difference approach. In: Canter D, Jesuino J, Soczka L et al (eds). NATO Advanced Research Workshop on Social and Environmental Psychology in the European Context: Environmental social psychology. Boston: G Kluwer, 1988, 149-159
21. Bullinger M: Psychological effects of air pollution on healthy residents - A time series approach. J Environ Psychol 1989; 9:103-118
22. Bullinger M: Relationships between air-pollution and well-being. Z Sozial Praventivmed 1989; 34:231-238
23. Zeidner M, Schechter M: Psychological responses to air pollution: Some personality and demographic correlates. J Environ Psychol 1988; 8:191-208
24. Rotton J, Frey J: Air pollution, weather, and violet crimes: Concomitant time series analysis of archival data. J Personality Social Psychol 1985; 49:1207-1220
25. Briere J, Downes A, Spensley J: Summer in the city: Urban weather conditions and psychiatric-emergency-room visits. J Abnormal Psychol 1983; 92:77-80
26. Wohlwill JF, Kohn I: Environment as experienced by the migrant: Adaptation level view. Representative Res Social Psychol 1973; 4:135-164
27. Rotton J: Affective and cognitive consequences of malodorous pollution. Basic Appl Social Psychol 1983; 4:171-191
28. Flacshbart P, Phillips S: Index and model of human responses to air quality. J Air Pollution Control Assoc 1980; 30:759-768
29. Evans GW, Colome SD, Shearer DF: Psychological reactions to air pollution. Environ Res 1988; 45:1-15

Nostalgia: A Neuropsychiatric Understanding

Alan R. Hirsch, Smell & Taste Treatment and Research Foundation, LTD.

Nostalgia, or the bittersweet yearning for the past has been eloquently analyzed in terms of society and consumerism, but what of its neuropsychiatric substrate and its implication? (Havlena, et al). It is these I shall address today.

Within the psychiatric framework, nostalgia may be considered a yearning to return home to the past -- more than this, it is a yearning for an idealized past -- a longing for a sanitized impression of the past, what in psychoanalysis is referred to as a screen memory -- not a true recreation of the past, but rather a combination of many different memories, all integrated together, and in the process all negative emotions filtered out. For a personal example of screen memory think of your first ever vivid memory. Although to you it seems a realistic recall of an early childhood event, it in fact is a compilation of memories all integrated into one. This can be demonstrated in psychoanalysis: during the analysis of the transference neurosis, the patient's earliest memory undergoes changes and divides into multiple components that are separate, definable childhood memories.

If one defines nostalgia as a yearning for an idealized past, the bittersweet nature of it becomes clearer. One can never return to this past, it never truly existed. And the present reality, no matter how good, can never be as good as an ideal -- which nostalgia has created. Thus the saying "you can't go home again."

Nostalgia, unlike screen memory, does not relate to a specific memory, but rather to an emotional state. This idealized emotional state is framed within a past era, and the yearning for the idealized emotional state manifests as an attempt to recreate that past era by reproducing activities performed then and by using symbolic representations of the past.

Idealized past emotions become displaced onto inanimate objects, sounds, smells and tastes that were experienced concurrently with the emotions. This same mechanism of displacement is utilized in medicine for its negative impact in the treatment of alcoholism. Disulfiram (Antabuse) is used as an adversive conditioning agent to inhibit recurrent use of alcohol in addicts. (Kaplan, et al 1988, p. 227).

The nostalgic urge to recreate the past within the present is, in many ways, a driving force for behavior -- how frequently we marry spouses with characteristics reminiscent of those of our parents. As other examples, we may adopt the political affiliations and prejudices of our forebears, become democrats, republicans, or even racists because our parents were.

Similarly, the nostalgic urge to recreate the past explains why so many abused children marry abusive spouses, and children of alcoholics marry alcoholic spouses -- not because their childhood was happy, but rather because they seek to recreate their idealized sanitized memories of their childhood by identifying with symbolic manifestations of the past which they find in their alcoholic or abusive spouses.

This same paradigm governs the repetition of failures on the part of "neurotics" who behave as if oblivious to logical rationale. This is seen in persons with recurrent failing relationships (those marrying seven or eight times), those with recurrent failures at business, and even those with recurrent experiences of being victimized.

Through daily behavior, the nostalgic urges may also be partially gratified -- food choices for example (hence the passing down from generation to generation of family recipes) -- with an actual primitive incorporation into the self of the nostalgic object.

Observing holidays precipitates nostalgic desires, while it simultaneously recreates past experiences, hence fulfilling the nostalgic yearning. Emotionally-laden rituals discharge nostalgic energies through the physical activity of the ritual, while forging linkages with the past. Religious practices may be viewed as an immersion in institutionalized nostalgia -- unchanged over the millenia, hence gratifying nostalgic wishes. This explains how the intertwining of religion with the major holidays (Christmas, Thanksgiving, Easter) achieves the greatest impact and relief of nostalgic drives.

Thus, nostalgia may be viewed in psychiatric terms as a driving force for actual behavior -- the attempt to recreate an idealized past in the present. By attempting to recreate this idealized past, one discharges psychic energies to fulfill nostalgic yearnings. Some results of these attempts throughout society may be seen in the production of sequels to movies, TV shows, and in the common practice of naming first-born sons after their fathers.

Nostalgia exists in the pathological, as well as the normal, states. Some severely regressed schizophrenics actually live within the delusional system of their idealized memories.(Hill). In pathological bereavement, obsession with loss of the idealized past causes depression.(Kaplan et al, 1988, p. 299). In senile dementia of the Alzheimer's type, or Wernicke-Korsakoff syndrome, where recent memory is markedly hampered, nostalgic memories are still available, hence substituting the past for the present.(Lishman;Hales et al).

On the other hand, in an antithetical state to nostalgia, those suffering from posttraumatic stress disorder do not yearn for the past but rather desire to eliminate memory for the past.(*Diagnostic and Statistical Manual of Mental Disorders*). However, in both nostalgia and in posttraumatic stress disorder immediate stimuli can precipitate emotionally-laden memories. These stimuli are context specific. For instance, many Viet Nam veterans with posttraumatic stress disorder describe odors of seafood or burning diesel fuel as precipitants for the flashback phenomena.(Kline et al). Flashbacks for those who were Korean veterans with posttraumatic stress disorder describe odors of beaches and wet canvas as precipitants. And Persian Gulf veterans describe gustatory-evoked recall from drinking ionized water.(Coombs).

Homesickness is not true nostalgia, but rather a geographic nostalgia -- a yearning for a different space rather than a different time -- for return to idealized memories of a location and people left behind.

All the senses may be used to precipitate the nostalgic experience -- hearing music (witness the popularity of "classics" of the '60s, '70s, '80s, etc.), seeing pictures (photo albums in fashion with their recurring trends), and possibly the most significant, smelling odors.

Even as early as 1908, Freud recognized a strong link between odors and the emotions.(Freud). Anatomically, the nose directly connects with the olfactory lobe in the limbic system -- that area of the brain considered the seat of the emotions. The olfactory lobe is actually part and parcel of the limbic system.(MacLean). Therefore, the most powerful impact upon the emotions is through the sense of smell. In a universal phenomena called olfactory-evoked recall, an odor can bring back a memory from the past. Often a vivid visual image is evoked along with an associated positive mood state. A classic example was described by Marcel Proust in the first volume of his novel A La Recherche Du Temps Perdu (English translation Remembrance of Things Past).(Proust). The aroma of madeleine dipped in tea evoked in the author a flood of memories and feelings of nostalgia.

The understanding that odors evoke more powerful reactions than the other senses do is not particularly new. It is well known that the aroma of freshly baked goods conjures up warm childhood memories. When an odor of baked bread was released in a U.S. supermarket, sales in the bakery section increased threefold. Movie theater managers infuse the air in their lobbies with the aroma of popcorn to entice patrons to buy. The smell of chocolate chip cookies released into the air in front of cookie stands induces the people to salivate and buy cookies. The unique, leathery "new car scent" is an exciting enticement to most customers and a positive inducement to make a purchase. Victoria's Secret, a successful women's underclothing chain, uses a special floral potpourri throughout its stores. Many of the customers say that the aroma lifts their spirits.

Some odors, however, can have a negative impact. Among 1002 people queried in a 1989 Gallop poll throughout the United States, the most disliked odor was the odor of fish.(unpublished study, 1989). We might well expect any store located next to a seafood market to have their sales negatively affected by the odor.

An ordinary person can smell 10,000 odors.(Ackerman). But no two people react in exactly the same way.

In general women are more sensitive to odors than are men.(Doty et al). Ethnicity and geographical background strongly affect odor sensitivity. Japanese perfume may not be a popular sales item in North America. Among sample populations taken across the U.S., Korean-Americans had a keener ability to identify odors than either black or white Americans. Native Japanese were least able to identify the odors used in the study.

As might be expected, our judgement as to the pleasantness or the unpleasantness of various odors depends too upon who we are and where we live. In one study, sample populations from 20 nations were asked to evaluate 22 different fragrances.(Davis et al). The populations with similar odor preferences could be grouped geographically. One group with similar odor preferences included residents of California, Kansas, Japan, West Germany, Taiwan, Canada, Italians in Brazil, Phillipines and Taiwanese in California. A second group with similar preferences included residents of Australia, Sweden, France, Norway, East Germany, Finland, Mexico, Japanese in Brazil and Africans in Brazil. This clustering of odor preferences implies a similar clustering of preferences with regard to foods and perfumes.

Among the 1002 people mentioned previously, the particular area of the United States from which they came had a decisive influence on their responses to odors (Table 1).(unpublished study, 1989). Although in general, baked goods were the most common precipitant of an olfactory-evoked recall, among persons from the east coast, the smell of flowers prompted an olfactory-evoked recall of their childhoods. Among persons from the south, the smell of fresh air prompted a similar recall - among those from the midwest, the smell of farm animals, and among those from the west coast, the smell of meat cooking or barbecuing. Evoked memories of childhood are usually associated with a positive emotional state which may then be transferred to the place where the evoked memories are experienced -- the store and the items for sale. The makers of certain oriental perfumes already take advantage of this effect by adding the smell of baby powder to their formulas, baby powder being associated in most persons' minds with a safe, clean environment.

In order to further investigate olfactory-evoked recall, in September of 1991, 989 English-speaking individuals selected at random in Water Tower Place shopping mall in Chicago consented to be interviewed in person for this Institutional Review Board approved study. Respondents reported basic demographic data including the decade of their birth and their predominant geographic location during childhood. Psychological data revealed the existence of olfactory evoked recall, the particular smells that precipitated childhood memories and the overall level of happiness with the individual's childhood.

Demographic Profile: 478 were male, 511 were female. Decades of birth ranged from the 1900s to the 1970s as follows: 1900s - 3, 1910s - 16, 1920s - 43, 1930s - 70, 1940s - 118, 1950s 204, 1960s - 338, 1970s - 197 (Table 2). In order to achieve statistical significance, data for people born in the 1900s, 1910s and 1920s were combined into a single grouping. While most were reared in Chicago (325) or its suburbs (176), 45 states were represented and 39 countries as well.

TABLE 1
QUESTION:
"What smells or odors remind you of your childhood?"

Childhood Smells and Odors
(n = 1,002)
(Three Responses)

Percent of Response	Who Gave Total	Percent of Those Specific Response
Baking bread, cookies, cakes, etc.	18	23%
Fresh air, rain, outdoors	5	7
Baby powder, powder	4	6
Chicken	4	5
Flowers	4	5
Farm smells	4	5
Meat cooking	4	5
Cut grass	3	5
Burning leaves, wood	3	4
Popcorn	2	3
Apples	2	3
Spaghetti	2	3
General food cooking	2	3
Apple pie	2	2
Cleaning products	2	2
Bacon	2	2
Soup	2	2
Fish, seafood	2	2
Other (1% or less)	50	65
Don't know	20	

Statistics were analyzed using Chi-square test on contingency tables or Z-test for the difference between pairs of proportions.

Results: Overall, 85.2% displayed olfactory evoked recall, a generational effect was demonstrated in this regard (Table 3).

Eighty-six and eight tenths percent of those born after 1930 displayed olfactory-evoked recall, whereas only 61.3% of those born before 1930 displayed it. This implies that the marketing of products through nostalgia with odors would be more efficacious in a target consumer group born after 1930. This is not surprising since olfactory ability decreases with age: one-half of those over 65 and three-quarters of those over 80 years of age have a reduced ability to smell.(Doty et al). In addition, memory worsens with age further explaining our findings in the elderly.(Bartus et al).

As mentioned, women have better olfactory ability than do men. Yet in our study at Water Tower, no statistically significant difference was shown between the genders in their self-reports of odor-evoked nostalgia (Table 4). Hence, regardless of sex, aroma is an important nostalgia inducer. Based on the Z-test for the difference between two proportions, a statistically significant generational difference was found (Table 5). Those born from the 1930s on were more likely to have nostalgia induced by food odors and less likely to have nostalgia induced by nature odors than those born before the 1930s.

Those born before the 1930s cited smells of nature including pine, hay, horses, sea air and meadows, whereas those born in 1930 to 1979 were reminded of their childhood by such smells as plastic, scented markers, airplane fuel, vaporub, sweet tarts, and playdough. This shift away from natural odors and toward artificial ones may portend future problems for society. If we are concerned about ecology partly out of nostalgia for nature odors, then 50 years from now, how will the environmental movement be of much concern to the people who are nostalgic only for manmade chemicals?

TABLE 2

DECADE OF BIRTH (ALL DECADES)	POSITIVE SMELL PERSONS	NO SMELL PERSONS	TOTAL
1970's	171	26	197
1960's	290	48	338
1950's	186	18	204
1940's	98	20	118
1930's	60	10	70
1920's	28	15	43
1910's	8	8	16
1900's	2	1	3
TOTALS	843	146	989

TABLE 3

DECADE OF BIRTH	PERCENT OF PERSONS IN EACH BIRTH DECADE WHO ARE "POSITIVE SMELL."
1970's	85.8% - 171/197
1960's	85.8% - 290/338
1950's	91.2% - 186/204
1940's	83.1% - 98/118
1930's	85.7% - 60/70
1920's	65.1% - 28/43
1910's	50.0% - 8/16
1900's	66.7% - 2/3

TABLE 4

MALE	COMBINED TOTAL	FEMALE
83.7%	85.2%	86.7%

TABLE 5

	Combined 1930's - 1970's	Combined 1900's - 1920's
Food or Cooking Smells	40.2%	26.3%
Nature-related Smells	30.6%	44.7%

TABLE 6

	UNHAPPY CHILDHOOD	HAPPY CHILDHOOD
Foul Smell-Evoked Nostalgia	19.7%	7.8%

Clearly, in targeting a younger consumer group, food smells would be more efficacious than would nature smells, but the opposite would be true in targeting an older group. Odors were divided into foul and nonfoul smells. Foul smells (i.e. garbage, urine, manure) were defined by a panel of olfactory experts. Eight and eight tenths percent of those who reported olfactory-induced nostalgia said that foul smells were the precipitant. Eight and seven tenths percent (or one person in 12) reported an unhappy childhood. This was independent of birth decade or gender. And whether one had a happy childhood influenced which kind of smell evoked a childhood memory. The one person in 12 who reported having an unhappy childhood, was more than twice as likely to describe such foul odors as mothballs, body odor, dog waste, sewer gas, bus fumes, and mother's menstrual cycle (Table 6). This suggests that psychotherapists might well inquire into what odor induces childhood memories as a further method of gaining insight into personality.

Interestingly, happiness in childhood did not correlate with ability for olfactory evoked recall -- suggesting the universal nature of this phenomenon.

About equal numbers, 91% of men and 92% of women, reported a happy childhood.

Implications of our findings for marketers are: 1) approximately 85% of both men and women report smell-induced nostalgia -- suggesting smell is an important tool in marketing, 2) consumers under 60 years old are better targets for marketing nostalgia than older consumers, 3) while a wide range of smells could be utilized to induce nostalgic recall, food smells are a more effective stimulus for the younger consumer while nature smells are more effective for the older consumer, 4) in attempting to sell a product now, odorize it to maximize nostalgia of present-day consumers, 5) the product now odorized may come to be the focus of nostalgia for future consumers, 6) use of nostalgia through activation of the limbic system through the sense of smell will produce the strongest emotional appeal as a means of product marketing.

Through odors, nostalgia may be induced with greatest ease. One may speculate that nostalgic desires will increase in the coming decade since it seems likely that the more dissatisfied we are with the present, the more we idealize the past (a temporal equivalent of "the grass is greener on the other side" or as Richard Llewellyn wrote, "how green was my valley").(Liwellyn). Therefore, in the hard times ahead, it will be easier to sell nostalgia.

REFERENCES

Ackerman, D.: *A Natural History of the Senses*, p. 5 New York: Random House, 1990.

Bartus, R. T., Dean, R. L., III, Beer, B., and Lippa, A. S., The cholinergic hypothesis of geriatric memory dysfunction. *Science* 217:408-417. 1982.

Coombs, K., personal communication, 1991.

Davis, R. G. and Pangborn, R. M.: "Odor pleasantness judgments compared among samples from 20 nations using microfragrances." *AChemS VII: Abstracts*, p. 413.

Diagnostic and Statistical Manual of Mental Disorders,Washington, D.C.: American Psychiatric Assocation, 1987, p. 427-251.

Doty, R. L., Shaman, P. Applebaum, S. L.: Smell Identification Ability, Changes with Age. *Science* 226:1441, 1984.

Freud, S. Bemerkungen Uber Einen Fall Von Zwangs Neuroses, *Ges. Schr., VIII:* 350, 1908.

Hales, R. and Yudofsky, S., *Textbook of Neuropsychiatry*, Washington, D.C.: American Psychiatric Press, Inc., 1987, p. 128.

Havlena, W. and S. Holak (1991), "The Good Old Days': Observations on Nostalgia and Its Role in Consumer Behavior," *Advances in Consumer Research, 18*, Rebecca H. Holman and Michael R. Solomon, eds., Provo UT: Association for Consumer Research, 323-329.

Hill, L., *Psychotherapeutic Intervention in Schizophrenia*, Chicago: The University of Chicago Press, 1955.

Kaplan, H. and Sadock, B. *Synopsis of Psychiatry*, Baltimore: Williams & Wilkins, 1988, p. 227, 299.

Kline, N., Rausch, J., Olfactory Precipitants of Flashbacks in Post Traumatic Stress Disorder: Case Reports. *J. Clin.Psychiatry*, 46: 383-384, 1985.

Lishman, W., *Organic Psychiatry*, London: Blackwell Scientific Publications, 1978, p. 530.

Llewellyn, R. *How Green Was My Valley*. London: M.Joseph, Ltd, 1939.

MacLean, P.D., *A Triune Concept of the Brain and Behavior*. University of Toronto Press, Toronto, 1973.

Proust, M. *Remembrance of Things Past*. Vol. 1 Swann's Way Ch. 1, p. 36. New York, Random House, 1934. Translated by C. K. Scott Moncrieff.

Unpublished study, 1989.

PSYCHOSOMATIC
MEDICINE

Journal of the American Psychosomatic Society

1434

EFFECTS OF GARLIC BREAD ON FAMILY INTERACTIONS

Alan R. Hirsch, Smell & Taste Treatment and Research Foundation, Chicago, IL

This study assessed the effects of the odor and ingestion of garlic bread on family interactions.
Fifty families were given 2 identical spaghetti dinners, randomly presented with and without garlic bread. Average family size was 3.6 (range 2 to 12). At each dinner, the number of interactions both positive and negative were recorded during 3 one-minute intervals. The 1st minute served as a baseline. During the 2nd minute the garlic bread aroma was presented. During the 3rd minute the bread was ingested. Three minutes of interactions were also recorded during the control dinner. Significance was determined using the Wilcoxan Sign Rank Test for comparison of nonparametric means.

Smelling and eating garlic bread decreased the number of negative interactions by an average of 0.174 per family member per minute or 22.7% ($p=0.05$) and the number of pleasant interactions increased by an average of 0.25 per family member per minute or 7.4% ($p=0.04$). The decrease in negative interactions was more pronounced among older males who both liked and had nostalgic feelings evoked by the aroma.
Serving garlic bread at dinner enhanced the quality of family interactions. This has potential application in promoting and maintaining shared family experiences, thus stabilizing the family unit, and also may have utility as an adjunct to family therapy.

J Neurol Orthop Med Surg (1999) 19:14-19
Editorial Office: 2300 S. Rancho Dr., Suite 202, Las Vegas, NV 89102-4508, USA
14

Human Male Sexual Response to Olfactory Stimuli

Alan R. Hirsch, M.D., F.A.C.P.[1] and Jason J. Gruss[2]

[1]Smell and Taste Treatment and Research Foundation, Chicago, Illinois
[2]University of Michigan, Ann Arbor, Michigan

Abstract: Folk wisdom has it that various aromas are sexually enticing but no data exists demonstrating actual effects of specific odors on arousal. The present study reports the effects of 30 different scents on sexual arousal of 31 male volunteers by comparing their penile blood flow, measured by brachial penile index, while wearing scented masks and while wearing nonodorized, blank masks. Odors found generally pleasant in previous surveys were selected for this study. Each produced some increase in penile blood flow; the combined odor of lavender and pumpkin pie produced the greatest increase (40%). A multitude of mechanisms may mediate these effects. A potential application of odorants to increase penile blood flow in patients with vasculogenic impotence deserves study. Odors that may decrease penile blood flow have yet to be found for possible use in treating sexual deviants.

Key Words: Odors, Sexual Response.

Introduction

Historically, certain smells have been considered aphrodisiacs, a subject of much folklore and pseudoscience. In the volcanic remnants of Pompeii, perfume jars were preserved in the chambers designed for sexual relations. Ancient Egyptians bathed with essential oils in preparation for assignations; Sumarians seduced their women with perfumes. A relationship between smell and sexual attraction is emphasized in traditional Chinese rituals, and virtually all cultures have used perfume in their marriage rites. In mythology, rose petals symbolize scent, and the word "deflowering" describes the initial act of sex. Farcical stock characters in the popular Italian *Commedia dell'Arte* of the Renaissance wore long-nose masks to symbolize their phallic endowment, a tradition that lingers in the figure of Punch. Dramatic literature abounds with sly references to nasal size as symbolic of phallic size, as in the famous play *Cyrano De Bergerac*.

Psychoanalysis has made much of these associations. Fliess, in his concept of the phallic nose, formally described an underlying link between the nose and the phallus.[1] Jungian psychology also connects odors and sex.

In the modern world the pervasive promoting and use of perfumes, colognes and after-shaves as romantic enticements have produced a multibillion dollar business.[2] And the popular arts as well have seized on the theme linking olfaction and sex. The movie *Scent of a Woman* portrays the importance of smell and sexual attraction in our society, as does the recent novel *Perfumery*.

The prominent connection between odors and sex among diverse historical periods and cultures implies a high level of evolutionary importance. Freud[3] suggested that odors are such strong inducers of sexual feelings that repression of smell sensations is necessary to civilization.

Anatomy bears out the link between smells and sex: the area of the brain through which we experience smells, the olfactory lobe, is part of the limbic system, the emotional brain,[4] the area through which sexual thoughts and desires are derived.[5] Brill[6] suggests that people kiss to get their noses close together, so that they can smell each other (the Eskimo kiss). Or possibly they kiss to get their mouths together so they can taste each other since most of what we call taste is dependent upon olfaction.[7]

In discussing odors and sex we must begin with the birds and the bees. Classically, bees, moths, and other insects are known to release pheromones, aerosolized odorants that attract the opposite sex.[8] A female moth can release a pheromone into the air that attracts a male as far as a mile away, enhancing her chances of procreation. Similarly, pheromones exist throughout the animal kingdom in insect, subhuman primate, and primate genera[9] to the evolutionary benefit of the species. Whether human pheromones exist is unclear, but theoretic grounds support their presence, since structures that exist throughout the animal kingdom seem likely to be present in humans as well. Inside the human brain, near the top of the nose is an anatomical feature that gives us reason to believe that human pheromones exist: the vomeronasal organ.[10] Its function is unknown, but in subhuman primates, this is the area where pheromones act to

Address correspondence and offprint requests to: Dr. Alan R. Hirsch, Smell & Taste Treatment and Research Foundation, Water Tower Place, Suite 990W, 845 North Michigan Avenue, Chicago, Illinois, 60611
ISSN 0890-6599

increase the chance of procreation. This is where human vomeropherins bind.[11,12]

When we exercise, we sweat through endocrine glands.[13] But when we are embarrassed or sexually excited, we sweat through apocrine glands that release high-density steroids[14] under the arms and around the genitalia; their role is unknown. In subhuman primates, the same apocrine glands release pheromones.[14] If these glands function similarly in humans, this might explain why when a woman raises her arms to her head exposing her axillae, her gesture is considered sexually provocative; "this charming grotto is full on intriguing surprises."[13]

Physiologic evidence of the importance of odors in sexual excitation is two-fold: First, during sexual excitation, engorgement of the nose induces development of eddy currents (like small tornadoes). Then, since less of the air goes directly to the lungs,[15] more pheromones or sexual attractants can reach the olfactory epithelium[16] and smell is more acute. Breathing from the mouth during sexual excitation is evidence of nasal engorgement and maximizes contact with stimulants and pheromones. Second, olfactory ability in women, generally better than that of men[16-19] is at its peak during ovulation, perhaps to detect any pheromones present. Increased olfactory ability at this time may explain why periovulatory women tend to have more sexual experiences. Possibly increased olfactory stimulation prompts an increase in sexual activity.[20]

Clinical observation supports the existence of pheromones in humans, as manifested by the college roommate effect.[21,22] Women who move into all-women's dormitory halls have, by mid-term, synchronized their ovulating cycles with the other women in the hall. This indicates that a pheromone released by one woman may entrain the others in a pattern of dominance. The same phenomenon exists in small offices where women work together.

As further evidence of phermones' existence, male college students were asked to rate pictures of women while wearing masks either with no odor or with a postulated female pheromone (androsterone). The men with postulated female pheromone in their masks described the women as appearing friendlier and prettier than did those wearing unodorized masks.[23]

During a study in England, a possible male pheromone was placed beneath certain desks in a classroom; then pictures were taken continually to monitor where students sat. Female students tended to sit near the desks where the postulated male pheromone was placed.[24] Asked why they sat there, the girls said "it just seemed like the right place to sit."

Pheromones may be not only sexual attractants, but also territorial markers, e.g., a dog establishes dominance in his yard by urinating there.[25] In a study of a men's college dormitory room, a postulated male pheromone was placed beneath specific toilet stalls which were then monitored.[24] Men tended to avoid the stalls where the postulated male pheromone was placed, which seems suggestive that the scent had the effect of a territorial marker.

These experiments, of course, do not prove human pheromones exist. Yet perfume companies market their interpretations of pheromones, often containing musk, a pheromone of the male musk deer. Marilyn Miglan named a perfume "Pheromone," however its scent is a floral mixture.[26]

Various cultures favor various odors. In the U.S., women cut their axillary hair because this bodily smell is considered unclean. But in Eastern Europe, the smell is considered sexually provocative, and the axillary follicles ar left virginal. Alex Comfort calls it the woman's bouquet.[27]

Medical evidence links smell and sexual response. In one study, over 17 percent of patients with olfactory deficits had developed a sexual dysfunction.[28]

A relationship undoubtedly exists between the olfactory and sexual functions; its mechanism, however, remains to be discovered. In the present experiment, we investigate the impact of ambient olfactory stimuli upon sexual response in the human male.

Method

Participants

Subjects literate in English were recruited through solicitation on classic rock radio broadcasts. Thirty-one males, aged 18 to 64 years volunteered.

Measures

All subjects underwent olfactory testing with the University of Pennsylvania Smell Identification Test (UPSIT), a 40 item, forced choice, scratch and sniff odor identification test[29] and the Chicago Smell Test, a three odorant detection and identification test.[30-32] They were queried as to sexual preference, sexual practices, and odor hedonics.

During the experiment, subjects' sexual arousal was determined using the brachial penile index[33] with the Floscope Ultra Pneumoplethysmograph following manufacturer's protocol.[34] With this instrument, both penile and brachial blood pressures were measured and their ratio calculated, hence controlling for systemic effects. This allowed specific noninvasive assessment of penile blood flow.

Procedure

Twenty-four different odorants were chosen for this study based on their generally positive hedonics in previous surveys. In addition, 6 combinations of 2 of the most well-liked of these were chosen. The effects of the 30 odors on penile blood flow were assessed by comparing a subject's brachial penile index while wearing an odorized mask to his average index while wearing an unodorized blank mask. This was done for each subject for each odor.

Subjects underwent assessment as follows: after being attached to the plethysmograph, three minutes were allowed for acclimation, then a blank control mask was applied for one minute and brachial penile index recorded. The blank mask was then removed and an odorized mask applied. Thus 30 odorized masks were randomly applied in double-blind fashion, with a three minute hiatus between masks to prevent habituation to the odors. Each mask was worn for one minute and brachial penile index recorded. Finally, an additional blank mask was applied for one minute and brachial penile index again recorded.

Statistical Analysis

Statistical significance is defined by a ρ value ≤ 0.05. Data analysis includes these nonparametric tests: Signed Rank test, Wilcoxan Rank Sum test, and Spearman's Rank correlation coefficient.[35-36]

Results

Participants' Characteristics

All subjects lived in Chicago or suburbs. Most (77%) were single and their mean age was 30 years, median 29 years with a range of 18 to 64 years. Most (87%) were heterosexual, had a regular sex partner (74%), had intercourse four times in the 30-day period just prior to the experiment and considered their sex lives fairly satisfactory (Table 1).

TABLE I
Sexual Characteristics of 31 Male Subjects

Table I. Sexual Characteristics of 31 Male Subjects

	No.	%
Marital Status		
single	24	77.4
married	5	16.1
divorced	2	6.5
Heterosexual	27	87.1
Homosexual	4	12.9
Had a regular sex partner	23	74.2
Had more than one partner	2	6.5
30-Day sexual history:		
Erection difficulties	0	0
No. of times of intercourse		
median - 4 times		
range -		
none	6	19.3
25 times	2	6.5
Level of sexual satisfaction on a scale of 1 - 5:		
median - level 3		
range -		
1 (poorest)	2	6.5
5 (greatest)	7	22.6
Frequency of morning erections on a scale of 1 - 5:		
median - level 3		
range		
1 (absent)	1	3.2
5 (every AM)	2	6.5
Ever had odor-induced erection?		
No	26	83.9
Yes	5	16.1

To assess their physiologic erectile function, subjects were asked to rate the frequency of their morning erections on a scale of 1 (absent) to 5 (every morning). Their median response was 3 (Table I). Most (84%) stated that they had never experienced an odor-induced erection (Table I).

Subjects' olfactory characteristics are shown on Table II. UPSIT scores were graded based on published norms for age and sex. Given these, 52% of subjects scores were normal and 48% were microsmic, i.e., hyposmic (deficient in odor sensitivity) or anosmic (without a sense of smell). Over half the subjects (55%) had experienced odor-evoked recall, a phenomenon wherein an aroma triggers memories and associated feelings.[37] More than half (61%) were nonsmokers. Most (71%) used cologne, and of those who had a regular sex partner, 83% of the partners used scent.

TABLE II
Smell Characteristics

Table II. Smell Characteristics

All Subjects (n = 31)	No.	%
UPSIT scores		
Normal	16	51.6
Microsmic, Anosmic	15	48.4
Experienced odor-evoked recall	17	54.8
Smoked		
No	19	61.3
Yes	12	38.7
1 - 2 pks/da	3	9.7
< 1 pk/da	9	29.0
Used cologne	22	71.0
Subjects with a regular partner (n = 23)		
Partner used scent	19	82.6

Effects of Odors on Penile Blood Flow

Each of the 30 odors produced an increase in penile blood flow (Table III). The combined odor of lavender and pumpkin pie had the greatest effect, increasing median penile-blood flow by 40%. Second in effectiveness was the combination of black licorice and doughnut, which increased the median penile-blood flow 31.5%. The combined odors of pumpkin pie and doughnut was third, with a 20% increase. Least stimulating was cranberry, which increased penile blood flow by 2%. None of the odors reduced penile-blood flow.

Men with below normal olfaction did not differ significantly from those with normal olfaction, nor did smokers differ significantly from non-smokers. However, among subjects with normal olfactory ability, several correlations are significant: higher brachial penile indices correlate with greater age and with greater responses to the odor of vanilla (ρ = 0.05); self-assessed level of sexual satisfaction correlates with greater responses to the odor of strawberry (ρ = 0.05); and frequency of sexual intercourse correlates with greater responses to the odors of lavender (ρ = 0.03), oriental spice (ρ = 0.02) and cola (ρ = 0.03).

TABLE III
Increases in Penile Blood Flow Produced by Various Odors on 31 Subjects

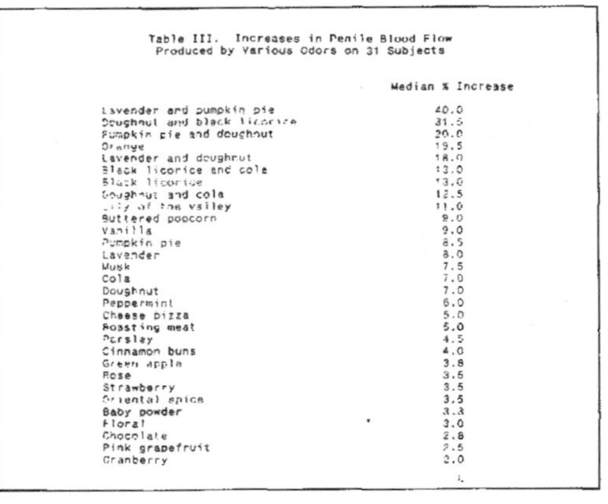

Table III. Increases in Penile Blood Flow Produced by Various Odors on 31 Subjects

	Median % Increase
Lavender and pumpkin pie	40.0
Doughnut and black licorice	31.5
Pumpkin pie and doughnut	20.0
Orange	19.5
Lavender and doughnut	18.0
Black licorice and cola	13.0
Black licorice	13.0
Doughnut and cola	12.5
Lily of the valley	11.0
Buttered popcorn	9.0
Vanilla	9.0
Pumpkin pie	8.5
Lavender	8.0
Musk	7.5
Cola	7.0
Doughnut	7.0
Peppermint	6.0
Cheese pizza	5.0
Roasting meat	5.0
Parsley	4.5
Cinnamon buns	4.0
Green apple	3.8
Rose	3.5
Strawberry	3.5
Oriental spice	3.5
Baby powder	3.3
Floral	3.0
Chocolate	2.8
Pink grapefruit	2.5
Cranberry	2.0

Discussion

We hypothesized that hedonically positive odors, since they have other behavioral effects,[38-40] would increase penile blood flow. Our data support this hypothesis.

A multitude of mechanisms exist by which this might occur. The odors could induce a Pavlovian conditioned response reminding subjects of their sexual partners or their favorite foods.[41] Among persons raised in the United States, odors of baked goods are most apt to induce a state called olfactory-evoked recall.[37] Possibly, odors in the current study evoked a nostalgic recall with an associated positive mood state that affected penile blood flow.[38-40] Or the odors may simply be relaxing. In other studies, green apple was thought to reduce anxiety, as was lavender, which increased alpha waves posteriorly, an effect associated with a relaxed state.[42-43] In a condition of reduced anxiety, inhibitions may be removed and thus penile blood flow increased.

It has been shown that the odor of jasmine increases beta waves frontally, which is associated with alertness.[42] Possibly odors may awaken the reticular activating system, making subjects more alert to any sexual cues, thus increasing penile blood flow.

An another possibility, odors may act neurophysiologically. MacLean[5] demonstrated that stimulation of the septal nucleus in the squirrel monkey induces erection. A direct pathway connects the olfactory bulb to the septal nucleus,[44] hence, it seems anatomically correct that odor could impact upon the septal nucleus to induce erection with increased penile blood flow. This seems a strong possibility in our study, since the one subject who slept through the entire experiment showed the greatest increase in penile-blood flow in response to the combined odors of lavender and pumpkin pie.

We suspect a direct physiologic mechanism, yet we cannot rule out a possible impact of odors upon the dreams of the subject who slept through the experiment, perhaps with his dream content influencing penile blood flow.

Possibly odors can increase aggression, through septal nucleus stimulation. Increased penile-blood flow may be a measure of a "neighborhood effect" of induced aggression rather than of direct sexual excitation.[45]

Nor can we rule out a generalized parasympathetic effect, increasing penile blood flow rather than specific sexual excitation.[46] As much as possible, we controlled for this by measuring brachial blood pressure coincident with penile blood flow.

The specific odors that affected penile blood flow in our experiment were primarily food odors. More directly, Rediwhip® has been used perigenitally, again indicating a strong relationship between sex, food and smell. Does this support the axiom that the way to a man's heart (and sexual affection) is through his stomach? An evolutionary hypothesis explains why this may be so. After a successful hunt, humans in primitive tribes congregated around the food.[47] There, perhaps they had most opportunities to procreate. An increase in penile-blood flow in response to food odors, then would be an advantage. A recent finding about the Bonobos—that when they found a plentiful food source they stopped to have sex before they ate, perhaps to reduce quarreling over food—provides another explanation for the association between food and sex.[48]

Humans can detect approximately 10,000 odors.[8] Studies indicate that many of them affect behavior, i.e., certain floral smells can enhance learning[49] and buying behavior;[50] green apple odor may ease claustrophobic feelings,[51] barbecue smoke may induce a flight response[51] and inhaling certain food odors may help effect weight loss.[52] Odors other than those examined in this study could possibly have a greater effect on penile-blood flow.

Olfactory sensation can influence the sexual reflex arc; as mentioned, human pheromones, which trigger sexual response through direct olfactory-limbic interconnections, are speculative.[53-55] Penile erection, the measure of male sexual arousal[56] is a manifestation of outflow from the septal nuclei within the limbic system, and end organ for olfactory fibers.[57] As a function of the autonomic nervous system,[58] penile engorgement is controlled by arterial flow through the pudendal artery and the smaller arteries to the penis. The first physical sign of sexual excitation is a change in penile-blood flow. Blood flow to the penis increases with sexual excitement and decreases with sexual inhibition.[59]

We certainly cannot consider the odors in our experiment to be human pheromones, therefore we believe they acted through other pathways than do pheromones, which are thought to cause an endocrinologic effect upon the brain. A postulated pheromone, androstenol, a high-density steroid, is said to act very slowly on the endocrine system.[60] Odors that affect penile-blood flow act immediately on the brain or have an immediate psychological effect, unlike the postulated pheromones.

These preliminary data suggest potential uses of odors as a treatment modality. Impotence, in 10-15% of cases, is organic, the most common cause being vasculogenic, usually due to diabetes.[57,61] Current investigations should determine whether noninvasive treatment with odors can enhance penile blood flow in diabetics.

Although we found no odor to reduce penile blood flow. We hypothesized that such an odor might be found, possibly a trigeminal stimulant with a very negatively hedonic odor. Such an odor might be utilized to decrease penile blood flow in sex offenders, such as pedophiles, as part of their deconditioning or aversion training.

While we studied only male subjects, undoubtedly analogous odors might be found to affect women. Parallel studies of vaginal blood flow are being undertaken.

References

1. Freud S. Report on my studies in Paris and Berlin (1886). Extracts from the Fliess papers. Standard Edition, Vol. 1, London, Hogarth, 1892-99, 173-280
2. Dichter P. Second hand scents. Drug & Cosmetic Industry 1995; 156:72-75
3. Freud S. Civilization and Its Discontents (1930). In: Strachey J, (ed). Standard Edition, Vol. 21, London, Hogarth, 1961, 100
4. MacLean PD. Limbic system and its hippocampal formation: Studies in animals and their possible application to man. J Neurosurg 1954; 11:29-44
5. MacLean PD. Cerebral evolution of emotion. In: Lewis M, Haviland JM (eds). Handbook of Emotions. New York, Guilford, 1993, 66-67
6. Brill AA. Sense of smell in the neuroses and psychoses. Psychoanalyt Quart 1932; 1:7-42
7. Hirsch AR. Smell and taste: how the culinary experts compare to the rest of us. Food Technology 1990; 44:96-102
8. Ackerman D. Natural history of the senses. New York, Random House, 1990, 5:26-27
9. Durden-Smith J, deSimone D. Sex and the brain. New York, Arbor House, 1983; 216
10. Moran DT, Monti-Bloch L, Stensaas LJ, Berliner DL. Structure and function of the human vomeronasal organ. In: Doty RL (ed). Handbook of Olfaction and Gustation. New York, Marcell Dekker, 1995, 794
11. Monti-Bloch L, Grosser BI. Effect of putative pheromones on the electrical activity of the human vomeronasal organ and olfactory epithelium. J Steroid Biochem Mol Biol 1991; 39:573-582
12. Monti-Bloch L, Jennings-White C, Dolberg DS, Berliner DL. Human vomeronasal system. Psychoneuroendocrinology 1994; 19:673-686
13. Gower DB, Nixon A, Mallet AI. Significance of odorous steroids in axillary odour. In: Van Toller S, Dodd GH (eds). Perfumery: Psychology and Biology of Fragrance. New York, Chapman and Hall, 1988, 47, 49
14. Russell MJ. Human olfactory communication. Nature 1976; 260:520-522
15. Schneider RA, Wolf S. Relation of olfactory activity to nasal membrane function. J Appl Physiol 1960; 15:914-920
16. Parlee MB. Menstrual rhythms in sensory processes: Review of fluctuations in vision, olfaction, audition, taste, and touch.
17. Lanza DC, Clerico DM. Anatomy of the human nasal passages. In: Doty RL (ed). Handbook of Olfaction and Gustation. New York, Marcel Dekker, 1995, 53
18. Hirsch AR. Scentsation: Olfactory demographics and abnormalities. Internat J ARoma Ther 1992; 4:16-17
19. Deems DA, Doty RL. Age-related changes in the phenyl ethyl alcohol odor detection threshold. Trans Penn Acad Ophthalmol Otolaryngol 1987; 39:646-650
20. Adams DB, Gold AR, Burt AD. Rise is female-initiated sexual activity at ovulation and its suppression by oral contraceptives. N Engl J Med 1978; 299:1145-1150
21. McClintock M. Menstrual synchrony and suppression. Nature 1979; 229:244-245
22. Graham CA, McGrew WC. Menstrual synchrony in female undergraduates living on a coeducational campus. Psychoneuroendocrinology 1980; 5:245-252
23. Kirk-Smith MD, Booth DA, Carroll D, Davies P. Human social attitudes affected by androstenol. Res Commun Psychol Psychiatr Behav 1978; 3:379-384
24. Gustavson AR, Dawson ME, Bonett DG. Androstenol, a putative human pheromone, affects human (Homo sapiens) male choice performance. J Comp Psychol 1987; 101:210-212
25. Ackerman D. Natural history of the senses. New York, Random House, 1990, 26
26. Moran J. Fabulous Fragrances. California, Crescent House, 1994, 183
27. Comfort A. Likelihood of human pheromones. Nature 1971; 230:432-433
28. Hirsch AR, Trannel TJ. Chemosensory dysfunction and psychiatric diagnoses. J Neurol Orthop Med Surg 1996; 17:25-30
29. Doty RL, Newhouse MG, Azzalina JD. Internal consistency and short-term test-retest reliability of the University of Pennsylvania Smell Identification Test. Chem Senses 1985; 10:297-300
30. Hirsch AR, Cain DR. Evaluation of the Chicago Smell Test in a normal population [Abstr.]. Chem Senses 1992; 17:642-643
31. Hirsch AR, Gotway MB. Validation of the Chicago Smell Test (CST) in subjective normosmic neurologic patients [Abstr.]. Chem Senses 1993; 18:570-571
32. Hirsch AR, Gotway MB, Harris AT. Validation of the Chicago Smell Test (CST) in patients with subjective olfactory loss [Abstr.]. Chem Senses 1993; 18:571
33. Laws DR, Pithers WD. Penile plethysmorgraph. In: Schwartz BK, Cellini HR (eds). Practitioner's Guide to Treating the Incarcerated Male Sex Offender. Washington, DC, U.S. Department of Justice, National Institute of Corrections, 1988, 85-93
34. LifeSigns Corporation. PC Compatible FLOSCOPE ULTRA. Minneapolis, MN, Vascular Lab, 1994

35. Lehmann EL. Nonparametrics: Statistical Methods Based on Ranks. New York, Holden-Day, 1975
36. Colton T. Statistics in Medicine. Boston, MA, Little Brown, 1974
37. Hirsch AR, Nostalgia: neuropsychiatric understanding. Advances in Consumer Research 1992; 19:390-395
38. Warm JS, Dember WN, Parasuraman R. Effects of olfactory stimulation on performance and stress in a visual sustained-attention task. J Soc Cosmetic Chemists 1991; 42:119-210
39. Dunn C, Sleep J, Collett D. Sensing an improvement: Experimental study to evaluate the use of aromatherapy, massage, and periods of rest in an intensive care unit. J Advanced Nursing 1995; 21:34-40
40. Baron RA. Environmentally induced positive affect: Its impact on self-efficacy, task performance, negotiation, and conflict. J Appl Soc Psychol 1990; 20:368-384
41. Baron RA. Psychology 3rd ed. Boston, MA, Allyn and Bacon, 1995, 177
42. Sugano H. Effects of odors on mental function [Abstr.]. JASTS 1988; XXII:8
43. King JR. Anxiety reduction using fragrances. In: Van Toller S, Dodd GH (eds). Psychology and Biology of Fragrance. London, Chapman and Hall, 1988, 157-165
44. MacLean PD. Triune Concept of the Brain and Behavior. Toronto, University of Toronto, 1973, 14
45. Donatucci CF, Lue TF. Psysiology of penile tumescence. In: Hasmat AI, Das S (eds). Penis. Philadelphia, PA, Lea and Febiger, 1993, 19
46. Adams RD, Victor M. Principles of Neurology, 4th ed. New York, McGraw-Hill, 1989, 418
47. Diamond J. Third Chimpanzee: Evolution and Future of the Human Animal. New York, Harper Collins, 1992, 68
48. Blount BG. Issues in bonobo (pan paniscus) sexual behavior. American Anthropologist 1990; 92:702-714
49. Hirsch AR, Johnston LH. Odors and learning. J Neurol Orthop Med Surg 1996; 17:119-126
50. Hirsch AR, Gay S. Effect of ambient olfactory stimuli on the evaluation of a common consumer product. Chem Senses 1991; 16:535
51. Hirsch AR. Odors and perception of room size [Abstr.]. 148th Annual Meeting Am Psychiatr Assoc, Miami, FL 1995
52. Hirsch AR, Gomez R. Weight reduction through inhalation of odorants. J Neurol Orthop Med Surg 1995; 16:28-31
53. Filsinger EE, Fabes RA. Odor communication, pheromones, and human families. J Marriage and Family 1985; May, 349
54. Filsinger EE, Monte WC, Braun JJ, Linder DE. Human (homo sapiens) responses to the pig (sus scrofa) sex pheromone 5 alpha-androst-16-en-3-one, J Comp Psychol 1984; 98:219-222
55. Kirk-Smith M, Booth DA, Carroll D, Davies P. Human social attitudes affected by androstenol. Research Communications in Psychology, Psychiatry and Behavior 1978; 3:379-381
56. Hirsch MS, Melman A. Overview of evaluation of impotence. In: Hashmat AI, Das S. (eds). Penis. Philadelphia, PA, Lea and Febiger, 1993, 129-153
57. Kolodny RC, Masters WH, Johnson VE. Textbook of Sexual Medicine. Boston, MA, Little Brown, 1979, 10-11, 507-508
58. Cayaffa JJ. Rhinencephalon and the limbic system. Lecture Notes: Cook .County School of Medicine Basic Review Course 1981
59. Weiss MD. Physiology of human penile erection. Ana Int Med 1972; 76:793-799
60. Gustavson AR, Dawson ME, Bonett DG. Androstenol, a putative human pheromone, affects human (homo sapiens) male choice performance. J Comp Psychol 1987; 101:210-212
61. Pogach LM, Vaitukaitis JL. Endocrine disorders associated with erectile dysfunction. In: Krane RJ, Siroky MVB, Goldstein I (eds). Male Sexual Dysfunction. Boston, MA, Little Brown, 1983, 73

COVER ARTICLE

By Alan R. Hirsch, MD, FACP

Scent and Sexual Arousal

Could Fragrance Help Relieve Sexual Dysfunction?

In Western culture, it is common practice to eliminate body odors. Could this be part of the reason why so many people suffer from diminished sex drive or sexual dysfunction? Could star-crossed lovers be responding unwittingly to each other's scent? Scents can promote sexual enjoyment and might be useful for treating such problems as sexual dysfunction or menstrual irregularity.

Long, lingering kisses, the sensual texture of cool silk sheets, the sound of romantic music, and the sight of our lover's flesh—all are classic images of romance and sex. But something is missing from this fantasy, and it could be the most important element. Where are the fragrances that add so much to the mood we enjoy?

Virtually all cultures have, in one way or another, recognized the importance of all the senses in sexuality. In Western society, however, the importance of the sense of smell is given little attention.[1] Furthermore, the powerful emotional responses that odors evoke have provided even more incentive to repress our sense of smell.[2]

Medical researchers are just now beginning to understand the importance of the sense of smell in human sexuality. This research may lead to safe, noninvasive ways to enhance sexual experiences or manage sexual dysfunction.

LOVE IN THE AIR

In the animal world, mating habits are virtually ruled by pheromones. Pheromones are substances released by an individual that produce a change in the sexual or social behavior or physiology of another animal of the same species. As the study of pheromones has progressed, research is coming closer to establishing the existence of human pheromones. Early work shows that

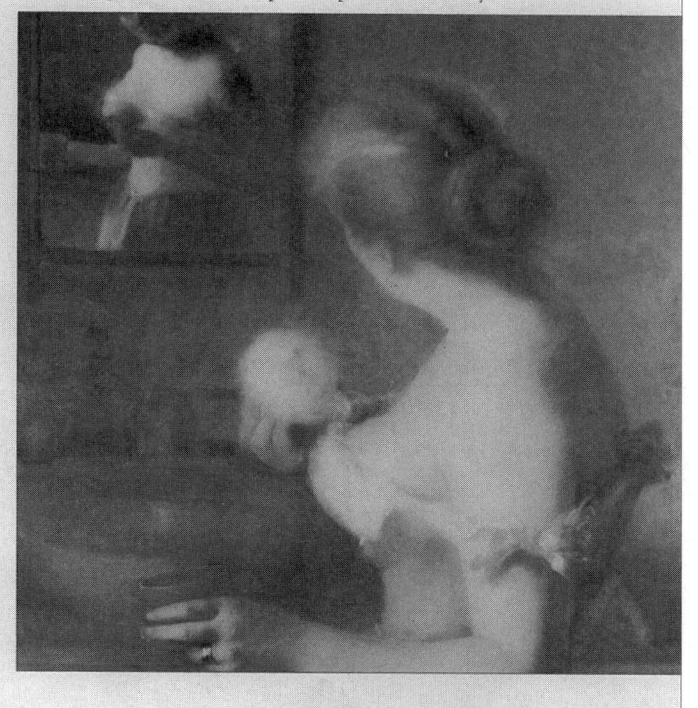

an unidentified constituent of women's perspiration could affect the timing of other women's menstrual cycles.[3] Until the actual pheromonal substances are definitely isolated, physicians can only infer their existence from a strong body of evidence.

Both androstenone and androstenol are believed to have pheromonal effects in humans.[4] The presence of androstenol has been shown to affect the territorial behavior of men as well as their assessment of the sexual attractiveness of a woman.[4] People who can perceive the odor of androstenol describe it as "musky." Women are about a thousand times more sensitive to the odor of musk than men are; at ovulation, women are about a hundred thousand times more sensitive to the odor.

Pheromones are probably byproducts of reproductive hormones and are probably produced by apocrine glands in the axilla and groin. Pheromones are believed to have a direct physiologic effect via the rhinencephalon (the "smell brain," through which the olfactory system is directly connected with the limbic system). Thus, it might not be necessary for an individual to perceive the odor of the pheromone in order for the pheromone to have its effect.

Physiologically, arousal is a complex neurologic process in which sensory signals reach the brain and stimulate the changes in the body that people associate with sexual excitement. Much of the experience of sexual arousal is related to involuntary nervous responses, as is the case in our response to food. If a hungry person perceives the aroma of baking bread, the message reaches the brain and he or she may begin to salivate. Even just thinking about food can cause a person to salivate. Similarly, sexual stimuli cause spontaneous, involuntary physiologic responses; and the stimuli may be self-generated, in that thinking—or dreaming—about sex can begin the arousal process.

If a woman complains that her partner's body odor turns her off, the complaint should be taken seriously.

Each sense is controlled by a specific area of the brain. Sensory signals are processed in that area and are then projected to the septal nucleus, which is the erection center in male and female brains. A lover's touch, for example, produces a message that travels through the spinal cord, is processed in the thalamus, and then is projected to the septal nucleus. Then, the signal travels back down the spinal cord and results in the physiologic changes we associate with arousal. Visual signals are processed in the occipital lobe before being projected to the septal nucleus.

Both the nose and the genitalia have erectile tissue that becomes engorged during sexual excitement.[5] This engorgement could improve olfactory acuity by increasing eddy currents in the nose. Also, regardless of the initial stimulus, sexual arousal tends to produce hyperventilation, which can also enhance olfactory acuity.

Odors may enhance female sexual arousal through dopaminergic, GABAergic, or serotoninergic effects on brain areas that induce sexual arousal (including the septal nucleus). Medications that have been reported to induce female sexual arousal include those with dopaminergic effects (e.g., L-dopa).

Direct effects on the rhinencephalon are not the only way in which odors can influence sexuality. Other possibilities include a pavlovian conditioned response or olfactory evoked nostalgia. Some scents could enhance sexual experiences by promoting relaxation or inducing a state of risk-taking or generalized pleasure seeking.

Studies of other species have shown that the female's sense of smell plays an important role in her selection of sex partners. For example, damage to the olfactory center reduces a female rat's ability to choose among mates: She will mate with any available male.[6] The sense of smell may play a similar role in a woman's sexuality and choice of sex partner. If a woman complains that her partner's body odor turns her off, this complaint should be taken seriously. Starting at puberty, women tend to have higher olfactory acuity than men have. Thus, men often dismiss women's complaints about odors that the men cannot perceive.

While pheromones do not rule humans, they should not be discounted when research attempts to explain human behavior. Those mismatched couples we often puzzle over may have liked each

TABLE 1.
Effects of Scents and Scent Combinations on Sexual Arousal

	Turn Ons*	Turn Offs*
Women	Good & Plenty® candy and cucumber (13%)	Cherry (–18%)
	Baby powder (13%)	Charcoal barbecue smoke (–14%)
	Good & Plenty® candy and banana nut bread (12%)	Men's colognes (–1%)
	Lavender and pumpkin pie (11%)	
	Baby powder and chocolate (4%)	
	Women's perfumes (1%)	
Men	Lavender and pumpkin pie (40%)	None have been found
	Licorice and doughnuts (32%)	
	Pumpkin pie and doughnuts (20%)	
	Cinnamon buns (4%)	

*The percentages represent the average increase in genital blood flow. The women's responses to the various scents were much more variable than the men's and seemed to depend on whether the women reported being aroused by manual genital stimulation.

other's pheromones so much that all the logical, rational reasons why they shouldn't be together were overcome. The question of homosexuality arises, too. We do not yet know why some individuals are attracted to members of the same sex or are bisexual if, theoretically, pheromones create sexual distance between members of the same sex. There is much about pheromones (and sexuality, of course) that we don't understand.

SMELL RESEARCH

For most of human history, there were no laboratory methods to prove that various kinds of sensory stimulation could alter mood and change behavior. However, recent research has confirmed what most people instinctively know: Odors can soothe frazzled nerves, promote sleep, wake us up, lift our spirits, and help us learn and work more efficiently.[7] Early evidence suggests that odors may also help treat some physical and psychological disorders, including sexual dysfunction. Most certainly, scents can enhance our sexual experiences.

At the Smell & Taste Treatment and Research Foundation, we have found that many patients who had lost their sense of smell also suffered from sexual dysfunction. This piqued our interest in the role of smells in sexual arousal. We hope that our work will contribute to the development of scents that can be used as safe, noninvasive treatments for erectile dysfunction as well as female arousal disorders and anorgasmia. Because of the role of olfactory cues in regulating menses, scents could eventually also help in treating menstrual irregularities.

Our most recent study examining the relationship between smell and sexuality involved 30 nonanorgasmic women between 18 and 40 years of age (average age, 31.8 years). Each was instructed not to have sexual stimulation, either by a partner or by masturbation, for 48 hours prior to testing. A sterile monitoring gauge, called a photoplethysmograph, was placed in each woman's vagina to measure pulse pressure, which indicates any change in blood flow to the vagina. The gauge was hooked up to a computer, and changes in pulse strength were recorded on a continuous basis.

A surgical mask, untreated with any additional odor, was placed over the nose and mouth. The woman's response was recorded. Then, in a double-blind, randomized manner, masks that were laced with eight different individual and combined odors were given to each woman and left in place for 1 minute. That was followed by a 3-minute "washout" period, during which blood flow was measured when no mask was in place. Results

TABLE 2.
Possible Causes of Olfactory Problems

Smoking
Alcohol consumption
Normal aging

of the study were applied in several categories, based on the kinds of sexual behavior and activities preferred (Table 1).

Many people have been amused by our findings; and I must admit, the idea of pumpkin-pie–scented condoms is amusing. Nevertheless, although our study seems lighthearted, we undertook it for serious reasons and the results have serious applications.

CLINICAL SIGNIFICANCE

Our research has shown that various fragrances have a measurable effect on markers of sexual arousal. Thus, they may represent an opportunity for clinicians to help patients who complain of sexual dysfunction, such as diminished arousal or anorgasmia.

Female sexual responses can be suppressed by a partner's unpleasant body odors. In these cases, the physician might help persuade the partner to take the woman's complaints seriously. Sometimes, the unpleasant odors are related to inadequate hygiene. In other cases, the odors result from a health problem that requires medical or dental treatment (e.g., halitosis).

Scents might even be useful in the management of sexual dysfunction that results from disease that impairs blood flow in the genitalia (e.g., diabetes mellitus). Because various scents have been shown to increase genital blood flow, they might help a diabetic man achieve firmer erections—without the side effects associated with other interventions. They might similarly promote sexual arousal in diabetic women.

Not only do individuals who lose their sense of smell frequently suffer from sexual dysfunction, the sense of smell tends to decline with age. Thus, stronger scents may help promote sexual arousal and sexual functioning in older people or others whose sense of smell is impaired (Table 2).

Some scents can help promote relaxation and enhance mood, thus promoting a setting conducive to love-making. If scents are frequently incorporated into sex play, they may help promote arousal through a conditioned response.

When advising patients about the use of fragrances to enhance sexual experiences, clinicians must keep in mind that women's responses to the fragrances we have tested are more variable than men's. Scents that were arousing for some women proved to be a turn-off for others. Some of these differences between women could be correlated with other features of the woman's sexuality. For example, among women who reported being frequently multiorgasmic, we found that the scent of baby powder *reduced* vaginal blood flow by 8%. Among women who reported being mono-orgasmic, in contrast, the scent of baby powder *increased* vaginal blood flow by 15%. Thus, women should be encouraged to experiment to find the scents that enhance their own sexual responses.

REFERENCES

1. Ellis H. *Sexual Selection in Man*. Philadelphia: FA Davis Co; 1906;65.
2. Freud S. Bermerkungen ueber einen Fall von Zwangs Neurosa. *Ges Schr*. 1908;VIII:350.
3. Preti G, et al. Determination of ovulation and alteration of menstrual cycle by human odors. Abstract. *188th Natl Meet Am Chem Soc*. 1984.
4. Kirk-Smith M, et al. Human social attitudes affected by androstenol. *Res Commun Psych Psychiatr Behav*. 1978; 3:379–384.
5. Cole P. *Respiratory Role of the Upper Airways*. St Louis: CV Mosby; 1993:8.
6. Moss RL. Modification of copulatory behavior in the female rat following olfactory bulb removal. *J Compar Physiol Psychol*. 1971;74:374–382.
7. Hirsch AR, Johnson LH. Odors and learning. *J Neurol Orthop Med Surg*. 1996;17:119–126.

Alan R. Hirsch, MD, FACP, is the Neurological Director of the Smell & Taste Research Foundation in Chicago.

Smell and Taste: How the Culinary Experts Compare to the Rest of Us

Ten top chefs were studied to determine whether they had greater than normal olfactory and gustatory abilities

Alan R. Hirsch, M.D.

☐ THE ABILITY to smell and taste is necessary to the enjoyment of food and drink. Taste buds in the tongue distinguish sweet, salt, sour, and bitter flavors, but it is the sense of smell that discerns the refinements that help us distinguish between fish and chicken, for instance, and appreciate a gourmet meal.

This is because most of what we call taste or flavor is really aroma. When we chew or swallow, odor-bearing molecules from our food or drink travel through the back of the mouth and into the upper nasal cavity. There they stimulate the olfactory cells, which are linked via nerves to the brain.

Ability to smell and taste varies widely among individuals, and even the same individual varies in sensitivity under different conditions. Approximately 2 million Americans have abnormalities in this area, and more than 200,000 individuals seek medical advice each year because of complaints regarding smell or taste (AAO, 1986).

In general, women have greater olfactory sensitivity than men, and their sensitivity is keenest at ovulation. Young people are more sensitive than old, nonsmokers more sensitive than smokers (Frye et al., 1990), and hungry people more sensitive than those who are satiated. Heavy eaters especially are much more sensitive to smell and taste impressions when they are hungry.

Chefs Studied

Obviously, tasting and smelling are at least as important in the cooking and preparation as they are in the eating and enjoyment of the delicacies of the table, yet information on the olfactory and gustatory abilities of culinary experts is sparse or nonexistent. This prompted us to initiate a study of chefs who have achieved recognition as culinary experts.

We hypothesized that the ability of chefs to sense odors would be normal but, based on their experience, their ability to identify odors would be superior. We further hypothesized that their gustatory ability would be normal. If chefs were hypersensitive to flavors and aromas, they might underseason their dishes, and diners would consider them bland. If chefs were hyposmic, they might overseason.

To assess our hypotheses, we selected ten restaurants which *Chicago Magazine* considered to be of high culinary excellence. The chefs agreed to participate in the study. We asked them before undergoing testing to abstain from (1) alcohol for 4 days, (2) caffeine and pastries for 48 hr, and (3) smoking, chewing gum, eating, drinking, and using toothpaste, scented soaps, cosmetics, deodorants, shampoo, shaving cream, aftershave, and colognes for 8 hr. We then gave the ten chefs the tests listed in Table 1.

The ten chefs were men ranging in age from 25 to 50 years with an average age of 32.5 years. This supports the general consensus that chefs tend to be young men. Their youth may give them a competitive advantage, since medical data show that in the general population, olfactory and gustatory abilities gradually decline with advancing age. More than half the people over 65 years of age have significant impairment in their sense of smell and among those over 80 years of age, the number impaired rises to 75%. Thus it would seem that these older diners might judge the dishes cooked by young chefs to be too bland and tasteless. Perhaps older chefs can better please older diners while younger chefs can better please younger diners.

Test Results Analyzed

Analysis of the test data revealed the following:

- **UPSIT Odor Identification Tests.** The ten chefs scored, on the average, 97.5% correct on these scratch-and-sniff tests. Their individual scores ranged from 95 to 100% correct. The older

The author is Director, Smell and Taste Treatment & Research Foundation, 845 N. Michigan Ave., Suite 930W, Chicago, IL 60611.

chefs scored no worse than the younger ones, but since their ages fell within a narrow range, they probably were not old enough to show deficits due to aging. Or perhaps their experience and familiarity with common substances enhanced their olfactory ability enough to overcome any mild effects of aging. Also, selective pressures may force olfactory-impaired older chefs out of premier restaurants, leaving only those older chefs who are superior in their olfactory ability.

Compared to thousands of normal persons who have taken the UPSIT, the ten chefs ranked, on the average, at the 81 percentile. Individual chefs ranged from the 29 to the 99 percentile. This means that ordinarily about 19% of the male diners in these chefs' restaurants can smell—and hence taste—significantly better than the chef and probably can detect flavor elements the chef is unaware of. If we apply these data to gourmet restaurants in general, we could say that no matter how hard the chef tries, up to one fifth of the male patrons may be displeased with the meal. And since women have a keener sense of smell than men, they may, with good reason, be more critical of restaurant meals than their male dining partners.

The chef with the lowest UPSIT score ranked among the lower third of the male population in olfactory ability, meaning that two out of three of his male diners may have a better sense of smell than he does. Yet he is considered one of the foremost chefs in the nation!

• **Connecticut Olfactory Tests.** The ten chefs earned scores ranging from 10 to 70% and averaging 32.5% on these tests. Three of the chefs scored so poorly that they met the criteria for a clinical diagnosis of hyposmia, i.e., abnormally decreased sensitivity to odors. The hyposmic chefs were unaware of any deficiency.

Among the general population, many individuals are also hyposmic and don't know it. Persons often complain to their doctors about anosmia, the absence of smell, or about phantosmia, a persistent odd smell, but they very rarely complain of hyposmia. Because of the insidious nature of hyposmia, sometimes originating at birth and sometimes slowly developing over decades, hyposmics among the general population, including chefs, may unconsciously learn to compensate for their deficit by using mint to stimulate the trigeminal nerve or by using spices to stimulate their taste buds.

Hyposmia brought on by trauma or acute infection is more likely to be noticed by the individual, but lifelong or chronic hyposmia undoubtedly seems normal and natural to its victims, just as color blindness seems normal and natural to persons with this problem. Color blindness, however, is usually detected because physicians screen patients for it and because traffic lights are red and green. But physicians do not screen patients for hyposmia, and there is no signal comparable to the traffic light in our society that depends on the sense of smell, except for the odorant added to gas to warn of leaks. In this case, a failure to perceive the signal could be disastrous. This is a matter of concern for old people, who, as mentioned, are likely to have some degree of impairment in the sense of smell.

Why are so many of our chefs mildly deficient in their sense of smell? Constant exposure or repeated exposures to an odor can cause a person to adapt to it, i.e., to lose the ability to perceive it. For instance, most persons cannot detect their own halitosis and most persons, a short time after applying perfume or aftershave lotion, can no longer perceive its fragrance.

Our study protocol had the chefs abstain from many odorants before testing in an effort to eliminate the effects of their adaptation to odors, but because of their habitual daily exposure, chronic adaptation may well persist, just as callouses persist on the hands of a laborer even though he has just taken a few days off.

Another possible explanation concerns the reasons people may decide to become chefs. It has been demonstrated that some extremely successful persons are motivated in their choice of a career by an unconscious desire to master their deficiencies. For example, a short person like Spud Webb becomes a basketball player; a shy person like Michael Jackson becomes a performer. A hyposmic person may become a chef because he unconsciously recognizes his deficit and is motivated to overcome it.

The wide variation in scores on the Connecticut Olfactory Tests—from 10% to 70% correct—suggests a reason why chefs may criticize one an-

Table 1—**Tests Administered to the Chefs**

Olfaction

University of Pennsylvania Smell Inventory Test (UPSIT)—a series of 40 scratch-and-sniff odor identification tests

Unilateral Connecticut Olfactory Tests—unilateral (one nostril at a time) identification tests of a series of 20 bottled odorants

Isoamyl Acetate Intensity Tests to determine sensitivity to various concentrations of this substance

Isoamyl Acetate Adaptation Tests to determine adaptation to odorants, i.e., failure to sense them after up to 15 sniffs

Smell Suprathreshold Detection Tests to determine ability to sense 10 odorants at concentrations above the minimal level required for detection by normal persons

Smell Suprathreshold Recognition Tests to determine ability to recognize 10 common odorants as familiar

Smell Suprathreshold Identification Tests to determine ability to name the 10 common odorants sensed in the recognition tests

Unilateral Carbinol Threshold Tests to determine sensitivity to various concentrations of this substance

Unilateral Pyridine Threshold Tests to determine sensitivity to various concentrations of this substance

Gustation

Taste Threshold Tests to determine ability to detect sweet, sour, salt, and bitter substances

Taste Suprathreshold Identification Tests to determine ability to distinguish among sweet, sour, salt, and bitter substances

other's cooking. Their criticism may stem not from mere jealousy, but from an actual physiological difference in their perceptions of the taste of foods—as the old saying puts it, "One man's meat is another man's poison."

- **Isoamyl Acetate Intensity Tests.** These tests measured the chefs' responses to varying concentrations of this chemical. Scores averaged 82%, with a range of 60–100%. Since these scores did not correlate with scores on the other tests, the isoamyl acetate tests may cover an aspect of olfaction not evaluated by the other tests, or they may not be valid as a general measure of olfactory ability.
- **Isoamyl Acetate Adaptation Tests.** In these tests, six of the ten chefs did not adapt but remained sensitive to the odorants after 15 sniffs. A seventh chef finally did adapt, but only after the 15th sniff. By not adapting, the chefs demonstrated that they could maintain the acuity of their sense of smell despite long hours spent in a kitchen filled with the aromas of food and spices. This may well be an important physiologic trait for a professional chef, assuring that the food he prepares for the last seating is of the same quality as that prepared for the first.
- **Smell Suprathreshold Detection Tests.** All ten chefs were able to detect all ten odorants in these tests, i.e., they detected the substances in concentrations higher than ordinarily required for detection by normal persons.
- **Smell Suprathreshold Recognition Tests.** In these tests, the chefs recognized as familiar the odors of the ten substances 70–100% of the time, with an average of 95%. They were not asked at this point to identify the substances, but simply to indicate whether they were familiar. The older chefs performed no better or worse than the younger ones on this test.
- **Smell Suprathreshold Identification Test.** The chefs were then asked to name the substances. Their scores ranged from 20 to 70%, with an average of only 48%. They were then given a list of 20 common substances, including the ten substances they were given to sniff. With the help of this prompting, their ability to name the substances improved dramatically: their scores averaged 79% correct and ranged from 60 to 100%. Even for culinary experts, apparently, knowing what to expect makes the recognition of it more positive. This suggests that reading a menu describing the taste of the food beforehand may enhance the enjoyment of the dinner.

Prompting improved the scores of the older chefs more markedly than the scores of the younger ones, a fact that suggests that the older chefs' loss of memory for the names of odors was more pronounced than their loss of ability to smell.

Except in the case of gross impairment of the olfactory sense, the ability to recognize an odor as familiar or to identify it is independent of the ability to smell it. This suggests that an internal construct exists for odors analogous to the internal construct for colors or for auditory pitch. The construct for odors, and hence for taste, may well be the significant attribute exercised by chefs in their production of a meal. Just as Beethoven could compose a symphony after he became deaf, a chef may be able to produce a gourmet meal even though relatively hyposmic.

Two memory systems may be postulated: First, a primitive one of recognition alone without an accompanying memory of identification, like meeting and recognizing an old friend without being able to recall his or her name. And second, a more developed one matching the name to the remembrance. It has been demonstrated that in the visual and auditory systems, the more primitive memory improves with age and experience, while the more advanced naming memory deteriorates with age. This is probably the case in the olfactory system as well (Doty et al., 1984).

- **Carbinol Odor Threshold Test.** Not surprisingly, all ten chefs showed normal sensitivity to carbinol. Two of the chefs, however, were more than two standard deviations from the mean for the normal population, in the direction of hyposmia. Again, this is not surprising. As mentioned, if chefs were hypersensitive to odors, restaurant patrons might complain that their dishes were underseasoned. The poorer olfaction was not related to age.
- **Pyridine Threshold Tests.** On these tests, the ten chefs averaged 11.75 decismells (a standard measurement of smell threshold), better than normal for their age. Since the Pyridine Threshold Test scores did not correlate with scores on the Smell Suprathreshold Tests, with or without prompting, this may be taken as further evidence that the ability to identify odors, beyond a certain minimal receptor threshold, is independent of odor perception and relies more on a different central nervous system process, namely, memory. It is probably more important for chefs to remember what a particular dish should smell like than to be able to sense minute amounts of an odorant.

Olfaction is related to handedness, the dominant nostril correlating with the dominant hand. In the general population, right-handed persons smell better with the right nostril. But among the professional chefs tested—eight of whom were right-handed, one left-handed, and one ambidexterous—the pyridine threshold values were 8.0 decismells for the left nostril and 5.0 for the right, indicating that the opposite is true: the chefs smell better with the left nostril.

How can we explain this finding? It is well known that the right hemisphere of the brain is the locus of musical and artistic sensitivity, while the left hemisphere is the locus of language and logical thought. Yet it is known that professional musicians' skills of reading, interpretation, and appreciation of music are located in the left rather than the right hemisphere. A similar situation may prevail with respect to olfaction and gustation. The ordinary diner experiences aromas and flavors with the right, more intuitive hemisphere of the brain, while the professional chef processes

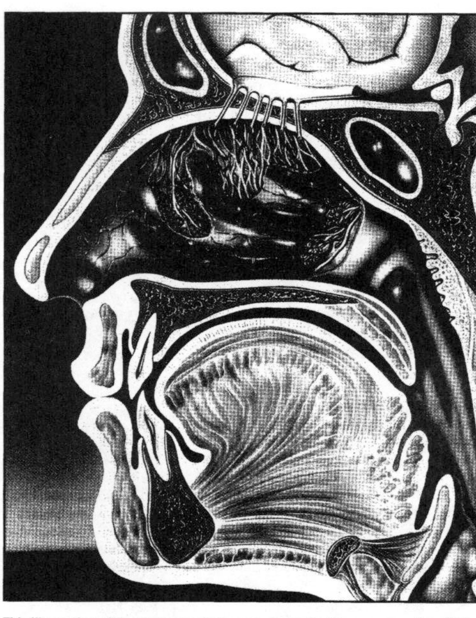

PHOTO: SCIENCE PHOTO LIBRARY

In January, FIRE INTERNATIONAL reported on an American study, believed to be the first of its kind, which tested firefighters in Chicago for any impairment in their sense of smell. Here, Dr ALAN R HIRSCH and MARIA L COLAVINCENZO present the results of their research

First study into smell loss among firefighters

This illustration of the structure of the nose shows the inner nasal cavity, which contains projecting bones called conchae (three curling plates), covered with a mucous membrane. This membrane has blood vessels (here coloured red and blue) which warm the air; and nerves (yellow, leading to the olfactory bulb of the brain) responsible for smell.

One-hundred-and-two Chicago firefighters who attended quarterly union meetings volunteered for this IRB-approved study. Their median age was 41 years, in a range from 24-69 years; 100 were white and two were black. After completing a demographic, hedonic, and occupational questionnaire, subjects were asked subjectively to rate their ability to smell. Their firefighting histories were taken, including frequency of firefighting and whether they used protective respiratory devices.

All subjects took the University of Pennsylvania Smell Identification Test (UPSIT), a self-administered, 40 question scratch-and-sniff test of olfactory ability.

Data was independently analysed by the Illinois School of Public Health using chi-square analysis, the Fischer Exact Two-tailed Test, logistic regression analysis, and the one-sample binomial test normal theory method with $p<0.05$ deemed the level of statistical significance. For some subjects, information was incomplete so analysis was based on the largest possible sample size for each variable.

Individuals were exposed to a mean number of 1,002 fires, with a range of 0 to 10,850. The mean years as a firefighter was 17, ranging from 1-43 years.

Almost half of the firefighters tested, 47.5 per cent ($n=48$), displayed abnormal UPSIT scores, as adjusted for age and sex, ie they were anosmic (suffering a loss of the sense of smell) or hyposmic (suffering a deficiency in the sense of smell). Olfactory impairment was directly related to the number of years as a firefighter ($p<0.02$).

***See News, page 9, FIRE INTERNATIONAL January 2000.**

Among our subjects, 82 per cent ($n=78$) routinely wore masks while fighting fires. Since use of masks is thought to ameliorate olfactotoxic impact, we believed those who wore masks through years of firefighting may not have incurred the same deficits as those who did not. However, we found olfactory ability did not correlate with the use of protective respiratory devices ($p=0.82$). For those who wore respiratory protective gear, impaired olfactory ability still correlated with years as a firefighter ($p=0.03$).

Among the 48 subjects with abnormal UPSIT scores (anosmic or hyposmic), 87.5 per cent ($n=42$) perceived their sense of smell as normal. Yet an awareness of olfactory loss is critical to firefighters not only in the performance of their work, but also at home. Most subjects – 98 per cent ($n=100$) – reported having gas furnaces at home, 38 per cent were the primary preparers of meals in their households, and 34 per cent ($n=35$) had experienced food poisoning once or more. The incidence of food poisoning did not correlate with UPSIT scores ($p=0.5$); however we did not assess the frequency, which might have.

Among the general US population, the

Dr Alan R Hirsch, MD, FACP

incidence of olfactory dysfunction is only about two per cent, so the incidence in our subject population, 47.5 per cent – nearly half – is extreme ($p<0.00001$). Various factors may account for this.

Firefighters are exposed to high levels of olfactotoxins, with risk of synergy, formed during pyrolysis (application of heat to cause chemical decomposition). Combustion of wood alone produces as many as 200 toxic chemicals. Hydrogen sulphide, for example, has been demonstrated to induce olfactory loss. Oxidation of such materials as diesel fuel and fabrics produces a mixture of nitrogen oxides, including nitrogen tetroxide, acute exposures of which are olfactotoxic at low levels. Thermal degradation of polyvinyl chloride produces at least 75 toxic chemicals, including the olfactotoxin chlorine. Other common olfactotoxins produced during combustion include: acrolein (from wood, at levels exceeding 3ppm), ammonia (from household furnishings), halogen acid gases (from flame retardant materials), isocyanates (from urethane isocyanate polymers), phosgene (from solvents), sulphur dioxide (at levels as high as 42 ppm), carbon monoxide (which ranges from 11-1087 ppm in fires), hydrogen cyanide (from paper and clothing, at levels up to 75 ppm), and heavy metals including cadmium, chromium, lead and zinc.

Several factors other than toxic chemicals may heighten the potential for olfactory damage to firefighters. Soot, ubiquitous in fires, may react with chemicals, possibly producing more dangerous particles. The high temperatures to which firefighters are exposed (fires can reach 1,000°F on the top floor of a burning building and inhaled smoke can be as hot as 260°F) may exacerbate the olfactotoxic effects of chemicals. Finally, the great physical exertion involved in firefighting requires a high respiratory rate, which increases the amount of inhalation.

Olfactotoxins may affect the olfactory system in a multitude of ways. They can be directly cytotoxic to the epithelium. Or, a pyrolytic chemical may combine with biological chemicals to produce an olfactotoxin. Ammonia, for instance, combines with water from the olfactory mucosa to form ammonium hydroxide, which can cause liquification of the mucosal surface. Another example is chlorine; this gas combines with water in the olfactory mucosa, inducing the formation of free radicals. Olfactotoxins may overwhelm xenobiotic mechanisms, so that ordinarily neutral endogenous or exogenous substances have toxic effects. Or, the olfactotoxins may act directly on olfactory nerve cells or stem cells, preventing the olfactory nerve from regenerating. Finally, the pyrolytic byproduct may inhibit the flow of mucous, impeding removal of all toxins in a cellular environment.

The number of years as a firefighter, a marker for exposure to olfactotoxins, directly relates to olfactory loss. One might expect that the firefighters' use of masks would protect them against olfactory damage, but this was not found to be the case. Our data indicates that wearing masks had no significant effect. Several explanations are possible:

- The toxic particles could be so small that the masks fail to filter them out, or do so insufficiently. Studies which have identified pulmonary impairment in firefighters despite their use of respiratory protection support this explanation since the same toxins that cause pulmonary dysfunction are also olfactotoxins;
- The mask does not protect against heat, which may be the chief olfactotoxin;
- Masks were not widely employed until 1981 – possibly by that time the olfactory damage had already occurred. This seems doubtful, however, since subjects employed within the past 17 years also displayed olfactory loss;
- Inappropriate use of the masks may have precluded their protective functioning. Anecdotally, firefighters describe the physical difficulty of firefighting while wearing a mask; they frequently do not use them. Furthermore, the masks are routinely discarded during the overhauling stage while fires still smoulder. The decision of when to remove masks is often based on the visual impression of low smoke density, which is misinterpreted as indicating the absence of toxins. Surveys indicate that 66 per cent of firefighters do not wear masks during this phase of the fire.

One question our data brings to mind: why do firefighters display the olfactory effects but not other neurological effects of toxins? Several explanations seem plausible:

- The olfactory epithelium and the olfactory nerve are directly adjacent to the external atmosphere and hence are most susceptible to its changes;
- Many pyrolytically formed toxins are highly water-soluble and dissolve in the mucus of the olfactory epithelium and upper respiratory tract, without necessarily dissolving in the alveoli of the lung for dissemination via the bloodstream to other organs;
- Through active pinocytosis the olfactory epithelium maximises the absorption of nonspecific chemicals, rather than barring their uptake;
- Since no evolutionary pressure existed to develop protective enzymes to degrade olfactotoxins not present in the natural environment, such toxins easily overwhelm the xenobiotic mechanisms of the epithelium;
- By the time a toxin has disseminated to other neurological areas of the body, its concentration is reduced through various mechanisms. After absorption, the toxin is diluted as it spreads through the bloodstream. It is also captured at specific storage and processing sites, such as adipose tissue and gut. Its concentration is further decreased by metabolism in the liver and lungs;
- Absence of the blood-brain barrier at the olfactory nerve allows otherwise excluded toxins to enter;
- Just as the majority of firefighters were not aware of their smell loss, they may have other neurological symptoms they are not aware of or that they attribute to other causes.

The fact that so many of our subjects with olfactory dysfunction were unaware of any problem suggests that firefighters, whether or not they have complaints, should be assessed for olfactory status. Industrial workers exposed to similar toxins at lower levels may also have olfactory deficits they are unaware of. One study, for example, found that half of anosmic workers exposed to cadmium were unaware of any problems.

Certainly our findings have far-reaching implications. If Chicago firefighters are representative of the estimated one million firefighters across the US, an occupation-specific epidemic of olfactory dysfunction exists. Olfactory loss entails particularly serious risks for firefighters. They need the ability to smell natural gas in order to prevent explosions. They need the ability to detect the rotten-egg odour of hydrogen sulphide so they can flee before losing consciousness. And they need the ability to detect olfactory indications of an underlying fire. Hence olfactory loss jeopardises these individuals and their performance on the job.

Whether firefighters' olfactory losses are permanent is unknown. If permanent, these losses would exacerbate the effects of ageing on olfaction of former firefighters, thus increasing the hazards to their personal safety, ie failure to detect leaking gas, spoiled food, and excessively salted food. Studies of the olfactory ability of retired firefighters may demonstrate this.

Particularly disturbing is the high incidence of cigarette smoking among this occupational group. Since smoking alone impairs olfactory ability, even without the olfactotoxic effects of their occupational exposure, firefighters should be aggressively targeted in campaigns to reduce cigarette consumption.

Methodological errors may possibly have contributed to our findings. If, for instance, the firefighters had smoked immediately before being tested, this could have impaired their olfactory scores. We do not believe this was the case, however, since subjects were occupied in answering a demographic survey for at least 15 minutes prior to being tested.

Sample selection may have been another source of error. We examined only 102 while G Barry of the Chicago Firefighters' Union estimated a membership of 4,000. Our sample population may have been biased, since it was a voluntary programme, and persons who perceive that they have smell losses might be more likely than others to volunteer for such a study. This is unlikely to have been the case, however, since there was no correlation among our subjects between perceived smell loss and measured olfactory deficits.

A further consideration is that industrial Chicago, with its high manufacturing density, may not be representative of the rest of the nation with respect to the kinds and amounts of furnishings, construction materials, and industrial products that form toxic gaseous compounds when they undergo pyrolysis. Firefighting techniques and equipment may also be regionally specific.

Other possible confounding factors include exposure to olfactotoxins unrelated to fires, such as alcohol, illegal drugs, petroleum and solvents used in the maintenance of firefighting equipment. However, since firefighters show evidence of end organ dysfunction in other systems, eg the pulmonary, or lungs, due to exposure to toxins related to fires – particulates, tars, acrolein, ammonia, hydrogen chloride, and nitrogen oxides – it is likely that the observed olfactory deficits are also the result of exposure to fires. Pulmonary impairment is a direct effect of exposure of the lungs to toxins and heat, thus the olfactory nerve, which is in direct conduit with the lungs and is exposed to environmental toxins before the lungs are, would suffer a similar exposure.

Our study has no intrinsic control group; the UPSIT, however, has been validated in over 1,819 normal male control subjects. The 47.5 per cent incidence of olfactory loss among our subjects is 24 times greater than the two per cent in the normal population, and far greater than we anticipated.

This is the first study of olfactory ability in firefighters, and since products such as polymers that produce cyanide upon pyrolysis and other building materials that produce olfactotoxins are now in more frequent use, this problem is apt to be of greater concern in the future.

The effect of a single exposure to olfactotoxins in fire victims has yet to be studied. Each year, about 25,000 civilians are injured in fires, a number which would certainly be higher if olfactory injuries were included. The fact that 90 per cent of fire survivors were found to have elevated blood cyanide levels indicates that they were exposed to substantial levels of olfactotoxins. With nearly two million fires in the US each year, the extent of olfactory damage could be epidemic.

Dr Alan R Hirsch, MD, FACP and Maria L Colavincenzo, BA can be contacted at the Smell & Taste Treatment and Research Foundation, 845 N. Michigan Avenue, Suite 990W, Chicago, Illinois 60611, USA. (Tel: +1 312 938 1047; Fax: +1 312 649 0458).

Sources

Olfaction and taste IX. Roper SD, Atema J, eds. *Annals of the New York Academy of Sciences, Vol. 510. Ninth International Symposium on Olfaction and Taste*. Snowmass Village, Colorado; 1986: 644-646. Kales SN, Aldrich JM, Polyhronopoulos GN, et al. Fitness for duty evaluations in hazardous materials firefighters. *J Occup Environ Med*. 1998; 40:925-931. Doty RL. *Smell Identification Test Administration Manual: 3rd Ed*. Haddon Hts, NJ: Sensonics; 1995: 6. Colton T. *Statistics in Medicine*. Boston: Little Brown; 1974. Public Health Service. *Report of the Panel on Communicative Disorders to the National Advisory Neurological and Communicative Disorders and Stroke Council (NIH Publication no. 79-1914)*. Washington, DC: National Institute of Health; 1973: 319. Treitman RD, Burgess WA, Gold A. Air contaminants encountered by fire fighters. *Am Ind Hyg Assoc J*. 1980; 41:799-802. Nelson GL. Regulatory aspects of fire toxicology. *Toxicology*. 1987; 47:185. Hirsch AR. Long term effects on the olfactory system of exposure to hydrogen sulphide. *Occup Environ Med*. 1999; 56:284-287. Hirsch AR. Neurotoxicity as a result of acute nitrogen tetroxide exposure. In: *International Congress on Hazardous Waste: Impact on Human and Ecological Health*. Atlanta, Georgia: U.S. Dept. of Health and Human Services, Public Health Agency for Toxic Substances and Disease Registry; 1995: 177. Hirsch AR. Chronic neurotoxicity of acute chlorine gas exposure. In: *13th International Neurotoxicity Conference, Developmental and Neurotoxicity of Endocrine Disrupters Proceedings*, Hot Springs, AR: 1995: 13. Dyer RF, Esch VH. Polyvinyl chloride toxicity in fires: hydrogen chloride toxicity in fire fighters. *JAMA*. 1976; 235:395. Brandt-Rauf PW, Fallon LF Jr, Tarantini T, Idema C, Andrews L. Health hazards of fire fighters: exposure assessment. *Br J Ind Med*. 1988; 45:606-610. Hung OL, Shih RD. Fire fighters. In: Greenberg MI, Hamilton RJ, Phillips SD, eds. *Occupational, Industrial, and Environmental Toxicology*. St. Louis: Mosby; 1997: 114-118. Amoore JE. Effects of chemical exposure on olfaction in humans. In: Barrow CS ed. *Toxicology of the Nasal Passages*. New York: Hemisphere; 1986: 155-190. Snow JB Jr, Doty RL, Bartoshuk LM, Getchell TV. Categorization of chemosensory disorders. In: Getchell TV, ed. *Smell and Taste in Health and Disease*. New York: Raven; 1991: 452. Hoponik EF. Clinical smoke inhalation injury: pulmonary effects. *Occup Med*. 1993; 8:436. Liu D, Okan KR. Smoke inhalation. *CMCC Crit Care Toxicol*. 1989; 1:203-210. Schwartz DA. Acute inhalational injury. *Occup Med*. 1987; 2:300. Lewis JL, Dahl AR. Olfactory mucosa composition, enzymatic localization, and metabolism. In: Doty RL, ed. *Handbook of Olfaction and Gustation*. New York: Marcel Dekker; 1995: 33-52. Hastings L. Sensory neurotoxicology: Use of the olfactory system in the assessment of toxicity. *Neurotoxicol Teratol*. 1990; 12:455-459. Morgan KT, Patterson DL, Goss EA. Responses of the nasal mucociliary apparatus to airborne irritants. In: Barrow CS, ed. *Toxicology of the Nasal Passages*. New York: Hemisphere; 1986: 123-141. Tepper A, Comstock GW, Levine M. Longitudinal study of pulmonary function in fire fighters. *Am J Ind Med*. 1991; 20:307-311. Berignus VA, Prah JD. Olfaction: anatomy, physiology, and behavior. *Environ Health Perspect*. 1982; 44:15-21. DeLorenzo AJD. Olfactory neuron and the blood-brain barrier. In: Wolsterholme GEW, Knight J, eds. *Taste and smell Vertebrates*. London: Churchill; 1970: 151-176. Baker H. Olfactory receptor neurons are a peripheral conduit for access of foreign substances to the central nervous system. *Soc Neurosci*. [Abstr]. 1984; 10:859. Adams RG, Crabtree N. Anosmia in alkaline battery workers. *Br J Industr Med*. 1961; 18:216-221. Morse L, Owen D, Becker CE. Firefighter's health and safety. In: Rom WN, ed. *Environmental and Occupational Medicine*. Boston: Little, Brown; 1992: 1197-1204. Stevens J, Cain W, Weinstein D. Aging impairs the ability to detect gas odor. *Fire Technology*. 1987; 23:198-204. Frye RE, Schwartz BS and Doty RL. Dose-related effects of cigarette smoking on olfactory function. *JAMA*. 1990; 263:1233. Ditraglia GM, Press DS, Butters N, et al. Assessment of olfactory deficits in detoxified alcoholics. *Alcohol*. 1991; 8:109-115. Cometto-Muniz JE, Cain WS. Influence of airborne contaminants on olfaction and the common chemical sense. In: Getchell TV, Doty RL, Bartoshuk LM, Snow JB Jr., eds. *Smell and Taste in Health and Disease*. New York: Raven; 1991: 765-779. Serby MJ, Chobor KL. *Science of Olfaction*. New York: Springer-Verlag; 1992: 451. Doty RL, Newhouse MG, Azzalina JD. Internal consistency and short-term test-retest reliability of the University of Pennsylvania Smell Identification Test. *Chem Senses*. 198; 10:297-300. Silverman SH, Purdue GF, Hunt JL, Bost, RO. Cyanide toxicity in burned patients. *J Trauma*. 1988; 28:172, 175. Karter MJ. *Fire loss in the United States during 1997*. Quincy, MA: National Fire Protection Association; 1998:i.

THE EFFECT OF INHALING GREEN APPLE FRAGRANCE TO REDUCE THE SEVERITY OF MIGRAINE: A PILOT STUDY

Alan R. Hirsch, M.D., F.A.C.P. and Chil Kang, M.D.

(*Headache Q.* 1998; 9:159-163)

ABSTRACT

Objective: Since certain ambient odors reduce anxiety — one such odor, green apple, affects emotions positively in other contexts — we hypothesized that if the patient sniffs its fragrance during an attack, the severity of migraine symptoms may be reduced.

Design: For three headache episodes, 50 patients with chronic cephalalgia were asked to rate the severity of their headaches at the onset and 10 minutes later. The first and third episodes served as controls. During the second, subjects sniffed green-apple fragrance from an inhaler.

Setting: Outpatient clinic.

Patient selection: Fifty chronic headache patient volunteers.

Main outcome measures: Patient's subjective ratings of severity of pain at onset and 10 minutes later.

Results: Those patients with normal olfactory abilities and who liked the fragrance, judged that it slightly reduced the severity of their symptoms ($p < 0.03$).

Conclusion: These data indicate that green apple odorant may be useful as an adjuvant therapy in managing chronic headache.

INTRODUCTION

Several studies document the fact that certain odors aggravate migraine. In a study by Blau and Solomon,[1] 50 migraine patients were interviewed, 20 of whom experienced osmophobia due to a variety of scents ranging from cooking odors to dishwashing liquid odors. Eleven reported that similar smells could trigger migraine. For others, perfume and cigarette smoke can trigger migraine.[2] In a 1992 study, Blau showed that for patients whose migraines were triggered by eating certain foods, these foods had no effect on other types of headaches.[3]

It also is well-known that odors can be part of migraine auras, as many authors attest. In one report, a woman experienced olfactory hallucinations of decaying animals before the onset of migraine.[4] Another report described a mother and daughter who smelled odors similar to burning wood chips as part of their aura.[5] A 1985 citation noted a case of a woman who smelled cigarette smoke before, during, and after her migraines even though she did not smoke nor did anyone around her.[6] A later study reported three migraine patients who smelled peanut butter and cigars.[7] Gustatory hallucinations are also known to occur during migraine attacks. In a 1989 report, the authors found that 13 percent of their subjects experienced these symptoms.[8]

For any positive effects of odors on migraine, there is a paucity of data. In a 1993 survey of 109 migraine patients, 50 could tolerate eating and drinking during headache episodes.[9] Twenty-seven reported that eating reduced the severity and duration of their symptoms, and five reported craving certain foods during attacks, preponderately starchy types. A deficiency of metabolites has been implicated in the triggering of migraine[9] — suggesting that if patients are able to tolerate eating, they should be encouraged to eat starchy foods with their headache medications. We further suggest that possibly some of the positive effects of eating may be due to smelling the food. Ninety percent of what we usually consider taste is, in fact, perceived through the sense of smell.[10]

Certain ambient odors are known to affect emotions and reduce anxiety.[10] In one study, patients conditioned to associate a designated odor with a relaxed state were able to reduce the severity of their episodes of anxiety by smelling their designated fragrance.[11] In a study by one of the authors relating ambient odors and perceptions of room

Doctor Hirsch is Neurologic Director, Smell & Taste Treatment and Research Foundation, Chicago, Illinois. Doctor Kang is in the Department of Medicine at Rush-Presbyterian-St. Luke's Medical Center, Chicago, Illinois

Address correspondence and reprint requests to Alan R. Hirsch, M.D., F.A.C.P., Smell & Taste Treatment and Research Foundation, 845 North Michigan Avenue, Suite 990W, Chicago, IL 60611

size,[12] subjects siting in a small isolation booth perceived the booth to be larger while inhaling a scent similar to green apples. We speculate that green-apple scent reduced the anxiety of being enclosed in a small space, thus the perceived size of the room was increased.

Since green-apple fragrance may reduce the anxiety of being enclosed in a small space, it may also help cephalalgia patients relax and thereby reduce the severity of their headaches. The present pilot study was undertaken, therefore, to examine the effect of inhaling green-apple fragrance on the severity of symptoms during migraine attacks.

METHODS

Subjects

Fifty chronic headache patients, 33 women and 17 men ranging in age from 18 to 67 years (mean: 39 years), volunteered for this Institutional Review Board-approved study. Their headaches, based on the subjects' histories, were classified into the following modified categories of the Headache Classification Committee of the International Headache Society:[13] traumatic (n = 20); common migraine (n = 14); atypical cephalalgia (n = 10); tension-type (n = 2); Costen's syndrome (n = 1)[14]; pseudomotor cerebri (n = 1); trichloroethylene-induced headache (n = 1);[15] and, mixed headache types (n = 4).

Instruments

Amoore's Olfactory Threshold Test for phenylethyl methylethyl carbinol (PM Carbinol)[16] was used to determine the minimal concentration of this standard odorant which subjects were able to detect. Odor intensity is expressed in decismels (ds), units which are modeled after the decibel units of sound intensity.

A pen-like device, its tip impregnated with an odorant that smells like green apples and which comprises one component of the Chicago Smell Test, [17,18,19] was provided to each subject as an inhaler.

Procedure

Following the administration of the Olfactory Threshold Test of Amoore to each subject, a survey sheet was to be completed by each, at home, during three consecutive migraine attacks. At the first attack, subjects subjectively rated the severity of their headaches on a scale of 1 to 10, from least to most severe. They would then lay in a dark, quiet room for 10 minutes after which they again rated the headaches.

During the second episode, subjects also rated the headaches, they reposed in a dark, quiet room for 10 minutes, but this time they inhaled green-apple fragrance from the pen-like device, breathing normally, and holding the pen approximately 2cm from their noses. At this time, they indicated whether they found the scent pleasant or unpleasant. After 10 minutes, they again rated their headaches. During the third episode, subjects rated the headache at onset and also after 10 minutes resting in a dark, quiet room. As in the first attack, the subjects did not inhale apple odor.

Statistical Analysis

The University of Illinois School of Public Health provided the statistical analysis of the data using the *t*-Test for correlation for significant difference from zero and the Signed-Rank Test.

RESULTS

In the olfactory tests, 31 subjects had normal olfaction, ie they were able to detect PM Carbinol odorant at a concentration of 25 ds. Seventeen subjects were hyposmic, ie able to detect it at the concentrations of 30 to 55 ds. Two subjects were anosmic, ie able to detect odor only at irritant level (greater than 55 ds) (Table 1). Thirty-five subjects did not like the green-apple odor while 15 rated it as pleasant (Table 1). Considering the group as a whole, inhaling the green-apple odor produced no statistically significant improvement over simple resting in a dark, quiet room. The 15 subjects who liked the odor, however, did experience a statistically significant reduction in the severity of their migraines ($p < 0.03$) (Table 1).

DISCUSSION

The efficacy of the green-apple odor in the present study hinged upon hedonics. Patients who liked the smell experienced a statistically significant reduction in the severity of their headaches while patients who disliked the smell experienced no significant effects, either for better or for worse.

Odors have been linked to hedonics in various other studies. Subjects who liked a scent were able, in its presence, to increase their speed of learning,[20] ability to lose weight,[13,21,22] and willingness to buy a common consumer product.[23]

The incidence of hyposmia and anosmia is higher among migraine patients than among the general population.[24] In the present study, the olfactory abilities of the positive and negative hedonic groups did not differ, thus amelioration of symptoms was not due to better olfactory ability among those who liked the green-apple scent.

It is unclear whether the positive response of the 15 patients was due to an organic effect of the odorant or to their psychological response to the smell through Pavlovian conditioning. These patients might have associated the green-apple odor with a past anxiety-or-pain-alleviating experience and such an association could have helped them relax during

TABLE 1
Effects on Migraine Patients of Sniffing Green Apple Scent During a Headache Attack

Pt	Sex	Age	HA* type	Olfactory thresholds	Hedonics	Headache Attacks: #1 Control Pre	Post	Delta**	#2 Green Apple Pre	Post	Delta**	#3 Control Pre	Post	Delta**
1	f	29	1	25	+	8	8	0	8	6	+2	8	8	0
2	f	46	2	25	−	7	7	0	8	8	0	7	7	0
3	m	52	3	35	+	10	10	0	10	1	+9	1	9	−8
4	m	42	1	25	−	7	7	0	6	2	+4	6	5	+1
5	f	32	2	25	−	7	7	0	8	8	0	8	8	0
6	f	44	1	25	−	5	5	0	5	2	+3	1	1	0
7	f	26	2	25	+	5	1	+4	6	0	+6	4	1	+3
8	f	50	3	25	−	2	0	+2	5	0	+5	6	1	+5
9	m	41	3	55	−	6	5	+1	6	7	−1	4	4	0
10	f	33	2	25	−	2	2	0	2	2	0	2	2	0
11	f	37	3	25	−	4	6	−2	3	1	+2	4	4	0
12	f	37	2	35	−	3	3	0	3	3	0	3	3	0
13	f	52	2	35	−	4	4	0	2	2	0	2	2	0
14	f	43	2	55	−	1	1	0	2	2	0	2	2	0
15	f	49	1	25	−	5	5	0	5	5	0	5	5	0
16	f	42	2	35	−	4	2	+2	7	4	+3	3	1	+2
17	m	33	1	35	+	8	8	0	8	6	+2	8	8	0
18	m	36	1	35	+	6	6	0	4	4	0	8	8	0
19	f	39	2	25	−	2	2	0	2	2	0	2	2	0
20	m	18	1	35	−	10	10	0	9	8	+1	9	7	+2
21	f	53	3	35	−	7	7	0	8	7	+1	8	8	0
22	m	34	3	35	−	4	3	+1	3	4	−1	3	3	0
23	m	46	4	25	−	7	7	0	7	7	0	7	7	0
24	f	40	4	25	−	4	4	0	3	3	0	3	3	0
25	f	46	1,4	25	−	4	4	0	3	3	0	5	5	0
26	m	32	1	25	+	8	6	+2	10	6	+4	7	5	+2
27	f	53	1	25	+	10	8	+2	10	5	+5	10	8	+2
28	f	49	5	25	+	4	4	0	5	5	0	5	5	0
29	f	45	3	25	−	8	7	+1	7	5	+2	8	7	+1
30	f	21	6	25	+	4	4	0	4	3	+1	3	3	0
31	f	34	1	25	−	8	3	+5	10	7	+3	10	5	+5
32	f	25	1	25	−	5	7	−2	3	5	−2	3	2	+1
33	m	33	1	25	+	7	8	−1	8	8	0	8	5	+3
34	f	31	1	25	−	7	7	0	7	8	−1	6	5	+1
35	m	38	1	25	−	8	8	0	7	5	+2	8	8	0
36	f	46	2	35	+	10	9	+1	10	4	+6	9	9	0
37	f	32	3	25	+	9	9	0	9	10	−1	9	9	0
38	m	55	1	25	−	8	8	0	8	9	−1	8	8	0
39	m	38	1	35	−	7	7.5	−.5	5	6.25	−1.2	5.5	5.5	0
40	f	58	3	35	+	1	1	0	1	1	0	2	2	0
41	f	27	2	35	−	5	7	−2	7	9	−2	7	7	0
42	f	20	2,4	25	−	6	5	−1	7	7	0	7	7	0
43	f	21	1	25	−	7	6	+1	7	8	−1	8	6	+2
44	m	67	7	35	−	0	0	0	0	0	0	0	0	0
45	m	25	1	35	−	4	4	0	6	4	+2	5	5	0
46	f	31	3	35	−	5	5	0	4	5	−1	6	6	0
47	f	34	2	25	−	5	3	+2	5	7	−2	3	3	0
48	f	46	4,5	25	+	8	8	0	5	4	+1	9	9	0
49	m	18	1	35	+	8	4	+2	8	2	+6	8	5	+3
50	m	37	2,4	25	−	3	5	−2	3	3	0	7	7	0

*Headache Types: 1-Traumatic, 2-Common Migraine, 3-Atypical Cephalalgia, 4-Muscle Contraction, 5-Costens, 6-Pseudomotor Cerebri, 7-Trichloroethylene-induced, 8-Mixed Types

**Positive Delta number indicates improvement, negative number worsening of symptoms.

their headache episodes.[25] In a study of olfactory-evoked recall, the phenomenon whereby an odor evokes memories and associated feelings, one of the authors demonstrated that food smells were the most common triggers of this response.[26] Memories evoked by food smells were usually pleasant and associated with a positive mood state. In the present study, the green-apple scent may have induced a positive mood state in the 15 patients, and such a state would tend to reduce perceptions of pain.[27]

The lack of response of our patients who did not like the green-apple scent suggests that odor hedonics were more important than the particular chemicals impregnated in the pen-tips. Still, this does not preclude the possibility of a neurophysiologic effect. Serotonin, dopamine, acetylcholine, norepinephrine, gamma amino butric acid, gastrin, beta endorphin, metencephalon, and substance P are all known to be both essential modulators of headache, including migraine, and neurotransmitters within the olfactory bulb, hence affected by odors.[28-43]

Possibly, the green-apple odor worked in a venue similar to that of pharmacologic agents used in the management of headache, eg amitriptyline or propranolol, by modifying the neurotransmitters involved in the pain pathway.[44,45] In those who disliked the odor, it may have induced a strong negative mood state that the odor's neurophysiologic effect was unable to overcome, thus there was no alleviation of pain. Further studies of this response would require a variety of odors.

CONCLUSIONS

Despite our present lack of understanding of the mechanism behind the green-apple's efficacy, research and therapeutic indications are clear. In addition to standard medical treatment of migraines, adjuvant therapy involving eating certain foods or inhaling certain odors may further benefit patients. Future studies of foods and fragrances should provide new treatment options of mitigating migraine, a special boon to patients who poorly tolerate conventional therapy.

CITED MEDICATIONS

AMITRIPTYLINE
Elavil® — ZENECA

PROPRANOLOL
Inderal®; Inderal LA® — WYETH-AYERST

REFERENCES

1. Blau JN, Solomon F. Smell and other sensory disturbances in migraine. *J Neurol* 1985; 232:275-276.
2. Raffaeli E, Martins O. Role for anticonvulsants in migraine. *Func Neurol* 1986; 1:275-276.
3. Blau JN. Migraine: Theories of pathogenesis. *Lancet* 1992; 339:1203.
4. Wolberg FL, Ziegler DK. Olfactory hallucinations in migraine. *Arch Neurol* 1982; 39:392.
5. Crosley CJ. Dhammon S. Migrainous olfactory aura in a family. *Arch Neurol* 1983; 40:459.
6. Diamond S, Freitag FG, Prager J, Gandhi S. Olfactory aura in migraine. *N Engl J Med* 1985; 312:1390.
7. Fuller GN, Guiloff RJ. Migrainous olfactory hallucinations. *Neurol Neurosurg Psychiatry* 1987; 50:1688-1690.
8. Morrison DP, Price WH. Prevalence of psychiatric disorder among female new referrals to a migraine clinic. *Psychol Med* 1989; 19:919-925.
9. Blau JN. What some patients can eat during migraine attacks: Therapeutic and conceptual implications. *Cephalalgia* 1993; 13:293-295.
10. Hirsch AR. Scentsation, olfactory demographics and abnormalities. *Int J Aromather* 1992; 4:16-17.
11. Schiffman SS. Aging and the sense of smell: Potential benefits of fragrance enhancement. In: Van Toller S, Dodd GH (eds). *Fragrance: The Psychology and Biology of Perfume.* London: Elsevier Applied Science; 1992; 57-58.
12. Hirsch AR. *Dr. Hirsch's Guide to Scentsational Weight Loss.* Rockport, MA: Element Books; 1997.
13. International Headache Society. Classification and diagnostic criteria for headache disorders, cranial neuralgias and facial pain. *Cephalalgia* 1988; 8(suppl 7):1-96.
14. Goldman AR, McCullough V. *TMJ Syndrome. The Overlooked Diagnosis.* New York: Simon and Schuster; 1987.
15. Hirsch AR, Rankin KM, Panelli PP. Trichloroethylene; exposure and headache. *Headache Q* 1996; 7:126-138.
16. Amoore J, Ollman B. Practical test kits for quantitatively evaluating the sense of smell. *Rhinology* 1983; 21:49-54.
17. Hirsch AR, Cain Dr. Evaluation of the Chicago Smell Test in a normal population. *Chem Senses* 1992; 17:642-643.
18. Hirsch AR, Gotway MB. Validation of the Chicago Smell Test in subjective normosmic neurologic patients. *Chem Senses* 1993; 18:570-571.
19. Hirsch AR, Gotway MB, Harris AT. Validation of the Chicago Smell Test in patients with subjective olfactory loss. *Chem Senses* 1993; 18:571.
20. Hirsch AR, Johnston LH. Odors and learning. *J Neurol Orthop Med Surg* 1996; 17:119-126.
21. Hirsch AR, Dougherty DD. Inhalation of 2-acetylpyridine for weight reduction. *Chem Senses* 1993; 18:570.
22. Hirsch AR, Gomez R. Weight redution through inhalation of odorants. *J Neurol Orthop Med Surg* 1995;; 16:28-31.
23. Hirsch AR, Gay S. Effect of ambient olfactory stimuli on the evaluation of a common consumer product. *Chem Senses* 1991; 16:535.
24. Hirsch AR. Olfaction in migraineurs. *Headache* 1992; 32:233-236.
25. Jacobson E. *Modern Treatment of Tense Patients.* Springfield, IL: Charles C. Thomas; 1970.
26. Hirsch AR. Nostalgia: A neuropsychiatric understanding. *Adv Consumer Res* 1992; 19:390-395.
27. Fields H. Psychology of pain. In: *Pain.* New York: McGraw-Hill; 1987; 171-203.
28. Halasz N. Shepherd GM. Neurochemistry of the vertebrate olfactory bulb. *Neurosci* `1983; 10:579-619.
29. Macrides F, Davis BJ. Olfactory bulb. In: Emson PC (ed). *Chemical Neuroanatomy.* New York: Raven Press; 1983; 391.
30. Haberly LB, Price JL Association and commissural fiber systems of the olfactory cortex in the rat. II. Systems originating in the olfactory peduncle. *J Comp Neurol* 1978; 178:781-808.
31. Mair RG, Harrison LM. Influence of drugs on smell function. In: Laing DG, Coty RL, Briephol W (eds). *Human Sense of Smell.* Berlin: Springer-Verlag; 1991; 336-355.
32. Zaborsky L, Carlsen J, Brashear HR, Heimer L. Cholinergic and GABA-ergic projections to the olfactory bulb in the rat. *J Comp Neurol* 1985; 243:468-509.
33. Sjaastad O. Cluster headaches. In: Vinken PJ, Bruyn GW, Klawans HL (eds). *Handbook of Clinical Neurology,* Vol 48 — *Headache.* New York: Elsevier Science; 1986; 217.
34. Gall CM, Hendry SHC, Seroogy KB, Jones EG, Haycock JW. Events for co-existence of GABA and dopamine in neurons of the rat olfactory bulb. *J Comp Neurol* 1987; 266:307-318.
35. Leston J. Barontini M, Mancini A, Rocchil V, Hershkovits E. Free and conjugated plasma catecholamines in cluster headache. *Cephalalgia* 1987; 7(suppl 6):331.
36. Foote S, Bloom F, Aston-Jones G. Nucleus locus coeruleus: New evidence of anatomical and physiological specificity. *Physio Rev* 1983; 86:844-914.
37. Shipley M, Halloran F, Torre J. Surprisingly rich projection from locus coeruleus to the olfactory bulb in the rat. *Brain Res* 1985; 329:294-299.
38. Igarashi H, Sakai F, Suzuki S, Tazaki Y. Cerebrovascular sympathetic nervous activity during cluster headaches. *Cephalalgia* 1987; 7(suppl 6):87-89.
39. Anselmi B, Baldi E, Cassacci F, Salmon S. Endogenous opioids in cerebrospinal fluid and blood in idiopathic headache sufferers. *Headache* 1980; 20:294-299.
40. Nattero G, Savi L, Piantino P, Priolo C, Corno M. Serum gastrin levels in cluster headache and migraine attacks. In: Pfaffenrath V, Lundberg PO, Sjaastad O (eds). *Updating in Headache.* Berlin: Springer-Verlag; 1985; 305-311.
41. Appenzeller O, Atkinson RA, Standefer JC. Serum beta endorphin in cluster headache and common migraine. In:

Rose FC, Zilkha E (eds). *Progress in Migraine*. London: Pitman; 1981; 106-109.
42. Hardebo JE, Ekman R, Eriksson M, Holgersson S, Ryberg B. CSF opioid levels in cluster headache. In: Rose FC (ed). *Migraine*. Basel: Karger; 1985; 79-85.
43. Moskowitz MA. Neurobiology of vascular head pain. *Ann Neurol* 1984; 16:157-168.
44. Baldessarini RG. Drugs and the treatment of psychiatric disorders. In: Goodman AG, Gilman S (eds). *Pharmacologic Basis of Therapeutics*. New York: Pergamon Press; 1990; 404-414.
45. Schoenen J. Beta blockers and the central nervous system. *Cephalalgia* 1986; 6:47-54.

Olfaction in Migraineurs

Alan R. Hirsch, M.D., F.A.C.P.

SYNOPSIS

Many investigators have described olfactory dysfunction among migraineurs. Olfactory stimuli can precipitate migraine, and olfactory hallucinations can occur as auras of migraines or as part of the symptom complex. Despite many reports linking olfactory phenomena and migraine, no evaluations of the olfactory abilities of migraineurs have been documented. To begin such assessments, sixty-seven consecutive migraine patients were given Pyridine odor threshold tests. Twelve of them (18%) scored as hyposmic or anosmic. In comparison, 1% of the general population of the U.S. is hyposmic or anosmic. Aside from possible diagnostic or methodological error, several possibilities may account for our result: migraine may induce olfactory pathology; olfactory pathology may induce migraine, or; a common pathogen may induce both olfactory dysfunction and migraine. The association of migraine with the emotional component of the limbic system has long been recognized, and our results strengthen its association with the olfactory component as well. Headache patients should be tested for olfactory loss and warned of such risks as inability to detect gas leaks and spoiled food.

Key words: olfaction, migraine

(*Headache* 1992; 32:233-236)

INTRODUCTION

In 1888, Gowers[1] noted that odors can precipitate headaches in susceptible migraineurs. More recently, Blau and Solomon[2] reported that 11 of 50 migraine patients had olfactory triggers to their headaches, the most common being the odor of cigarette smoke. Fifteen of eighty members of the British Migraine Association also had migraines precipitated by an odor, usually the odor of a perfume or paint. Raffaelli[3] described 31 patients with common migraine in which an odor, particularly perfume or cigarette smoke, induced their headaches. In 64.7% of them, treatment with diphenylhydantoin improved their osmophobia. Raffaelli suggested that odors may overexcite the migraineur by interacting with limbic structures to evoke an alarm response with associated release of neurotransmitters, thus stimulting the sensitive receptors of the scalp arteries and causing the headaches.

Olfactory hallucinations have been well described as auras of migraines. Bary[4] in 1895 and Flatau[5] in 1912 described olfactory hallucinations of a floral scent as auras to migraine. More recently, Wolberg and Ziegler[6] reported a case of a 32 year old woman who had an aura of the smell of "decaying animals" lasting for 20 minutes in association with visual scotomata and followed by headache. They suggested that ischemia in the temporal lobe produced an irritation, and thus the aura, in a process analogous to that in which visual scotomata arise from the occipital lobe. Crosley and Dhamoon[7] described two patients, a mother and daughter, both of whom experienced olfactory auras: the mother had the aura of "the smell of the inside of a pencil sharpener" and the daughter had various auras: "the odor of gas, burning cookies or wood chips". The perceptions were so realistic that several times they undertook a search for gas leakage. Sacks[8,9] noted that olfactory migrainous auras are often associated with déjà vu and other temporal lobe phenomena. Diamond et al[10] reported the case of a 30 year old woman, a nonsmoker, who had the aura of cigarette smoke which persisted after the headache began and continued for as long as an entire day. Fuller and Guiloff[11] described three migraineurs who had olfactory auras of a repulsive smell, an unidentifiable smell and a smell either of cigars or of peanut butter, respectively. The authors suggested that in some reported cases of migraine triggered by an odor, the odor was, in fact, an olfactory aura.

In addition to documentation as triggers and as auras, olfactory symptoms have also been documented as part of the headache symptom complex. Ardila and Sanchez,[12] in evaluating 200 consecutive patients with vascular headaches, found olfactory hallucinations in 1% of them. Morrison and Price[13] found that 13% of 46 female migraineurs had olfactory or gustatory hallucinations at the same time as the headache attacks. As with uncal olfactory hallucinations of temporal lobe epilepsy,[14] these hallucinations correlated with mood changes (depression and irritability). This link between depression and olfactory hallucinations in the migraineurs was postulated to be due to changes in regional cerebral blood flow. A spreading depression of EEG activity then results, disrupting limbic system function and causing both chemosensory hallucinations and mood changes.[15]

Reprint requests to: Alan R. Hirsch, M.D. F.A.C.P., Smell and Taste Treatment and Research Foundation Water Tower Place, Suite 930W, 845 N. Michigan Avenue, Chicago, Illinois 60611.
Accepted for Publication: December 17, 1991.

In a recent paper, Morrison[16] reported olfactory hallucinations accompanying their migraine headaches in 10.9% of 46 women studied. He attributed the hallucinations to uncinate gyrus irritation due either to temporal lobe ischemia or to spreading depression of Leão.

During a migraine attack, patients may experience an unusual sensitivity to odor as well as to sound and light.[17,18] This hyperosmia may be associated with the dislike of smells or osmophobia. Blau and Solomon[2] noted osmophobia in 40% of 50 migraineurs studied.

Dysosmia has even been described as a manifestation of amigrainous migraine.[19]

Despite this ample evidence of olfactory dysfunction among migraineurs, no systematic evaluations of olfactory abilities among migraineurs have been documented.

METHODS

To assess olfactory abilities of migraineurs, sixty-seven patients who presented consecutively at an urban headache center in 1990 and whose headaches met the diagnostic criteria for migraine as defined by the Headache Classification Committee of the International Headache Society[20] were selected as subjects. Their olfactory thresholds were tested using Pyridine threshold tests in the standardized protocol.[21] Each subject was given four squeeze bottles successively and asked to sniff and rate the odors (in a forced choice procedure) as more or less intense than the one sniffed previously. The four samples consisted of an odorless control and three concentrations of Pyridine (25 decismells, 55 decismells and the trigeminal irritant stimulus level).

Subjects were tested interictally so as to eliminate any competing stimuli of headache pain that might distract them from smelling the samples, and weaken both their ability to respond correctly and their desire to cooperate.

RESULTS AND DISCUSSION

Twelve of the sixty-seven migraineurs (17.9 ± 4.6%) were found to be hyposmic or anosmic in comparison with normal subjects for whom data has been established. We consider this a high incidence, since, in the normal population of the United States, the general incidence of hyposmia and anosmia is only about 1%.[22]

Epidemiologically, young people and women are over-represented among migraineurs. And since the young have better olfactory abilities than do the elderly, and women have better olfactory abilities than do men,[23,24] we might have expected our sample of migraineurs to show better olfactory abilities than the general population. But the opposite was the case: our migraineurs had considerably poorer odor detection thresholds than the general population.

We can interpret our finding in various ways. Diagnostic or methodologic error may account for it in whole or in part, or, it may represent a real relationship between olfactory loss and migraine, in which case several possibilities exist: 1) the migraine condition may induce olfactory pathology; 2) the olfactory pathology may induce migraine; or 3) according to a unified limbic system theory, a single pathogen may induce both olfactory loss and headache.

Diagnostic error may have skewed our results. Many diseases cause both nonmigrainous headaches and disturbances in smell. Sinusitis and olfactory groove meningiomas, for example, are both associated with olfactory loss and can present with headaches.[25,26] If these were misdiagnosed as migraines in our sample, true incidence of hyposmia and anosmia could be lower than reported.

Since all subjects were taking medications at the time of evaluation, and many common antimigrainous agents, including codeine, cause impaired olfaction,[27] our findings could have been skewed by the side effects of these medications.

Methodological error may have been introduced by our particular olfactory threshold test. Requiring that our subjects make a forced choice may have been inappropriate, given the perfectionistic and obsessive nature of the migraineur's personality.[28,29] In ambiguous situations, a migraineur may prefer to refuse to answer rather than to commit to a choice. And since any refusal to answer in this test is interpreted as an incorrect response, the data could be skewed towards the pathologic.

It is also possible that migraineurs' behavior unrelated to their headache condition is responsible for their olfactory loss. The use of cigarettes and drugs, or the existence of concomitant illnesses, for example, have been implicated in olfactory loss.[31,32,33,34]

However, our finding may represent a real relationship between olfactory loss and migraine. The olfactory loss may be due to the migraine and associated conditions. The recurrent small vascular insults of complicated migraine are known occasionally to result in a persistent neurologic deficit[30] and such insults may possibly also result in olfactory deficit.

Lacrimation and rhinorrhea, which often accompany migraine, may engorge the nasal passages, obstructing air flow to the olfactory epithelium and preventing odorant molecules from stimulating the olfactory nerve, as in acute rhinitis.[35] If such nasal engorgement were present during our testing, this could affect our findings.

Alternatively, a lack of olfactory sensibility can be a learned response. Through a Pavlovian method of self-conditioning, migraineurs with olfactory triggers can learn to tune out environmental odors just as, in an analogous manner, the narcoleptic can inhibit emotional response to prevent cataplectic attacks.[36] Conversely, an olfactory loss may have led to the development of migraines. An individual whose olfaction is impaired is more likely to be exposed to substances — toxins and spoiled foods — which can precipitate vascular headaches.[37]

The hyposmic migraineur may be unable to detect odors that are nonetheless strong enough to cause headaches. The effects of these odors can be analogous to the effects in normosmics of subliminal odors that can induce both EEG and behavioral changes.[38] While a normosmic migraineur can learn to avoid suprathreshold odor precipitants, the hyposmic migraineur cannot even detect offending odors, let alone avoid or remove them to prevent developing headaches.

Since approximately 90% of what we perceive to be taste or flavor is, in fact, smell, a lack of olfactory ability impairs the perception of taste and flavor, and changes the dysosmic individual's food preferences. A migraineur can by this same process lose any appetite for foods perceived as tasteless and thus succumb to a nutritional deficiency, a state that is associated with headaches.[39,40]

Alternatively, an olfactory loss can act as a form of sensory deprivation syndrome. Lack of sensory input can induce hallucinations and neurologic symptoms,[41] and similarly, a lack of olfactory input may possibly induce headaches.

A unifying theory may explain our findings: a single common pathogen can affect both the olfactory system and the structures responsible for migraine. Such trauma as head injury or toxic exposure, for example, can cause both olfactory loss and headache.[42,43]

Neurotransmitters of the olfactory bulb — dopamine, GABA, acetylcholine and serotonin — all have been implicated in migraine.[44,45] Thus an insult to any of these neurotransmitters can cause both pathologic states.

Moreover, the anatomy of olfaction further strengthens the concept of an olfactory-migraine link. According to MacLean's[46] definition, the olfactory lobe is part of the limbic system. And, as has long been recognized, migraine is associated with the emotional component of limbic system function. As many as 60% of migraines occur during stressful situations and are associated with emotional upheaval.[47] Emotional discharge is recognized as a common aura and accompaniment of migraine.[48] Autonomic discharge of an emotional type, such as blushing or lacrimation, helps to define the migrainous event.[49] Moreover, the treatment of psychiatric disorders overlaps with that of migraine and includes the use of such medications as tricyclic antidepressants and monoamine oxidase inhibitors, as well as biofeedback and stress reduction techniques.[50] And, according to Morrison and Price,[13] migraineurs have an increased incidence of interictal psychiatric disturbances. Since an integral component of the limbic system is the olfactory lobe, migraineurs may display either emotional or olfactory symtomatology as a manifestation of their limbic system dysfunction.

Like migraineurs, those with chemosensory complaints also display limbic system dysfunction.[51] Freud[52] noted the integral relationship between olfaction and the emotions. In investigating depression, Deems et al[53] found an incidence of 35% among subjects with dysosmia and dysgeusia and an incidence of 24% among those with hyposmia or hypogeusia. Studies of olfactory bulbectomy as a model of depression strengthen this linkage.[54] In addition, patients with schizophrenia or depression, when queried, often admit to olfactory changes.[55] In my study with Trannel,[56] 96% of 46 consecutive patients complaining of chemosensory disorders had DSM IIIR Axis I or II diagnoses.

CONCLUSION

Our finding appears not only to further substantiate the migraine-limbic-olfactory link, but also to suggest issues of clinical importance. All headache patients should be queried regarding olfactory complaints and tested for olfactory loss.

Since an estimated 5-10% of Americans suffer from migraines, millions of persons as a result of their hyposmia may be at risk of failure to detect leaking gas and consequent explosions.[57] Hyposmic patients should be provided with gas detectors. They should also be warned of the risks of eating spoiled food. Specific anosmias, those that accompany certain types of headaches and those that occur at particular times within the headache cycle deserve further investigation.

REFERENCES

1. Gowers WR: A Manual of Diseases of the Nervous System. London: Churchill, 1988:788.
2. Blau JN, Solomon F: Smell and other sensory disturbances in migraine. *J Neurol* 1985; 232:275-276.
3. Raffaelli E, Martins O: A role for anticonvulsants in migraine. *Funct Neurol* 1986; 1:495-498.
4. Bary A: Zur Frage von den Aequivalenten der Migrane. *Neurologisches Centralblatt* 1895; 1:249-252.
5. Flatau E: Die Migrane. In: Alzheimer A, Levandowsky L, editors. Monographien aus dem Gesamtgebiet der Neurologie und Psychiatrie. Berlin, 1912:2.
6. Wolberg FL, Ziegler DK: Olfactory hallucination in migraine. *Arch Neurol* 1982; 39:382.
7. Crosley CJ, Dhamoon S: Migrainous olfactory aura in a family. *Arch Neurol* 1983; 40:459.
8. Sacks O: Migraine — Evolution of a Common Disorder. London: Pan Books, 1981:95-97.
9. Sacks O: Migraine — Understanding a Common Disorder. Los Angeles: University of California Press, 1985:75.
10. Diamond S, Freitag F, Prager J, Gandi S: Olfactory aura in migraine. *N Engl J Med* 1985; 312:1390.
11. Fuller GN, Guiloff RJ: Migrainous olfactory hallucinations. *Neurol Neurosurg Psychiatry* 1987; 50:1688-1690.
12. Ardila A, Sanchez E: Neuropsychologic symptoms in the migraine syndrome. *Cephalalgia* 1988; 8:67-70.
13. Morrison DP, Price WH: The prevalence of psychiatric disorder among female new referrals to a migraine clinic. *Psychology Medicine* 1989; 19:919-925.
14. Jackson HJ, Stewart P: Epileptic attacks with a warning of a crude sensation of smell and with the intellectual aura (dreamy state) in a patient who had symptoms pointing to gross organic disease of the right temporosphenoidal lobe. *Brain* 1899; 22:535-547.
15. Hansen AJ, Lauritzen M, Tfelt-Hansen P: Spreading cortical depression and antimigraine drugs. In: Amery W, et al editors. The Pharmacological Basis of Migraine Therapy. London: Pitman, 1984:161-170.
16. Morrison DP: Abnormal perceptual experiences in migraine. *Cephalalgia* 1990; 10:273-277.

17. Bruyn GW: Migraine equivalents. In: Vinken PJ, Bruyn G, Klawans HL, editors. Handbook of Clinical Neurology. New York: Elsevier Science Publishers, 1985:155-171.
18. Adams R, Victor M: Principles of Neurology. New York: McGraw-Hill, 1989:183-189.
19. Debney LM, Hedge A: Physical trigger factors in migraine — with special reference to the weather. In: Amery WK, Wauquier A, editors. The Prelude to the Migraine Attack. London: Bailiere Tindall, 1986:8-24.
20. Headache Classification Committee of the International Headache Society. Classification and diagnostic criteria for headache disorders, cranial neuralgias and facial pain. *Cephalalgia* 1988; 8 suppl 7:1-96.
21. Amoore J, Ollman B: Practical test kits for quantitatively evaluating the sense of smell. *Rhinology* 1983; 21:49-54.
22. Public Health Service. Report of the Panel on Communicative Disorders to the National Advisory Neurological and Communicative Disorders and Stroke Council (NIH Publication no. 79-1914). Washington, D.C.: National Institute of Health, 1979:319.
23. Doty RL, Shaman P, Applebaum SL, Giberson R, Sikorski L, Rosenberg L: Smell identification ability: changes with age. *Science* 1984; 226:1441-1443.
24. Doty RL, Applebaum S, Zusho H, Settle G: Sex differences in odor identification ability: a cross-cultural analysis. *Neuro-psychologia* 1985; 23:667-672.
25. Fein B, Kamin P, Fein N: The loss of sense of smell in nasal allergy. *Ann Allergy* 1966; 24:278.
26. Bakay L: Olfactory meningiomas. *JAMA* 1984; 251:53-54.
27. Shifman SS: Taste and smell in disease. *N Engl J Med* 1983; 308:1275-1279 and 1337-1343.
28. Fine BD: Psychoanalytic aspects of head pain. In: Friedman AP, editor. Research and Clinical Studies in Headache, Vol. 2. Basel: Karger, 1969:169-194.
29. Dalsgaard-Neilsen T: Migraine and heredity. *Acta Neurol Scand* 1965; 41:287-300.
30. Bradshaw P, Parsons M: Hemiplegic migraine: a clinical study. *Q J Med* 1965; 34:68-85.
31. Frye R, Schwartz B, Doty R: Dose-related effects of cigarette smoking on olfactory function. *JAMA* 1990; 263:1233-1236.
32. Pray S: How to help patients with taste and smell disorders. *U S Pharmacist* 1989; Jan:30-31.
33. Doty RL: A review of olfactory dysfunctions in man. *Am J Otolaryngol* 1979; 1:57-74.
34. Brown I: The widespread influence of olfaction. *Neurosurg Nursing* 1985; 17:273-279.
35. DeWeese DD, Saunders WH: Textbook of Otolaryngology, 6th Ed. St. Louis: C.V. Mosby Company, 1982: 184-185.
36. Lishman WA: Organic Psychiatry: The Psychological Consequences of Cerebral Disorder. Osney Mead, Oxford: Blackwell Scientific Publications, 1978:846.
37. Saper JR, Magee KR: Freedom from Headaches. New York: Simon and Schuster, 1978:144-146.
38. Hirsch AR, Gay S: The effect of ambient olfactory stimuli on the evaluation of a common consumer product. *Chem Senses* 1991; 16:535.
39. Lishman WA: Organic Psychiatry: The Psychological Consequences of Cerebral Disorder. Osney Mead, Oxford: Blackwell Scientific Publications, 1978: 676-677.
40. McBurney DH: Taste, smell, and flavor terminology: taking the confusion out of fusion. In: Meiselman HL, Rivlin RS, editors. Clinical Measurement of Taste and Smell. New York: Macmillan, 1986:118.
41. Schultz DP: Sensory Restriction. New York: Academic Press, 1965:99-108.
42. Hirsch AR, Wyse JP: Posttraumatic dysosmia: central versus peripheral. *South Med J* 1990; 83:2S-34.
43. Schwartz BS, Ford DP, et al: Solvent associated olfactory dysfunction: not a predictor of deficits in learning and memory. *Psychiatry* 1991; 148:751-756.
44. Halasz N, Shepherd GM: Neurochemistry of the vertebrate olfactory bulb. *Neuroscience* 1983; 10:579-619.
45. Olesen J: The pathophysiology of migraine. In: Vinken PJ, Bruyn GW, Klawans HL, editors. Handbook of Clinical Neurology. New York: Elsevier Science Publishers, 1986:59-84.
46. McLean PD: The limbic system (visceral brain) in relation to central gray and reticulum of the brain stem: evidence of interdependence in emotional processes. *Psychosom Med* 1955; 42:355-366.
47. Henryk-gutt R, Rees WL: Psychological aspects of migraine. *Psychosom Research* 1973; 17:141-153.
48. Moersch FP: Psychic manifestations in migraine. *Psychiatry* 1924; 80:697-716.
49. Hirsch AR: Neuroanatomic mechanism: the limbic system and migraine. *Cephalalgia* 1987; 7:191-192.
50. Lance JW: Headache: classification, mechanism and principles of therapy, with particular reference to migraine. *Recenti Prog Med* 1989; 80:673-680.
51. Hirsch AR: The nose knows. *Chicago Med* 1990; 93:27-31.
52. Freud S: Bemerkungen uber einen Fall von Zwangs Neuroses. *Ges Schr VIII* 1908:350.
53. Deems DA, Doty RL, Settle RG, Moore-Gillon V, Shaman P, Mester AF, Kimmelman CP, Brightman VJ, Snow JB Jr: Smell and taste disorders: a study of 750 patients from the University of Pennsylvania Smell and Taste Center. *Arch Otolaryngol Head Neck Surg* 1991; 117:519-528.
54. Richardson JS: Brain output dysregulation induced by olfactory bulbectomy: an approximation in the rat of major depressive disorder in humans? *Int J Neurosci* 1988; 38:341-365.
55. Levenson J: Dysosmia and dysgeusia presenting as depression. *Gen Hosp Psychiatry* 1985; 7:171-173.
56. Hirsch AR, Trannel T: Comorbidity of psychiatric and chemosensory disorders. *Chem Senses* 1991; 16:536.
57. Adams RD, Victor M: Principles of Neurology. New York: McGraw-Hill, 1989:138.

J Neurol Orthop Med Surg (1998) 18:98-103
Editorial Office: 2300 S. Rancho Dr., Suite 202, Las Vegas, NV 89102-4508, USA

ORIGINAL ARTICLES

Ambient Odors in the Treatment of Claustrophobia A Pilot Study

Alan R. Hirsch, M.D., F.A.C.P.,[1] and Jason J. Gruss[2]

[1]Smell & Taste Treatment and Research Foundation, Ltd., Chicago, IL 60611, USA
[2]University of Michigan, Ann Arbor, MI, USA

Abstract: Since-certain ambient odors can ameliorate anxieties, we theorized that the presence of such odors may ease claustrophobia and expand perceptions of room size. To measure the effects of various odorants on perceptions of room size as a first step, we recruited 8 volunteers. Each sat in a space-deprivation booth in the absence of any odorant while they completed questionnaires and analog scales rating their feelings about the room size. They then repeated the procedure in the presence of each of 10 different odors. One odor, that of barbecue smoke, affected all subjects' perceptions, making the room seem smaller-($p<0.05$). Another odor, that of green apple affected the 7 subjects with normal ability to smell, so that they perceived the room as being larger ($p< 0.02$). Experimentation with selected odors holds promise for use in MRI scanners to make claustrophobics more tolerant of the imaging procedures and to minimize the anxieties of the substantial proportion of the population who have subclinical components of claustrophobia.

Key Words: Claustrophobia, Odors, Space Perception

Introduction

Riding in crowded buses or trains bothers many people. Those with subclinical claustrophobia stand stiffly in packed elevators, stare straight ahead and avoid touching, talking, looking or even breathing on one another. Those with severe claustrophobia avoid such situations altogether. The disorder is disabling to roughly 10% of the population.[1]

For psychological wellbeing, a room must feel neither cramped nor immense. Thus to put their occupants at ease, various techniques are used to make small offices feel spacious, convention halls less huge.[2]

It is well known that our sensations mediate our space perceptions. The sight of mirrors, windows and furniture positioned along the periphery of a cramped room enlarge our visual image of it while curtains, dim lights and furniture placed amid open areas break up the image of vastness. Sounds reverberate against bare walls making a room seem larger, while carpets and padded walls dampen sounds making a room seem smaller. The tactile hardness of wood floors enlarges the perceived size of an area while plush carpeting and oversized furniture reduces the perceived spaciousness. The felt warmth of a fireplace imparts coziness to a large room.

Conspicuous for its absence in the literature, however, is any mention of effects of odors on space perceptions, since theoretically, odors could have a significant influence.

The question of the relationship between odors and space perception arose in the clinical setting when patients in group therapy for olfactory problems reported developing claustrophobia coincident with their loss of ability to smell.[3] We know that certain odors can reduce anxiety,[4] which led us to postulate the existence of an ambient odor that expands perceived space; the inability to detect this postulated odor would lead hyposmics (those with olfactory deficits) to develop claustrophobia.

As a first step in testing our hypotheses, we decided to measure the effects of various odors on ordinary persons' perceptions of room size.

Methods

Evaluation of Subjects

In this Human Investigational Review Board approved study, 8 volunteers, 4 of each sex, aged 18 to 64 years (mean = 30.9, median 19) underwent olfactory and psychological tests: Amoore's Unilateral (one nostril at a time) Thiophane Threshold Test[5] and University of Pennsylvania Smell Identification Test (UPSIT),[6] a series of 40 scratch-and-sniff odor identification tests, performed according to standard procedures.

Standardized self evaluations were administered — Zung Self Rating Depression Scale,[7] Zung Anxiety

Please address correspondence to: Dr. Alan R. Hirsch, Smell and Taste Treatment and Research Foundation, Ltd., Water Tower Place, Suite 990W, 845 North Michigan Ave., Chicago, IL 60611
ISSN 0890-6599

TABLE 1

Indoor	vs.	Outdoor
Barbecue Smoke		Evergreen
Vanilla		Tranquilities
Buttered Popcorn		Seashore
Charcoal Roasting Meat		Cucumber
		Coconut
		Green Apple

Food	vs.	Non-Food
Barbecue Smoke		Evergreen
Vanilla		Tranquilities
Buttered Popcorn		Seashore
Charcoal Roasting Meat		Green Apple
Cucumber		
Coconut		

Inventory,[8] and Beck Depression Inventory[9] — as was an informal questionnaire devised from various sources[10-15] to assess claustrophobia, phobia and spatial anxiety.

Selection of Odors

An independent panel at the Smell & Taste Treatment and Research Foundation selected 10 odors for their hedonics. A blinded panel at the Foundation then classified the 10 in two ways: indoor versus outdoor and food versus nonfood (Table 1).

Procedure

Subjects sat for a minute in an odor-free, cylindrical space-deprivation booth 2.5 ft. in diameter by 4.5 ft. in height, after which they completed a questionnaire including a 9 cm. analog scale rating their feelings about the room size. They then donned unperfumed surgical masks which they wore for 30 secs. before again completing the analog scale. Masks were removed for a 2 min. hiatus before repeating the procedure 10 times using 10 different surgical masks, each with a different fragrance applied.

One to two drops of fragrance were used on each mask to produce odor levels considered pleasant by the Smell & Taste Treatment and Research Foundation sensory panel. The perfumed masks were presented in random, double blind fashion.

Subjects completed a final questionnaire while wearing another unperfumed mask.

Results

Subject Data

Of the 8 subjects, 4 were single and 4 had partners. One smoked cigarettes; all denied use of drugs or medications.

On a scale of 1 to 10, subjects rated their olfactory abilities, on average, as 7, range 3 to 10. One subject considered his sense of smell excellent and all others considered themselves normal in this regard.

As to their perceptions of their personal odor, 5 subjects felt it was pleasant and the other 3 felt it was neutral or did not answer the question.

Regarding their use of scented personal products, the subjects divided into two groups: 6 used commercial perfumes or colognes, scented deodorant, breath freshener, mints and mouthwash; 2 used unscented deodorants and none of the other products.

Subjects divided also in their feelings about external odors, i.e., those not from their own bodies or personal perfumes: 5 subjects thought people around smelled pleasant, 2 felt neutral about others' odors and 1 thought others smelled unpleasant.

As for their use of external fragrances: 4 subjects used potpourri or room fresheners, 3 did not and 1 did not answer the question.

Olfactory and Psychological Test Data

Seven of the 8 subjects were normosmic, i.e., scored as normal on tests both for odor detection and odor identification (Table 2). One subject, #2, was hyposmic on the UPSIT (odor identification) as adjusted for age and sex.

Psychological test scores show that 4 subjects were at least somewhat anxious, subject #6 was depressed as well and subject #3 was somewhat depressed (Table 3).

Results of questionnaires to assess claustrophobia, phobia, and anxiety disorders were negative for all subjects.

Effects of Odors

Table 5 shows the shifts in perceptions of room size in the presence of each odor compared to the average perception with the odorless masks for each subject.

We calculated the effect of each odor on each subject's perception of room size as follows: First, the subjects' scores on analog scales of room size while wearing the two blank masks were averaged. This figure was the baseline for determining any shifts attributable to the presence of one of the odors. The average shift induced by each odor was then calculated 1) for all 8 subjects; 2) for the 7 with normal scores on both odor tests; and 3) for the 6 who used personal fragrances (Table 5).

For each subject, the change from the odor-free baseline with each odor was contrasted with the median change from

TABLE 2

Subject	Odor detection Amoore's Unilateral Thiophane Threshold* (decismels) Right	 Left	Odor identification UPSIT** no. correct of 40
1	-5	15	36
2	15	10	19
3	20	10	29
4	10	10	35
5	10	15	36
6	5	5	37
7	15	20	37
8	10	10	34

*Normal = -25 to +25 decismels. The decismel scale of cdor level is modeled after the decibel scale of sound level.

**Normal = 29-37

TABLE 3

	Anxiety	Depression	
	Zung	Zung	Beck
Normal =	<36	<40	<15
Subject			
1	39	35	11
2	20	24	0
3	42	43	10
4	37	32	6
5	32	33	4
6	42	46	16
7	33	34	4
8	31	25	2

TABLE 4

Shifts on analog scale of room size attributable to the presence of an odor

Subjects	1	2	3	4	5	6	7	8	Averages		
Normal olfaction	Yes	No	Yes	Yes	Yes	Yes	Yes	Yes	All	7	6 use
Use perfume	No	No	Yes	Yes	Yes	Yes	Yes	Yes	8	Norm.	Perf.
Odors											
Evergreen	-.25	0	-1.0	-2.5	2.0	.25	2.5	0.5	.19	.21	.29
Barbecue Smoke	-.25	0	-1.0	-0.5	-1.0	-.25	-1.0	0.5	-.44*	-.50	-.54
Tranquilities	.25	0	0.0	-2.0	0.0	-.75	3.0	0.5	.13	.14	.13
Vanilla	.25	0	-1.0	-1.5	-1.0	-.75	3.0	0.0	-.13	-.14	-.21
Buttered Popcorn	-.25	0	0.0	-2.5	-0.5	-.25	3.5	0.5	.06	.07	.13
Seashore	-.25	0	-0.5	-2.0	0.5	-.75	2.5	2.0	.19	.21	.29
Charcoal Roasting Meat	-.25	0	-0.5	-1.5	-0.5	-.75	2.5	0.5	-.06	-.07	-.04
Cucumber	-.25	0	-1.0	-1.5	-1.0	.25	3.0	0.0	-.06	-.07	-.04
Coconut	-.25	0	-0.5	2.0	-2.0	-.25	-3.0	0.5	-.44	-.50	-.54
Green Apple	-.25	0	0.5	-0.5	1.5	.25	3.0	0.5	.63	.71**	.88***

Note: Positive values indicate the odor made the room seem larger and negative values indicate the odor made the room seem smaller compared to the nonodorized condition.

*statistically significant. $p = 0.0469$
**statistically significant. $p = 0.0156$ for normosmics and
***statistically significant. $p = 0.0313$ for fragrance users

baseline with the other nine odors. The difference between the analog shift with each odor and the mean of the analog shifts with the other nine odors was calculated for each individual. Thus the median change for each odor was determined across all subjects, and the significance of the differences calculated.

Only one odor caused a statistically significant perceptual shift for all subjects: the odor of barbecue smoke, which diminished the perceived size of the room ($p < 0.05$).

Data were further analyzed for the 7 normosmics and the 6 who used personal fragrances. For these groups, the perceptual shift was statistically significant also for the odor of green apple, which expanded the perceived size of the room ($p = 0.0156$ and 0.0313 respectively).

Medians were further compared for indoor versus outdoor odors and for food versus nonfood odors for all 8 subjects, for the 7 normosmics and for the 6 perfume users. Differences were not significant (Table 4).

Statistical analysis was based on Signed-Rank Test for pair differences.[16]

Discussion

We know that ambient odors can create a mood: The aroma of Thanksgiving dinner usually induces a positive feeling and may lessen concern about surroundings. On the other hand, the smell of smoke may trigger fear and the impulse to flee. Odors can influence evaluation of consumer products,[17] speed of learning[18] and ability to lose weight,[19] thus it is not surprising that odors may influence perceptions of room size.

The cortical integration of odor at any of innumerable neuroanatomic circuits might alter perception of room size. Spatial size is Interpreted in the nondominant parietal lobe.[20] Various pathologic states can affect such interpretations and concern about space and size.[20-23]

The olfactory bulb directly projects to the dorsal medial nucleus of the thalamus.[24,25] Secondary thalamic projections to the neocortex include the parietal lobe,[26] hence odors might affect perception of room size directly via sensory integration in these areas.

Alternatively, odors might distract from other sensory stimuli and their integration, either by inducing a cognitive dissonance, as something to attend to rather than to room size, or by inhibiting cognition, so that the subject daydreams instead of attending to room size.

Odors can act affectively, changing the subject's emotional state.[27] A subject may become aware of hunger, for example, and concentrate on food rather than room size, or become reflective, and focus on another time or place.

Indirect anatomic effects of odors through secondary limbic system projections also may be possible. In describing the limbic system, MacLean included the olfactory lobe as part and parcel of it, indicating the importance of smell on emotions and behavior.[28] Freud discussed the importance of odors on emotions[29] and odors that increase or decrease anxiety may increase or decrease the discomfort of being in a small space.[4,30,31]

Odors can trigger memories. In a 1992 study,[32] 85% of individuaLs questioned indicated that they had experienced olfactory-evoked recall. The emotional state induced in this way is usually a positive one, which would decrease concern about room size. However, an olfactory evoked recall could be negative or even alarming. In our experiment, any evoked state would be superimposed upon the experience of being in the space-deprivation booth, with problematic consequences for our results.

We might assume some subcomponents of claustrophobia in our subjects that would manifest when they entered the space deprivation booth, then increase or decrease due to the odor. Difficulty breathing, for instance, a subcomponent of suffocating claustrophobia[15] might be exacerbated merely by wearing the mask, then further exacerbated by the odor. A relaxing odor, however, might reduce feelings of restriction.

The presence of a trusted individual can ease discomfort in claustrophobia as in other simple phobias. A subject may interpret a familiar odor as evidence that friendly, trustworthy persons are nearby.[14]

An odor may induce a direct sympathetic response as occurs in the auditory sphere when fingernails are scraped across a chalkboard. A limbic-flight-or-fight reaction could make an individual in the booth feel trapped.

Like hallucinogens, which can cause synesthesias[22] and various sensory distortions, an experimental odor might alter perceptions or their interpretation.

Animal behavior exhibits evolutionary evidence that odors can affect spacial perceptions: In response to the odors of members of the herd, animals travel close together. Since there is safety in numbers, the effect is protective of individuals. Possibly an experimental odor could act on our subjects' primitive brains to produce a comfortable herd effect.

Of the 10 odors we tested, however, only that of barbecue smoke significantly affected all subjects. This odor could have induced subclinical suffocative claustrophobic feelings either through a learned or emotional response. The odor of smoke in a small room could prompt thoughts of fire and a wish to escape the closed-in space, hence our experimental result is not surprising.

However, it seems surprising that of the outdoor smells, only the green apple significantly enlarged perceptions of the room size and only for the 7 normosmic subjects. The apple odor perhaps evoked memories of picking apples in an open orchard and feelings of ease and freedom. A study with more subjects of varied backgrounds might show significant effects with the other outdoor odors.

Although ours was a double-blind study with odors randomly presented, a placebo response might have been possible had our subjects recognized the odors and anticipated our belief that outdoor odors would be expansive and indoor odors claustrophobic. The results, however, were not statistically different for-indoor and outdoor odors.

We expected our results to support various studies that imply an odor's hedonics contribute to its effects.[17-19] The 10 odors in our experiment, however, selected for their hedonics by our independent panel, did not bear this out. We also expected that food odors, which can cause hunger or satiety,[19] might compete with and distract from perceptions of confinement. But our results for food versus nonfood odors did not differ significantly. A study of a larger number of subjects might demonstrate effects due to odors' hedonics or relation to food.

Most significantly, the subject who scored poorly on the UPSIT was unaffected by any of the odors, which validates our results with the normosmic subjects. Had any accidental factors been responsible for our findings, the subject with poor olfaction would have shown the same effects as the others.

The 75% of our subjects who found odors pleasant and used perfumed products were not necessarily superior in olfactory ability, but perhaps were more responsive to the odors in our experiment.

The effect of our subjects' ages is problematic. Younger subjects were more responsive to the odors than older ones. In general, younger people have better olfaction, but this was not true of our subjects according to our test data.

The effect of sex also is problematic. Women, in general, have better olfaction than men,[6] but our male and female subjects' responses did not differ significantly. Again, the number of subjects may have been too small to show differences due to age and sex.

Conclusions

The use of ambient odors to ameliorate anxieties of the substantial proportion of the population afflicted with claustrophobia appears to be a fruitful area to explore.

As many as 5-10% of patients undergoing imaging procedures suffer such intense discomfort in the confined space that the procedures must be stopped. Neurosurgeons, orthopedic surgeons and other medical practitioners who conduct MRI scans may be able to use particular odors such as green apple to minimize patients' anxieties so that claustrophobic individuals can tolerate the procedure and those with subclinical component can be made more comfortable with it.

References

1. American Psychiatric Association: Diagnostic and statistical manual of mental disorders, 4th ed. Washington DC: American Psychiatric Association, 1994, 399, 402, 403, 408
2. Green WR. Retail store. In: Design and construction, 2nd ed. New York: Van Nostrand Reinhold, 1991
3. Hirsch AR, Scott JM, Koch SH. Efficacy of group therapy in the treatment approach to chemosensory disorders. Chem Senses 1992; 17:643
4. King JR. Anxiety reduction using fragrances. In: Van Toller S, Dodd GH (eds). Perfumery. Psychology and biology of fragrance. London: Chapman and Hall, 1988, 147-165
5. Amoore J, Ollman B. Practical test kits for quantitatively evaluating the sense of smell. Rhinology 1983;21:49-54
6. Doty RL, Newhouse MG, Azzalina JD. Internal consistency and short-term test-retest reliability of the University of Pennsylvania Smell Identification Test. Chem Senses, 1985;10:297-300
7. Zung WWK. Self-rating depression scale. Arch Gen Psychiatry 1965;12:63-70
8. Zung WWK. Rating instrument for anxiety disorders. Psychosomatics 1971;12:371-379
9. Beck AT, Beamesderfer A. Assessment of depression-Depression inventory: Psychological measurements in psychopharmacology, 9th ed. Basel: S. Karger, 1974
10. Bystritsky A, Lim LS, Were JE. Development of a multidimensional scale of anxiety. Journal of Anxiety Disorders 1990;4:99-115
11. Derogatis LR. SCL-90R. Baltimore: Clinical Psychometric Research, 1977
12. Scrignar CB. Stress strategies. Treatment of the anxiety disorders. Basel: S. Karger, 1983, 6-7
13. Clarke JC, Jackson JA. Hypnosis and behavior therapy. Treatment of anxiety and phobias. New York: Springer, 1983, 320-321
14. World Psychiatric Association. Panic anxiety and its treatments. Klerman GL, Hirschfeld RMA, Weissman MM, Pelicier Y, Ballenger JC, Costa e Silva JA, Judd LL, Keller MB (eds). Washington DC: American Psychiatric Press, 1993, 7
15. Rachman S, Taylor S. Analyses of claustrophobia Journal of Anxiety Disorders. Pergamon Press, 1993, 281-291
16. Lehmann EL. Nonparametrics: Statistical methods based on ranks. Holden-Day, 1975
17. Hirsch AR, Gay S. Effect of ambient olfactory stimuli on the evaluation of a common consumer product. Chem Senses 1991;16:535
18. Hirsch AR, Johnston LH. Effect of floral odor on learning. AChemS-XVI 1994, No. 142
19. Hirsch AR, Dougherty DD. Inhalation of 2-acetylpyridine for weight reduction. Chem Senses 1993;18:570
20. Diamond S, Dalessio DJ. Practicing physician's approach to headache, 2nd ed. Baltimore, MD: Williams and Wilkins, 1978, 15-16
21. Adams RD, Victor M. Principles of neurology, 4th ed. New York: McGraw-Hill, 1989, 252, 363
22. Winger G, Hofmann FG, Woods JH. Handbook on drug and alcohol abuse-Biomedical aspects, 3rd ed. New York: Oxford University Press, 1992, 101-105
23. Strub RL, Black FW. Organic brain syndromes: Introduction to neurobehavioral disorders. Philadelphia, PA: F.A. Davis, 1981, 238-242
24. McLean JH, Shipley MT. Neuroanatomical substrates of olfaction. In: Serby MJ, Chobor, KL (eds). Science of olfaction. New York: Springer-Verlag, 1992, 158
25. Shipley M, Reyes P. Anatomy of the human olfactory bulb and central olfactory pathways. In: Laing DG, Doty RL, Breipohl W (eds). Human sense of smell. New York: Springer-Verlag, 1991, 54

26. Carpenter MB. Core text of neuroanatomy, 2nd Ed. Baltimore, MD: Williams and Wilkins, 1978, 212
27. Hirsch AR. Sensory marketing. Internatl J Aromatherapy 1993;5:21-23
28. MacLean PD. Triune concept of the brain and behavior. Toronto, Canada: University of Toronto Press, 1973
29. Freud S. Bemerkungen uber Einen Fall von Zwangs Neuroses. Ges Schr 1908;VIII:350
30. LeDoux JE. Emotional networks in the brain. In: Lewis M, Haviland JM (eds). Handbook of emotions. New York: Guilford Press, 1993, 109-118
31. Wolpe J. Psychotherapy by reciprocal inhibition. Stanford, California: Stanford University Press, 1958
32. Hirsch AR, Nostalgia: Neuropsychiatric understanding. Advances in consumer research 1992;19:390-395

Resources

If you suffer from smell loss as a result of head trauma or from other causes, or if you would like information about weight loss, please call our foundation. We currently have eighty-five active studies in many areas of human behavior and the use of medications for smell and taste disorders. My two previous books, *Scentsational Weight Loss* and *Scentsational Sex*, are also available by calling our foundation.

Smell & Taste Treatment and Research Foundation
Water Tower Place
845 N. Michigan Ave., 990W
Chicago, IL 60611
(312) 938-1047
Fax (312) 649-0458
Website: www.smellandtaste.org

SA for Men and SA for Women are the first fragrances created for the purpose of increasing sexual arousal. Certainly, other scents have been promoted and advertised as sensuous, perhaps having the ability to add to one's attractiveness to the opposite sex. However, the SA products are the first to be formulated based on scientific evidence that specific odors increase penile and vaginal blood flow. Currently, these products are available by calling (800) 951-0939 or through the website: www.esexualarousal.com.

Selected References

Barer-Stein, T., *You Eat What You Are* (Firefly, Ontario, Canada) 1999.

Bruinsma, K., Taren, D., "Chocolate: food or drug?" *Journal of the American Dietetic Association*, 10/1999, Vol. 99, No 10, 1252-1256.

Capaldi, E., editor, *Why We Eat What We Eat* (American Psychological Association, Washington D.C., 1996).

Glanville, E.V., Kaplan, A.R., "Food preference and sensitivity of taste for bitter compounds," *Nature*, 2/27/65, 851-853.

Harris, M., *Good to Eat* (Simon and Schuster, New York, 1985).

Hetherington, M, Macdiarmid, J., "Chocolate Addiction: A prelmiminary study of its description and its relationship to problem eating," *Appetite*, 1993, 21, 223-246.

Hirsch, A., "Listening to patients with chemosensory dysfunction," *Chicago Medicine*, 1/21/98, Vol. 101, No.2, 14-17.

Jerzsa-Latta, M., et al, "Use and perceived attributes of cruciferous vegetables in terms of genetically-mediated taste sensitivity," *Appetite*, 1990, 15, 127-134.

Martin, G. N., "Human electroencephalographic (EEG) response to olfactory stimulation: two experiments using the aroma of food," *International Journal of Psychophysiology*, 1998, 30, 287-302.

Michener, W., Rozin, P., "Pharmacological versus sensory factors in the satiation of chocolate craving," *Physiology & Behavior*, Vol 56, No. 3, 419-422, 1994.

Rozin, P., Levine, E., Stoess, C., "Chocolate craving and liking," *Appetite*, 1991, 17, 199-212.

Rozin, P., "Family resemblance in food and other domains: the family paradox and the role of parental congruence," *Appetite*, 1991, 16, 93-102.

Shepherd, R., Farleigh, C., "Attitudes and personality related to salt intake," *Appetite*, 1986, 7, 343-354.

Stone, L., Pangborn, R., "Preferences and intake measures of salt and sugar, and their relation to personality traits," *Appetite*, 1990, 15, 63-79.

Tisdale, S., *The Best Thing I Ever Tasted* (Riverhead/Penguin-Putnam, New York, 2000).

Visser, M., *Much Depends on Dinner* (Grove, New York,1986).

Index

About the Author

Alan Hirsch, M.D., F.A.C.P., is a neurologist and psychiatrist who specializes in the treatment of smell and taste loss. He is the neurological director of the Smell & Taste Research and Treatment Foundation in Chicago. Dr. Hirsch is certified by the American Board of Psychiatry and Neurology in Neurology, Psychiatry, Pain Management, Geriatric Psychiatry, and Addiction Psychiatry. He has appeared multiple times on *Good Morning America*, *Oprah*, and *CNN*. His studies have appeared on *Saturday Night Live* and *The Tonight Show*. Dr. Hirsch has been featured in *The New York Times*, *Cosmopolitan*, *Redbook*, *Entrepreneur* and hundreds of newspapers and radio interviews. His prior books include *Scentsational Weight Loss* and *Scentsational Sex*.